More Heavenly Treasures

Written and

Compiled

by

Rayola Kelley

Hidden Manna Publications

More Heavenly Treasures

Copyright © 2024 by Rayola Kelley

ISBN: 978-1-7347503-5-5

Except where otherwise indicated, all Scripture quotations in this book are taken from the King James Version of the Bible.

Hidden Manna Publications
P.O. Box 3572
Oldtown, ID 83822
www.gentleshepherd.com

Facebook:
https://www.facebook.com/HiddenMannaPublications/

Contents

INTRODUCTION

This is the sixth book in the collection of inspirational stories, sayings, and poems written and compiled by the author Rayola Kelley. Again, it was the author's purpose to bring out the gems of wisdom that can grace our lives with heavenly blessings and riches.

As in the past the material in this book is what the author considers nuggets from heaven. It is important to remember nuggets of truth and wisdom can be found in the most unusual places and stand alone in the midst of the corrupt and worthless rhetoric of this world. For example, there are some who shared a nugget here or there that may not even be an heir of salvation. There are those who are considered heretics, or someone I would never find any place of agreement with, but like the donkey in Balaam's case it is up to us as believers to discern if such a nugget is of a heavenly inspiration, and if so, we must receive its truth or instruction regardless of who handled it.

To the best of the author's abilities, she has identified the sources. She has written the stories and prayers unless otherwise noted, and identified her own sayings with her initials (RJK). Many of these inspired sayings were found circulating on Facebook (FB) and since they are passed around it is hard to say who the source is behind them.

The simplicity of these treasures can be handled by those with a child-like heart and embraced by the pure in heart. Their wisdom can be appreciated by those desiring to go deeper with the profound, and those seeking the clarity of truth.

These nuggets have been marked by banners and are designed to challenge, inspire, and encourage people in this dark world to consider the text of the subject. There are various ways people assimilate these riches into their treasure chest. There are those who, like Jonathan of the Old Testament, that during times of battle seek to taste a bit of honey to inspire them on to see the present battle through to the end.

There are those like Mary, the mother of Jesus, who hides treasures in her heart so she can ponder them later. There are the Benjamins who with wonder and trepidation consider what it means when they discover a silver cup among their possessions. There are those like a perplexed Job who sought for the wisdom to recognize and know how to handle such heavenly treasures.

Regardless of whether we are seeking such treasures or come upon them, they can, and will, enrich our lives once we see the wisdom of them, embrace them by faith, and with joy take pleasure in their unique, heavenly beauty and design of God.

Salvation

Immortality

Man was created to live forever. The first man, Adam was clothed in glory as one who would maintain the garden in service and keep it from all that would create discord between him and his Creator. He was called to walk with God in sweet fellowship, given dominion over creation to maintain the right environment and given a help-meet that would remind him of God's abiding care and provision.

It was a glorious paradise, but due to deception, in one act, man lost it all, except his immortality. Granted, his body would die, but where his soul and spirit would reside would come down to what he did with the God/Man, the Christ, the Son of the Living God, the Lord Jesus Christ.

Due to the sin of the first man, there is a great gulf between man and his Creator. No matter how many bridges man attempts to construct with his religious attempts or good deeds to get to God, it never can close the gulf. As Howard E. Kershner pointed out in his book, our lives are like suspension bridges, hanging between the past and the future but without something of the present linking them together, we have nothing to bring the cursed past together with a hopeful future. We are in essence doomed to fall into the abyss before we connect with any real future. After all, wishful thinking or fantasy may cause us to look forward to the future but they are nothing more than paper links that might connect with each other until reality of man's sinful plight tears them apart.

However, God brought the necessary links forth to connect the past with the future by sending His Son. Jesus would close the spiritual gulf with the ladder of the cross and the bridge of His redemption. He would be lifted up on the cross in order to spread out His arms as a means to bring in and embrace all who would believe on His work of redemption that has ransomed souls from the grip of death, the cursed claims of the world and the works of darkness.

Man was made for eternity: that of eternal life or damnation. The Bible speaks of heaven and hell. Hell is a temporary holding place for those who refuse to receive God's provision of eternal life. It's a place of darkness, ongoing torment, and utter hopelessness and despair for it is appointed unto man to die once, then judgment. Hell is not forever, but will be cast into the Lake of Fire along with death, but what that existence will look like is a matter of debate. Such debate is a waste of breath because what will be will be regardless of the theological debates.

The Bible is clear that there are two gates and they are narrow, but past one gate is a narrow hard path and past the other one is a broad path. I did not choose heaven to avoid hell; rather, I chose heaven because I believe in God's provision, and love Him for it. He gave His Son, and it is only right I give my all. Jesus gave His life and it is only fair I offer my body, my life in love, service, and worship. It is easy to choose the broad path because up front it offers the easy way, but I choose the hard, narrow path because it prepares me for heavenly bliss.

Kershner points out that those who become aware that they are immortal creatures, who are building for eternity, need to keep in mind that every thought, word, and deed acquires enormous significance. He goes on to say that such a person begins to measure their confidence in their immortality, knowing they have been reconciled to God and that the yardstick of their life must be scaled to everlasting values. (DPS, pgs. 136-137)

* Do not make a savior out of your morality. You can never be righteous enough. That office belongs to Christ alone.

-FB

* The door of heaven will be closed to all who have never opened the door of their heart to Jesus.

-J. Haley

* How could anyone have peace who believed that salvation depended on his own efforts? How could he be certain that he had paid enough attention to the demands of the law or ritual? It is the gospel of the grace of God which believed gives men full assurance.

-H.A. Ironside
(GE, (G) pg. 29)

* I came to Jesus and I drank of that life-giving stream; my thirst was quenched, my soul revived, and now I live in Him.

-Horatius Bonar

* There is a problem when sin doesn't offend us, but correction does.

-FB

* We have no right to preach unless we present the Gospel; we have not to advocate a cause or a creed or an experience, but to

present the Gospel, and cannot do that unless we have a personal testimony based on the Gospel.

-Oswald Chambers
(CWC, pg. 12)

- Salvation is a legal matter. The reason we need to be saved is because we are under a death sentence according to a holy Law. As a righteous judge who must execute this Law, the Lord cannot intervene or help us unless He has the grounds to do so. This means we must understand our plight in order to seek His intervention on our behalf. The truth is a righteous judge desires to show mercy where He can, but unless one sincerely seeks it, what is left for any righteous judge is to execute the sentence pronounced on the offender by the law. For those who have not received a pardon for their sins, it is separation from God who is life.

-RJK

- We need preachers who preach that hell is still hot, that heaven is still real, that sin is still wrong, that the Bible is God's Word, and that Jesus is the only way to salvation.

-FB

The Called

As believers we all have been called to work in the various harvest fields of the world. The reason is God is committed to save sinners. He does not want to see anyone taste His wrath. We clearly see this in His longsuffering with rebellious man, He is giving them time to repent so they will not perish in their sins.

In the Garden of Eden, the LORD God called out to Adam and Eve who hid from Him because they no longer had priestly glory surrounding them as described in *Ezekiel 28:13*. They stood naked in their flesh, exposed in their wretched spiritual state, and guilty and without recourse before their Creator.

The Lord continued to call individuals, Noah, Abram, Moses, Samuel, and David to name a few. Noah obediently built an ark in an environment of pure wickedness before the flood, Abram was called out from idolatry and paganism, Moses was driven out of the courts of Pharaoh to be prepared in the wilderness of God. Samuel was called as a boy to warn of pending judgment, and David learned to be a soldier in the darkness of night before facing a giant, but they were all called.

Spurgeon once said the highland soldiers were prepared in the low places of humility. I know that as a Gentile, I am saved and part of the universal body due to the preaching of a man named Paul who was called to take the Gospel to the Gentiles. This apostle established many churches, as well as a lasting legacy of God's faithfulness to send forth His servants into the various fields of the world. Jesus stated, as the Father sent Him, He sends us.

Throughout the book, missionary stories from such books as *Adventures of Missionary Heroism* will be highlighted. The consistent thread that runs through these stories is the willingness of these individuals to offer up their all, their lives to take the great message of the Gospel into the darkest regions of the world. To many it came with a great cost, but in their minds, it was the least they could do for One who gave it all for them to receive, know and gain the gift of eternal life. Today we call those who are sent forth, missionaries.

One such missionary was **Dr. Jacob Chamberlain**. He was born April 13, 1835 in Connecticut and at an early age felt the call of God to be a missionary. His response was delayed due to a commitment to his father to take care of his aging parents on the family farm. After experiencing many narrow escapes at home, Chamberlain sensed it was time to go to India as a missionary. With his father's blessing to pursue his calling, he attended seminary and earned a medical degree. He married Charlotte Close Birge in September of 1859.

The couple arrived on the mission field in India on April 12, 1860. Chamberlain did not minister in places where missions were already present; rather, he went to remote areas of the jungle to reach native groups and explore lands never before reached by the Gospel. In fact, one trek he traveled was 1,200 miles through a native kingdom located in Central India. They summarize his experience as being as striking and thrilling as any that have come from the pen of Rudyard Kipling.

This missionary planted seeds where he could. God would afford him the most amazing opportunities to plant them. In one case a very sick man was brought to him that he had to operate on. During his recovery Chamberlain read a chapter from the Gospel every day and made its meaning plain to the hearers. When the time came for the now well man and those who came with him to leave, they begged the doctor for the book about the "the Divine Guru" so they might let their neighbors know about Him. They admitted they were illiterates but merchants who could read always came to their villages and they would ask them to read it before they settle on the payments for goods.

Three years later he met those men again. They were smiling and they shared how everyone in the place agreed to give up their idols if someone would come and teach them about Jesus. In the end the doctor took one of their biggest idols and exposed it as being lifeless and powerless.

In one incident a riotous crowd was ready to stone him and those with him, but he encouraged them to listen to a wonderful story. By the time it was over, the crowd had dropped their rocks, as their hearts were touched and many stood with tears in their eyes and every copy of the Gospel that was brought to the city was taken.

He escaped the strike of a huge coiled serpent above his head and used an umbrella while emitting a war-whoop to scare a tiger away. He survived various floods, proving that God indeed knows how to preserve His servants. He also was ravaged by jungle fever that left him partially paralyzed until his death, which shows how God will sustain His servants.

Dr. Jacob Chamberlain died on the mission field March 2, 1908 after working in the harvest field of India for 48 years. He was called to India where he spent his life, and it was for countless Indian souls that he ultimately gave up his life. (AMH, pgs. 21-38)

———————

- If you think you're saved because there is something in you worth saving, then you're not saved.

-J. Haley

- Those who have a high opinion of themselves cannot be saved, it takes humility and brokenness to realize a need for Christ.

-FB

Prayer: Lord, in my ungodly state I knew things were wrong in my life and that I needed intervention. As a sinner, I realized I needed a Savior, and as a struggling soul, I knew I needed a Mediator. Thank You Lord for being my All in All; now I must let You become all things to me to realize the fullness of Your work, the greatness of Your earthly mission, and the majesty of Your glory. Amen.

- When it comes to our common salvation, God kept it simple so no one could complain that it was overly complicated and beyond the comprehension. Individuals who attempt to complicate it needlessly do so either out of pride and self-importance or a vested interest.

Michael Boldea Jr.

(EJ, pg. 7)

- The gospel doesn't require obedience, it produces obedience.

-Voddie Baucham

- Death is not a tragedy! Death is our passport to glory! Death without Christ is tragedy.

-FB

- To whom does God communicate eternal life? To all who put their trust in His blessed Son.

-H. A. Ironside

(GE, (G) pg. 128)

- The Gospel of the New Testament is based on the absoluteness of revelation, we cannot get at it by our common sense. If a man is to be saved it must be from outside. God never pumps up anything from within.

-Oswald Chambers

(CWC, pg. 14)

- The evidence that you have truly passed through the narrow gate is that you are now walking in the narrow way.

-FB

- If your faith is misplaced, perverted, or otherwise skewed, any talk of salvation must be tabled until we get the faith right.

-Michael Boldea Jr.

(EJ, pg. 27)

- The purpose of God in redemption is not just to save us *from* hell. The purpose of God in redemption is to save us *unto* heaven.

    -A. W. Tozer
    (WOG, pg. 27)

- As long as a man thinks he can save himself, he remains lost.

    -M.L. Jones

- The Gospel is neither a discussion nor a debate. It is an announcement.

    -FB

- The gospel of Jesus Christ does not present what men want; it presents exactly what they need.

    -Oswald Chambers
    (CWC, pg. 161)

The Gospel

Many Christians are looking for Jesus to come. I too keep looking up for I know the signs tell me His coming is near. However, there is one prophetic condition that must be fulfilled and that is the one surrounding the Gospel. It is found in Matthew 24:14, "And this gospel of the kingdom shall be preached in all the world for a witness unto all nations; and then shall the end come."

I was reading some interesting statistics gathered by the missionary organization, Ethnos360. Sixty percent of unreached people groups (UPG) in the world today are found in communities where the dominant worldviews are Islamic (3,400 UPGs), Hindu (2,288 UPGs), and Buddhist (530 UPGs often mixed with animism).

I don't always know what would constitute to the Lord the Gospel being preached in all the world for a witness unto all nations, but I do know it must happen before He comes and when the Gospel has been delivered in fulfillment of the prophetic, HE WILL COME.

It seems to me more people are emphasizing His coming rather than preaching the Gospel. However, what will bring Him forth is not how many people are looking for Him, but that a witness has been established by the preaching of the Gospel among all nations.

Our hope rests in Jesus, but the power to save is found in the Gospel and the source of overcoming is established in our testimony based on the good news. We must not forget we are commissioned to preach the Gospel and make disciples of Christ. It is easy to get caught up with the blessed hope of Jesus coming for His Church, but before He comes, a witness has to be established through the preaching of the Gospel.

Perhaps we need to come back to the commission and be faithful to our commission and calling, knowing in the end we have faithfully occupied while looking for our blessed hope until the Gospel establishes the witness among all nations to ensure no one can declare they never knew such a witness existed.

Revelation 14:6-7 tells us,

> And I saw another angel fly in the midst of heaven, having the everlasting gospel to preach unto them that dwell on the earth, and to every nation and kindred and tongue, and people, Saying with a loud voice, Fear God and give glory to him for the hour of his judgment is come: and worship him that made heaven, and earth, and the sea, and the fountains of waters.

- We take our salvation and our sanctification much too cheaply. We ought to rejoice when a man says he is saved, but remember what it cost God to make His grace a free gift.

  -Oswald Chambers

  (CWC, pg. 235)

- In short, many of today's Christian leaders, influenced by social justice, retain a portion of the legalistic gospel of modern liberalism that underlaid the social gospel movement of a century ago. While they may articulate forgiveness by grace though faith in Christ's finished work, they also add a systemic, institutional, or corporate salvation through law keeping to their gospel message.

  -Jon Harris

  (CSJ, pg. 44)

- The Gospel is meant to offend those in sin, not defend them living in it.

  -FB

- The business of the Gospel is to bring people to God, and to reconcile them to God. It is not to fill churches, not to have good statistics! But to reconcile men to God, to save them from the wrath to come.

  -Martyn Lloyd Jones

- It is not your hold of Christ that saves you, but His hold of you.

  -Charles Spurgeon

- Never separate the Incarnation and the Atonement. The Incarnation was not for the Self-realization of God, but for the purpose of removing sin and reinstating humanity into communion with God. Jesus Christ became Incarnate for one

purpose, to make a way back to God that man might stand before Him as he was created to do, the friend and lover of God Himself.
-Oswald Chambers
(CWC, pg. 220)

- The Gospel is not God hatefully saying, "Turn to me or I'll send you to hell." The Gospel is God's Mercy and Grace saying, "You're already on your way to Hell, turn to me and I'll save you."
-FB

How Far Would You Go?

How far would you go to see a soul saved? What kind of offering are you willing to make to the Lord to see the furtherance of His kingdom in the lives of people? We often have romantic ideas about our commitment to the Lord, but I have learned that so much of that notion is based on fantasy. It is often about our idea of personal greatness, and that upon presenting our sacrifice in the name of God, we want to make sure it will leave us in the end looking noble and not some witness that is mocked. We want a cross that allows us to be a suffering saint on it instead of a dead martyr, and a narrow path we can adjust enough to make it convenient for us to gain some type of recognition and glory along the way.

It all comes down to our level of consecration and faith, but there is something else we must have and that is a call from God that is loud and clear, a love that is compelling, and an urgency that never subsides with time. This is the passion behind many such believers who tread where others would never dare to go.

One such man was a Scotsman by the name of **James Gilmour**. He ended up in one of the darkest places, spiritually speaking, that covered a territory of 1,300,000 square miles. It is the second largest landlocked country in the world and its history was largely of a nomadic and pagan country that shared its borders with Russia and China.

The customs of the people were generally unknown until Gilmour took up the torch that was burning in his soul and accepted the call of God on his life to go into the foreign mission field. He ended up in a very unwelcoming harvest field that was made up of vast collections of tribes which had lost their former greatness. The leader that was associated with this greatness was Genghis Khan. They are known as the fierce Mongolians.

Gilmore arrived in Peking around the time that the Tientsin massacre took place in 1870 in China. This massacre was a prelude to the Boxer Rebellion. While many were fleeing for their lives, Gilmore set his face northward to see if there was an opening for Christian work among the Mongols. How often the circumstances around us can close doors while presenting a small narrow window of opportunity that leads the way into our very calling.

When Gilmore first arrived, he devoted much of his time in learning the language, while at the same time learning to live among them as he crossed the paths of these nomadic people. He spent months traveling through the vast countryside, which ended with him spending two decades to bring the light of the Gospel to them.

His adventures among the people are many. He traveled on camel and horse and by foot through the land, but his preference was horse. He was known to cover 300 miles in seven and half days, an average of 40 miles a day on foot. He juggled cultures as he also dealt with both Russians and Chinese. He took on the dress customs of the people to survive extreme temperatures and his equipment was minimal that included his weapon, a rough stick to fight off the dogs. In fact, he was known as the "Robinson Crusoe of Missionaries."

Gilmore was married to Emily Prankard who shared his vision and served with him for ten years until her death. He faithfully continued his work as he traveled, preached, and taught throughout

Mongolia and parts of China until he contracted a malignant strain of Typhus fever and died at age 48.

James Gilmore recorded not only his adventures but the customs and ways of the Mongols. In fact, his book, *Among the Mongols* had such insight about the Mongols that it has been preserved by libraries as part of historical artifacts and can be scanned and reproduced.

His book left a valuable and exciting record, but his life left an incredible witness. For the most part his ministry would not be considered a success because there were few converts due to the challenging field, but the life he poured out on his beloved people planted seeds. When he passed from this world into glory, the fierce Mongolian men even broke down in tears. It was clear that Gilmore had made the people his people and in turn upon his death, it was clear that he had become the Mongol's Gilmore, and sorrow gripped their hearts as they realized that now he was no longer among them. (AMH, pgs. 3-19)

- The emphasis to-day is being put on the fact that we have to save men; we have not. We have to exalt the Savior Who saves men, and then make disciples in His Name.

    -Oswald Chambers
    (CWC, pg. 226)

- Any gospel that preserves the flesh and does not teach you to deny yourself is anti-Christ because it leaves man in control.

    -FB

- My voice has no power to save unless Christ shall use my voice and make it the echo of His own.

  -Charles Spurgeon

- Bestir yourself to purpose for your soul before it be too late. Search your conscience as with candles. Be jealous of yourself. Consider now is your time. What you do, you must do quickly. The patience of God is waiting; Christ is knocking; the Spirit of God is striving, and death is at the door.

  -Joseph Alleine
  (TK, pg. 40)

- We often have a tendency to think that salvation is strictly associated with saving the soul. However, this is not true. God must save us from many things. He has to save us from our own devices because they lead to ruin. He must deliver us from the wicked tides of the world to ensure our testimony. He must preserve our sanity in the pit of hopelessness. The Lord must guide our steps down rocky, slippery slopes to ensure our very life.

  -RJK

- We are apt to mistake the sovereign works of Grace in salvation and sanctification as being final—they are only beginnings.

  -Oswald Chambers
  (CWC, pg. 221)

- There is no greater message, no greater thought than what CHRIST has done for us on the CROSS.

  -FB

They Must Hear God

There are so many things we can get caught up with when it comes to religion. However, the best of religion can prove to become the greatest hindrance when following and serving Jesus. We can get caught up with methods instead of learning to be led by the Spirit. We can get fixated with numbers instead of focusing on what is important to God: that of lost souls. We can become quite rigid in our religious practices and duties and fail to see our love for Christ becoming cold.

We also want a formula to ensure success. After all, who wants to fail God? We want to see God's kingdom furthered here on earth, while advancing forward. However, what has happened is that the numbers may be growing here but there is no evidence of salvation happening in many churches.

Jonathan Goforth had a successful ministry as a missionary in China, but it was not because of any of his doing but because God brought forth a revival. Goforth accredits it to the move and work of the Holy Spirit.

He was asked in his later years by young missionaries about the secret behind his power to win converts. This is his reply, "Because I just give God a chance to speak to souls through His own Word. My only secret in getting at the heart of big sinners is to show them their need and tell them of a Saviour abundantly able to save." (TK, pg. 142)

Repentance

If Man Repents

Repentance is a complete change in attitude and a complete turnaround in lifestyle practices. Jesus stated repent or perish in Luke 13:3 and 5. It is God's will that all come to repentance instead of perishing in their sins. We are told in Hebrews 12:17 that repentance is actually a place one must spiritually come to, to experience its benefits.

In God's economy such a place represents true humility and brokenness before Him that comes out of a complete utter desperation. In such desperation He will be sought with one's whole heart. It is clear that repentance not only changes the inward man, but it sets him on a complete opposite course from the path he has been walking.

If man repents, then God is able to bestow on him an act of grace by way of the cross: That of eternal life. The cross is a visible manifestation of grace, while grace is channeled through mercy at the point of repentance through forgiveness. Mercy allows God the opportunity to show His grace through deliverance or salvation, as He gives man space to repent.

People who do not understand how sin works will often show contempt towards God by abusing His grace. God shows grace with one goal in mind—to save people. In fact, mercy and judgment came together on the cross to produce the outward evidence of grace that results in eternal life for all who will come to Jesus. To toy with sin, while hiding behind a perverted concept of grace, is to put God to a foolish test.

———————

- Few are standing up for God's Word. Few are picking up their cross and following Jesus Christ. Few are giving the Gospel with REPENTANCE for the remission of sins. It's a narrow way and few find it.

  -FB

- Repentance is to seek to become a new person, to open the heart to the incoming of moral wisdom, to seek to be like the most excellent wisdom. It is to seek to live and have an affinity toward Jesus Christ the Lord.

  -A. W. Tozer
  (WOG, pg. 140)

- People are waiting on God to heal the land. When in reality God is waiting on the people to repent and turn from their wicked ways.

  -FB

- The key to righteousness begins with true repentance that turns from sin, humility that is a product of brokenness over sin, and true conversion that comes out of seeing a matter according to God's holiness.

  -RJK

- We repent enough to be forgiven, but do we surrender enough to be changed?

  -FB

- The bedrock of Christianity is repentance...Repentance means that I estimate exactly what I am in God's sight and I am sorry for it, and on the basis of the Redemption I become the opposite.

  -Oswald Chambers
  (CWC, pg. 83)

What Are You Searching For?

What is man seeking? He is seeking perfection in himself, utopia in this world, and an eternal existence that centers around his idea of happiness and well-being outside of acknowledging his need and intervention of his Creator. The problem with man's search is that in his attempt to rationalize, socialize, and adjust his existence to such things as science, he has created a greater spiritual vacuum.

In his book, *Game of Gods,* Carl Teichrib identifies the problem biblically. As he points out, the human condition is not due to biological or cognitive or technical limitations, but *positional* separation from the One who created us.

Teichrib goes on to point out that *rational severance* occurred when Mankind chose to pursue aggrandizement, to be anything other than Man. It was an act opposed to the position God had ordained, to be His representatives or image bearers on Earth. He goes on to say, "*Positional perfectibility* remains out of our hands; because of our sinful nature we are incapable of fixing this dire situation on our own. In fact, that is the point. Yet we long for perfectibility, a return to our previously unfallen state but without recourse to God's exclusive mandate - *salvation through Jesus Christ alone.*" (pgs. 450-451)

Man's search for paradise in this world is going to prove as useless as his attempts to reach perfection according to his wisdom, knowledge, and personal strength by establishing any valid merits, or reforming himself. He must recognize that saving himself is beyond any of his abilities, and it is clear he is miserably lost in a state that is void of any real satisfaction, contentment, and hope.

As pointed out there is only one way to be saved and there is only one act that will allow it to happen and that is "repentance" turning from all futile attempts of creating our own "Paradise" and facing the true Savior who ensures a lasting Garden of Eden in His presence.

- We are in the end days when accepting sin is normal and preaching holiness is heretical.

  -FB

- A repentance that does not produce a change in conduct is a sham.

  -E. M. Bounds

- If we could all see into hell for just one second…Every altar in every church would be flooded with repentance today.

  -FB

- Where repentance is genuine, the disposition to repeat sin is gone.

  -Charles Finney

- Repentance doesn't mean anything if you don't stop what you are sorry for.

  -FB

- It is not an affair,
  > It is adultery.
  It is not casual sex,
  > It is fornication.
  It is not gay love,
  > It is Sodomy.
  It is not veneration,
  > It is idolatry.
  It is not pro-choice,
  > It is murder.
  It is not exaggeration,
  > It is lying.
  It is not concern,
  > It is gossip.
  It is not admiration,
  > It is lust.
  Don't neutralize your sin.
  Repent of it and get right with God.

  -FB

- The only repentant man is the holy man, i.e., the one who becomes the opposite of what he was because something has entered into him.

  -Oswald Chambers
  (CWC, pg. 83)

27

The Epitome of Foolishness
in Action

If you could describe the source of foolishness besides it being bound in an unregenerate heart, these sources would include the absence of any thought of paying consequences for wrong decisions, wicked ways, unlawful practices, and foolish attitudes. We are clearly living in lawless times.

We watch leadership at every level including the justice systems be complicit towards what is right, true, and just. In fact, the victims are left traumatized, the righteous are mocked and persecuted, society as a whole will be left with the damming effects of ruin, and the home will be left in shambles, destroyed by spiritual neglect, moral corruption, and decaying decadence.

How can a society survive such foolishness? It can't, and eventually it will collapse on itself. How can society ignore such foolishness? For the most part it hides behind the lie of tolerance and love. It tolerates moral corruption and in the name of love placates lawlessness. However, if there are no consequences to pay for such destructive ways, there is no healthy fear that refrains a person from being foolish, selfish, and wretched. The lawless will see no need to do anything right because evil has a way of benefitting the foolish for a season. Eventually, however, it will require the necessary wages of one's soul.

Mercy without repentance encourages sin. Each person, regardless of the state they are clinging to, needs Jesus to save them from their base selves, wrong spirits, foul attitudes, foolish thinking, wicked ways, and evil plans. They need to see that the way they are on is the means of committing spiritual suicide and they need to turn from it and face the light of Jesus in order to repent of their sins along with its deadly ways and be saved.

We need to keep in mind foolishness excuses away such repentance, the flesh hides from it, pride mocks it, the unbelieving run from it, and the religious downplay it. However, Jesus is clear, "REPENT (sinner) OR PERISH (a fool)." (Parentheses are mine.)

* * *

- Without genuine repentance there can be no genuine conversion.

    -FB

- When we water down the meaning of sin, we water down the sacrifice which paid for it.

    -Repentance Cry.com

- If your Christianity does not include turning from sin and living obedient to the Word, then your Christianity is false.

    -FB

- Repentance to be true must issue in holiness, or it is not New Testament repentance. Repentance means not only sorrow and distress for the wrong done, but the acceptance of the Atonement of Jesus which will make me what I have never been—holy.

    -Oswald Chambers
    (CWC, pg. 225)

- Repentance is a complete 180-degree turn. It never intends to look back because everything behind already has been judged. Another way of putting it is "Don't waste time looking back, there is nothing there and you are not going that way again."

    -RJK

- If a man preaches grace without repentance, he succeeds only in causing many to march towards hell with complete peace.

-FB

The Assurance of Heaven

The Gospel of Jesus Christ comes with much assurance. This assurance is confirmed by the power that is behind the message of the Gospel. This power is the Holy Spirit working on the hearts and minds of those who have been made receptive to the message.

As mature Christians we possess this assurance because we have had an ongoing revelation of this message. We know the Gospel is that Jesus died for our sins, was buried, and three days later rose from the grave. We can say this over and over, but the power behind this revelation possesses a revelation of God's character and redemption.

This revelation is ongoing. For example, as we come to terms with the depth of our sin, we will gain a greater revelation of His holiness. When we consider and grow in the reality of His death, we will gain a greater insight into His redemption. This redemption includes such issues as life, forgiveness, ownership, and service.

When it comes to His resurrection, we will gain a greater revelation of Jesus' deity, His priesthood, His power, and the victory wrought upon the cross. Resurrection also gives us insight into our hope or expectancy in the future. Obviously, His death dealt with our past sins, His burial puts our old way of living into perspective, and His resurrection points to our future hope.

Our life in Christ is complete, but we must walk it out by faith. We must become identified with it in utter abandonment to the old, through repentance, as well as be prepared to embrace the new at all times.

- Jesus didn't eat with sinners and tax collectors because He wanted to appear inclusive, tolerant and accepting. He ate with them to call them to repentance.

  -FB

- Anyone trying to steer you away from the foot of the cross, from the blood of Jesus, from repentance, regeneration, sanctification, and being born again isn't looking out for your best interest; they are looking out for theirs.

  -Michael Boldea Jr.
  (EJ, pg. 42)

- Man has substituted tolerance for longsuffering. God does not show tolerance towards sin; rather, He is longsuffering towards the sinner in order to give him the opportunity to repent of his sin.

  -RK

- True repentance hates sin. False repentance hates the consequences of sin.

  -FB

False Repentance

Satan counterfeits what is real to give a person a false sense of their spiritual state. There are many false gospels, false Christs, false lights, false humilities, and false repentances. These false presentations serve as rungs on a ladder. They appear to lead people up into the clouds as a means to reach heaven, when in reality the ladder leads to dead air.

We know there is only one ladder that stands sure, tall, and truly leads back to God. Jacob encountered that ladder at Bethel in Genesis 28:11-22. At the top of it was Jehovah and the unveiling of it brought dread to him because there was only one such ladder that stood between heaven and earth, and Holiness Personified stood at the top of it.

Jesus made reference to that ladder when He spoke to Nathaniel in John 1:40-51. Apparently, Nathaniel (also known as Bartholomew), was pondering the incident of Jacob at that time when Jesus saw him under the tree and His statement implied that He knew what Nathaniel was pondering, "And he saith unto him, Verily, verily, I say unto you, Hereafter ye shall see heaven open, and the angels of God ascending and descending upon the Son of Man." Jesus was making it clear that the ladder Jacob saw pointed to Him being that ladder where all answered prayers and promises would ascend and descend because of Him.

In today's religious attempts man has substituted the Gospel of Christ with many false lights that delude men as to the fact the ladder they are climbing leads to nowhere but destruction. As these deluded souls reach the heights of these ladders, there is nowhere to go but down. In most cases they will fall with their ladder since there is no truth to hold them firmly to their false philosophies, heresies, and volumes of deceptions, or they will fall when they get to the top and find nowhere to go but down.

These counterfeits mirror the trends of our society which is spiraling downward. False gospels simply reveal the political and liberal trends taking place. They walk side by side with the predominate worldly secular culture that wants to always be fashionable in order to be in the current of acceptance, influence, and importance.

It is clear that the latest false "everything" comes through corrupt worldly ways: culture (tolerance), philosophies (New Age), education (Communism), entertainment (liberalism and the occult), politics (Progressive Socialism), religion (humanism) and even on the shirttails of so-called "justice" that is a mockery of true justice or one that is going awry. This "justice" is known as "social justice."

Let me say that anything that has the word "social" attached to it, no matter how good or decent it sounds, is contrary to the true Gospel and work of God in the midst of humanity. There is nothing social about the move of God. He moves on individual hearts and He saves individuals: one person at a time. To try to make man's plight a "social" problem is to ignore or do away with the sin that plagues each individual. It overlooks the heart of the matter and makes it about surface issues that may express attitudes. In the end, it proves to be an empty way that creates greater prejudices and spiritual vacuums so man can become even more lost in the lies of Satan and caught up with the destructive waves of delusion that are rushing towards the shores of judgment.

It is important to realize that all of these false ways lead down the same path of destruction to the same source, the god of this world, Satan, who is the father of lies and a murderer. Each way is based on a lie or false promise. It even mixes a bit of religion or works to make it look honorable, but behind it all are sinister agendas, wicked practices, and evildoers that play on the ignorance, social psychic, and foolish ways of man.

In the introduction to Jon Harris' book, *Christianity And Social Justice,* Russell Fuller summarizes "social justice." It started from the French Revolution and is in all actuality socialism. The gospel it proclaims is the "Woke Gospel," which is not an add-on gospel but a replacement of the true Gospel. Within Social Justice you will find Marxism with a heavy dose of radical racist (that includes Black Lives Matter movement), feminist, homosexual theories, and postmodernism.

Marxism has created a new secular religion and it has worked itself into the church as Liberation Theology beginning a generation ago and presently it advocates the Woke Gospel. Needless to say, the Woke faith is contrary to Scripture, but how many Christians have enough Scriptural foundation to even recognize it?

This new gospel is a confusing mixture of the law and gospel. It has taken Jesus' teaching and ministry, and intertwined it with the perverted presentation of "social justice" to justify the terrible fruits of prejudice, hatred, oppression, and slavery of "the elite, white race" to exalt the "oppressed" minorities into the same place of tyranny because of the slavery and oppression of the past.

This insanity is being promoted through Critical Race Theory that is so outlandish there are no words to describe it. And, the words to describe those who advocate it are "deluded pawns and fools" who are indeed entangled in Satan's web of destruction. Voddie Baucham, who is a popular critic against this blatant heresy that is swallowing many in its deception, refers to it as "Ethnic Gnosticism" because it promotes, "the idea that people have special knowledge based solely on their ethnicity." (CSJ, pg. 69)

This is where the false repentance comes in. If you are "white" in order to show you are repenting for being white, regardless of the fact you didn't have anything to do with the actions of others of your race, gender, and status, you must bow before the altars of Baal, and ask forgiveness for being part of the "privileged," and for what the generations did before you. This is not only contrary to true justice, which makes it clear that a man answers for his own actions and not the actions of others, but to what Ezekiel 18:19-32 establishes.

You must become part of the "collective salvation" a lie of Socialism, by being willing to give up all you have worked for, even though you have been slaves of the wicked systems that have robbed you through taxes, but now you must become absolutely poor. Your state of poverty is necessary so those who have bought the lie of this age, or those who are wicked opportunists who now see a way to steal more, can put their foot on your neck and feel justified in their wickedness as they show you that they are just as hateful tyrants as they accused you of being. However, they are justified in their hypocrisy and wickedness now that the balances

34

have changed in their favor. They are not interested in addressing attitudes but in putting down the "injustice" of the past in order to justify the "injustice" taking place in the present.

How far have we as Americans fallen as a society? Jon Harris in his book about social justice made this statement, "Achieving social justice has gone from the redistribution of income to the redistribution of privilege, from the liberation of the lower classes to the liberation of culturally constructed identities, from lamenting victimhood to promoting victimhood, and from changing society through politics to changing politics through society." (CSJ, pg. 19)

Regardless of race or social standing, the poor, the oppressed from all cultures and races have always been among us. Man has been willing to merchandise souls by selling mankind as slaves since practically the beginning of time. The blacks sold the blacks, the whites the white, with each eventually selling the other, while the higher class in every society finds the means to make slaves of those in the lower class. Man has justified robbing, raping, and pillaging others because of culture, race, religious preference, and social status, but to our Holy God it is all wickedness, an abomination that He loathes, and one day He will judge it with His wrath, especially those who have mishandled His Word to justify such wickedness (Romans 1:18).

The wickedness and oppression found among mankind has never been a social issue but a sin problem. However, man puts it in the social arena so he can somehow save the oppressed, enlighten the ignorant, show his "goodness" to the poor, rule the masses, and prove his way is the honorable and right way regardless of the causalities and the types of fruit that are left behind. The truth is the pride of man wants to rule, exalt self to be an exception to the rule to avoid consequences, desire to be believed, followed, and worshipped to ensure he is the god of his kingdom. This is humanism.

As believers we must never agree with the spirit of this world by coming into agreement with the godless philosophies, practices, trends, and ways of it. We must come out and be separate from it if we are going to be the light of the world and the salt of the earth.

We must not buy the lies of this world. We must choose to love the truth so it can set us free from the subtle traps of lies, and keep us free from the seductive delusions that are now running amuck. We must keep in mind there is only one ladder between heaven and earth and that is Jesus Christ and Him crucified. As deity He stands as ruler over all, and as man who ascended by way of a cross, He provides the only rungs in which man can be assured of salvation.

It is because Jesus is the only ladder, we must turn from our wicked ways in repentance, bow before the altar of His cross, look up into His glorious light and confess our personal sins in order to be reconciled back into a relationship with God. It is this reconciliation that will close all chasms and provide the rungs of love, grace, mercy, and forgiveness in which we can ascend upward into the glorious promises of God. And, one day like Enoch of old, we will no longer be; rather, we will be in our Lord's presence seeing Him in His glory for who He is.

(If you would like to know more about Social Justice, you can obtain Jon Harris' book, *Christianity and Social Justice, Religions In Conflict.*)

God's Attributes and Ways

The Applause of Heaven

It is easy to take pride in what we know, but there is a story about the British actor, Richard Burton, that reveals that knowledge is often just surface. During one of his hometown visits, Burton attended the parish of his youth. Even the pastor who had greatly influenced his life was in attendance. After some fanfare was directed at the actor, the old pastor asked Burton if he would quote the 23rd Psalm, something that the famous actor memorized while under the pastor's watchful care.

Burton agreed upon one condition, and that was after he quoted the infamous psalm that the pastor would follow up with his rendition of it. With his famous voice and all the right tones and fluctuations, Burton exquisitely cited the psalm, holding the congregation spellbound, meeting with great applause after he was finished.

Next came the old pastor. How could this old man outdo the famous actor? However, it was not a matter of competition for the pastor. No doubt his emphasis of this psalm that was a requirement of all of his students through the years to memorize was because he had believed and lived this psalm all of his life. The pastor, who at the time was in a wheelchair, stood up and with a feeble voice quoted the psalm.

When he was done, he did not receive the applause of this world, but the type of applause that heaven embraces when hearts are touched; there was not a dry eye in the place. That is when the actor rose and his voice quivered as he said, "Ladies and gentlemen, I reached your eyes and ears, but my old pastor has reached your hearts. The difference is just this: I know the Psalm, but he knows the Shepherd."

The Bible is clear we can know God who is the great shepherd. Sadly, many people know of God, know about God, but few know Him. They see Him through doctrinal boxes, fleshly intellectual understanding, worldly philosophies, and sentimental notions and assume they know Him when in reality, they have erected their own ideas or images of Him, but they do not know Him for who He is.

The world will receive applause for its ability to reach the mind with great orators and performances, the wisdom of the world will cause one to pause and become spellbound because it makes sense out of what seems senseless, and the philosophies of the world will gain notoriety based on how popular they become. However, there is only one way to reach the tender, pure heart and the courts of heaven that results in the applause of heaven that comes in the form of tears, and that is when one in humility delivers what heaven has inspired with a worshipful attitude because the person personally knows God.

+————————•◄═══►•————————+

- If the love of God does not master us, the love of the world will.

  -FB

- Pentecost has made God spiritual to us. Jesus Christ was God Incarnate; Pentecost is God come in the Spirit. The essential nature of God the Father, of God the Son and of God the Spirit is the same.

-Oswald Chambers
(CWC, pg. 124)

- We often speak of and hide behind God's love but this important point was brought out by Lillian Harvey in her book, *They Knew Their God*, "Love cannot be so intense in its nature, however, without manifesting an equally intense hatred for evil; for the one, by its very nature, produces the other" (pg. 54). God hates sin for what it does to us and our relationship with Him, He is angry at those who insist on wickedness and in the end His wrath will fall on those who walk in the ways of unrighteousness.

- At Bethlehem, He (Jesus) became God with us. At Calvary He became God for us. At Pentecost, He became God in us.

-Unknown

- There are perverse people with perverse minds, speaking perverse things in the name of God, and it's your duty to know God and His Word well enough to know when what someone is saying isn't something God would have ever said! When that occurs, it is likewise your duty to contend for the faith, defend the truth, and stand on the Gospel.

-Michael Boldea Jr.
(EJ, pg. 11)

- Never put a question mark where God has put a period.

-FB

- Give God His glory by resting in Him, by trusting Him fully, by waiting patiently for Him. This patience honors Him greatly. It

39

leaves Him, as God on the throne, to do His work. It yields self wholly unto His hands. It lets God be God.

-Andrew Murray

- We have to find out God's methods, not try to get God to approve our methods.

-Oswald Chambers
(CWC, pg. 430)

- God's glory! It is a wondrous thing to consider God's majesty in light of His attributes, ways, and works. We want to wait in His presence, rest in His goodness, marvel at His great works, and stand on His promises, but each new discovery causes us to realize how little we know or even can comprehend about the One who is eternal, the One who is all-knowing, ever-present, and unchangeable.

-RJK

Prayer: Lord, I am so thankful that my times are in Your hands. You are trustworthy in Your ways, pure in Your intentions, righteous in Your works, and powerful in Your actions. I humble myself before Your blessed ways, as I choose to trust You with each moment of my life. Amen.

- God doesn't give us what we can handle; God helps us handle what we are given.

-FB

- God is not going to negotiate His holiness in order to accommodate us.

-R.C. Sproul

- God's kingdom, power, and glory are eternal. There is no end to His kingdom, no limit to His power, and no boundaries to His glory. We can bank on His kingdom, experience His power, and reflect His glory. This combination is meant to establish, enlarge, and exalt us to realize our life in heavenly places with Jesus. This place in Christ allows us to enjoy an inheritance, partake of the eternal, and walk by faith towards a God who never changes.

  -RJK

- I'm going to give the devil my best years and give God the last few months before the dementia really ramps up, and voila, I get to name and claim my mansion in the sky. It's the mindset far too many have today, and it is off putting to God.

  -Michael Boldea Jr.
  (EJ, pg. 16)

- Only God can turn a **Mess** into a **Message**,
  A **Test** into a **Testimony**,
  A **Trial** into a **Triumph**,
  A **Victim** into a **Victory**,
  God is Good—all the time.

  -FB

- This day, my God, I hate sin, not because it damns me, but because it has done Thee wrong. To have grieved my God is the worst grief to me.

  -Charles Spurgeon

- Thou (God) wouldest not have me accept Thy will because I *must* but because I *may*. Thou wouldest have me take it, not with

41

resignation, but with joy, not with the absence of murmur, but with the song of praise.

-George Matheson
(VS, pg. 54)

- In order to accept and submit to God's will, one must accept His sovereignty.

-RJK

- Yes, if Christianity is true, it is clearly not a theory. It is a love affair with life and its author. It is reality.

-Mary Poplin
(GG, pg. 539)

- Surely an all-wise loving God would not tantalize us with a glimpse of beauty, a hint of perfection, and then deny us the substance the harbinger makes us yearn for. Death then is emancipation, fulfillment; the beginning of the next stage in God's plan.

Howard E. Kershner
(DPS, pgs. 132-133)

- God measures everything by one rule; He looks at everything by one standard; He tries everything by one touchstone. That rule, that standard, that touchstone is Christ.

-J. Gregory Mantle
(COS, pg. 112)

- There's NO way you heard God say to: Promote such things as car, house, and various increases, BUT didn't hear obedience, humility and holiness.

-FB

Prayer: Lord, You are my all in all. You are my God who oversees every aspect of my life. You are the King who rules my life. You are the Lord who owns me. You are my place of safety that I hide in. You are my Defense that I run behind, my Rock I stand upon, my Hope that I cling to, and My Judge who will ensure justice when all is said and done. Thank You for being everything I need and ever will need in this present life and the next to come. Amen.

- The remarkable thing about fearing God is that when you fear God, you fear nothing else, whereas if you do not fear God, you fear everything else.

-Oswald Chambers

- **Trust** in His timing.
  Rely on His promises.
  Wait for His answers.
  Believe in His miracles.
  Rejoice in His goodness.
  Relax in His presence.

-Daily Walk

- God will never explain Himself; rather, He will reveal Himself. Man's logic demands explanation that will satisfy it to silence its cruel judgments. On the other hand, godly reasoning will satisfy the inner man with revelation that brings understanding and agreement in the spirit, and will cause the restless soul by faith to land on the Rock of ages.

-RJK

A Shallow Christianity

What does it mean for me to be **in** Christ and Christ to be **in** me. The word "**in**" in this concept points to Christ being all inclusive as far as

His life in us and our position in Him as believers. It is summarized in Christ as all in all. There is nothing of value that can be added to the fact that I am in Him and because of it I will be partaker of an eternal inheritance. And, since Christ is in me, I possess His life that is everlasting, powerful, and enduring.

Sadly, many Christians do not have any real revelation of this concept and as a result they fail to discover who Christ must be to them and who they are in Christ. Dr. Alexander MacLaren dealt with this subject.

MacLaren stated, "This thought, Christ in us and we in Christ—two sides of one truth—is far too little present to the consciousness and to the experience, to the doctrinal belief, and to the personal verification of that belief in the lives of the mass of Christian people. To me it is the very heart of Christianity, for which Christ for us is the preface and introduction. You may call it mysticism if you like. There is no grasp of the deepest things in religion without that which the irreligious mind thinks it has disposed of by the cheap and easy sneer that it is mystical.

"*Your Christianity will be a shallow one* unless the truths which these two great complementary thoughts—Christ in me and I in Christ—be truths verified in your experience. I am afraid that Christian people in this generation have a very imperfect belief in the actual, supernatural, and, if you like to call it so, miraculous manifestation of Jesus Christ, His very Self, to men that love and cleave to Him." (COS, pgs. 166-167)

It is clear that the revelation of the completeness of Christ in us and us in Him can only be embraced with child-like faith that does not seek understanding, but simply trusts the revelation of it. In doing so, the believer ends up walking in light of it with such sweet confidence that all is indeed well with their soul.

- If Reality is not to be found in God, then God is not found anywhere. If God is only a creed or a statement of religious belief, then He is not real.

  -Oswald Chambers
  (CWC, pg. 57)

- GOD'S LOVE IS ENOUGH...

  When I fall...He catches me.

  When I am sad...He holds me.

  When I cry...He wipes my tears,

  When I am broken...He puts me back together.

  Thank you, GOD, for always loving me.

  -FB

- God must not only be the source of our confidence, but the one we must always seek in order to discover our direction and purpose. After all, it is easy to leave God behind when we are trusting in our own strength. In such times, our ears are closed due to prideful presumptions, our eyes are clouded by arrogant assumptions, and our discernment is being drowned out by personal confidence.

  -RJK

- The Apostle Paul...rejected the Greek ideas and presented to them Jesus Christ, crucified, the Messiah. He taught that Jesus Christ is the fulfillment of the ancient Hebrew doctrine of eternal wisdom out of which came all things, and that His work is more than jewels and silver.

  -A. W. Tozer
  (WOG, pgs. 21-22)

- God always has something for you, a key for every problem, a light for every shadow, a relief for every sorrow, and a plan for every tomorrow.

-FB

God's Perspective

Isaiah 66:1 brings out God's perspective about heaven, the earth, and man. We are told that earth is God's footstool. Such a thought proves to be incredible. How big God must be for the earth to simply serve as His footstool upon which He can rest His feet. The other amazing consideration is that heaven is His throne, and a believer serves as His temple or dwelling place.

His throne is related to His sovereignty as God, His footstool to His kingship, and His temple to the presence of His Spirit. God's majesty Is brought out even more when we consider how He chose earth (His footstool) in the vastness of the universe to put man (His temple) in a perfect environment in the Garden of Eden.

- Many people say, "Try Jesus;" you don't "try Jesus." He's not there to be experimented with. Christ is not on trial, you are.

-A. W. Tozer

- If GOD is your treasure, He will be your pleasure.

-FB

- As believers, we must remember the Lord is our Rock. He not only serves as our foundation, but he stands before us as our fortress, to the side of us as our companion, behind us as our protector, and in front of us as our guide. In essence, we are covered from every direction by Him.

-RJK

Prayer: Lord, You are God and it is because You are a loving, just God, I can trust You with all matters. You are Almighty and I can rest in You, and it is because You are sovereign, I can be still before You, knowing that You are in control, and You will bring about Your perfect will and righteous plan for my life according to Your timing. Amen.

- God's strength is used for one means: to carry out His eternal plan in regard to His creation and man's salvation. We see His strength restrained in mercy, channeled in grace, disciplined in sanctification, powerful in miracles, and mighty in wrath.

  -RJK

- Holiness has never been a driving force of the majority. It is however, mandatory for anyone who wants to enter the kingdom.

  -Elisabeth Elliot

- There is no greater darkness than ignorance of God.

  -FB

- Can you know the width of God's grace, the depth of His incredible love, the length His promises will reach or how high His excellent ways are? No, we can't because every aspect of God is eternal and ongoing—there is no beginning and no end to any of His virtues.

  -RJK

- In light of the cross, THE GREATEST insult you can give God is TO DOUBT His love for you.

  -J.C. Ryle

- God invites us to partake of the tree of life by inviting us to follow Jesus to that life. Granted, the tree begins with a dead tree, the cross, but what has been lifted up on the cross (Jesus) possesses life. The more we walk in the righteous ways of God, as we become identified to the tree (work of redemption) in order to partake of its life (Christ), the more goodness will be imparted into us and then in turn emitted from our lives.

  -RJK

- When you talk with God, no breath is lost. When you walk with God, no strength is lost. When you wait on God, no time is wasted. When you trust in God you gain all.

  -FB

- God is beyond description. Our imagination could not comprehend His majesty. Our mind could not contain His wisdom. Our soul could not be enlarged enough to sense the majesty of His greatness. Everything about God is beyond our fleshly understanding. As a result, we need to stand in awe of who He is.

  -RJK

Prayer: Lord, You are beyond comprehension. I stand in awe of You as I learn to be still in communion with You, while I offer sacrifices counted as righteous in faith towards You because of Your greatness. Amen.

- **JESUS:** His peace is greater than trouble.
  His love is greater than hate.
  His shelter is greater than the storm.
  His hope is greater than uncertainty.

  -FB

- God's love is beyond comprehension. We will be spending a lifetime exploring it, discovering it through the ages to come, and experiencing it in its fullness for all eternity. The purpose and desire for this love is that ultimately, we will be filled with all the fullness of God, for God is love.

  -RJK

- There is His sovereignty, having all power. There is His omnipotence, overseeing all things. There is His omniscience, all understanding. There is His all-knowledge, His Holiness. It is the breath of the power of God and a pure influence flowing from the glory of the Almighty.

  -A. W. Tozer
  (WOG, pg. 24)

- We are reminded that our surety in Christ's redemption rests on three of His attributes: His unchangeable ways and character, His power to bring a matter about, and His faithfulness to see it through. There are so many attributes of our Lord that we rejoice in such as His mercy, grace, and longsuffering. But we stand sure on His unchangeable character, we withstand in His power, and we continue to stand because of His faithfulness.

  -RJK

- Satan is a master theologian. He talks to God, interacts with God, believes in God's existence and knows more about God's attributes and abilities than most...and yet Satan doesn't love God. Knowledge about God doesn't equal faith in God.

  -FB

- When Jesus rose from the grave, He told Mary not to touch Him for He had not yet ascended to the Father. The main treasure we must handle properly was covered in the darkness of the grave and raised in newness of life. Jesus now sits on the right hand of the Father, and because of the access made available to each of us we can touch Him in sincerity, embrace Him in humility, and become identified with Him in glory.

-RJK

- There are no ifs in God's world, and no places that are safer than other places. The center of His will is our safety.

-Corrie Ten Boom

- God is the God of the humble, the miserable, the afflicted, the oppressed, the desperate, and of those who have been brought down to nothing at all.

-Martin Luther

- Sometimes our plans need to fall apart for His to truly unfold.

-FB

- God is holy. His holiness is consuming to the ordinary. It can appear to be an overpowering and frightening darkness to the profane. It can come across as a pillar to those seeking His strength, a cloud to those who desire to follow Him, and a fire to those He is protecting.

-RJK

Prayer: Lord, being human can prove to be comical, being wrong is humbling, being realistic is sobering, but when it comes to sin, it is a deadly, serious matter of life and death. Lord, give me the right attitude towards the matters that will count for eternity. Amen.

- When I am alone, God is my comforter. When I am weak, God is my strength. When I am nothing, God is my everything.

-FB

This Is Our God

Faithful in all His ways,
Committed to His saints,
Perfect in all of His doings,
To bring forth uprightness in His church,
Longsuffering in His endeavors with men,
To bring them to repentance,
Quick to be merciful,
To pull back judgment,
Ready to open the gates of grace,
To save those who are heirs,
Willing to hear the cries of the outcast,
Swooping them up on eagle's wings,
To lift them to great heights of deliverance.
This is our God, this is His way,
This is the legacy He passes to each generation.

-RJK

God's Word

How Do You Handle God's Word?

"But unto the wicked God saith, What hast thou to do to declare my statutes, or that thou shouldest take my covenant in thy mouth? Seeing thou hatest instruction, and castest my words behind thee" (Psalm 50:16-17). When we think of the wicked, we sometimes think of the worst individual we have encountered. However, the wicked can prove to come in various forms, from those who wear religious cloaks to the ones who wear a veneer of decency.

To summarize in one word, a wicked person is simple enough. He or she is an utter fool. These individuals can use the right terminology, but they hate instruction that would expose their heart attitude towards life and God. They can come across as declaring the ways of God, but behind closed doors they cast such ways aside in disdain and mockery, revealing the utter hypocrisy of their religious pose.

The true test of character is how a person handles the Word of God. If God's Word is honored, adhered to, and obeyed, such an individual will be counted for righteousness, but the person who casts aside God's words must be considered wicked. For me, I not only want to honor His words, but tremble before them.

Prayer: Lord, it is easy to discern the imposter. It all comes down to how Your Word is handled. Lord, give me the discernment to see around the cloaks and through the veneers so that I can righteously judge the spirit of a person. Amen.

- Changes in culture and education do not change God's Word.
  -Marvin Rosenthal
  Zion's Fire
  July/August 2022

- The Bible is NOT about you or how to achieve your best life now. It's about Jesus and what He did to save sinners.
  -Jordan Riley Ministries

- Read the Bible to be **wise**.
  Believe the Bible to be **safe**.
  Practice the Bible to be **holy**.

  -FB

- There is no such thing as new truth; error might be old or new, but truth is as old as the universe.
  -Frederick Douglass

- If spiritual truths do not take root in everyday living, they never become reality in our lives.
  -RJK

- Truth is meant to wound.

  -Paul Washer

- Hating the messenger because you hate the message has become another one to those accepted practices of late that was rarely ever done in the past... That is the new standard of tolerance even among those who call themselves believers.

  -Michael Boldea Jr.
  (EJ, pg. 7)

- Conformity is doing what everyone else is doing regardless of what is right. Biblical obedience is doing what is right regardless of what everyone else is doing.

  -FB

- The Bible is the only Book that throws light on our physical condition, on our soul condition, and on our spiritual condition.

  -Oswald Chambers
  (CWC, pg. 153)

- The Word of God is the greatest gold mine that the world possesses, but it has been the most overlooked and neglected.

  -RJK

- No man has the authority to divide the truth and preach only a part of it. To do so is to weaken it and render it without effect.

  -A. W. Tozer

- If the Bible doesn't impact our behavior, then we're either NOT reading it or we don't believe what it says.

  -Jordan Riley Ministries

- Good intentions do not finish the race. Obedience to God and perseverance finishes the race.

  -FB

- Real love tells the truth, but if people don't want the truth, they will mistake love for hate.

  -A.J. Johnson

- The Bible is no longer the final arbiter in any spiritual argument; it's how some individual or other interpreted what the Bible says and what biases they use.

  -Michael Boldea Jr.
  (EJ, pg. 7)

- Keep in mind you can't take hold of promises if you are clinging to the fragile limb of theology.

  -RJK

- We must quit bending the Word to suit our situation. It is we who must be bent to that Word, our necks that must bow under the yoke.

  -Elisabeth Elliot

- Morals have changed. Churches have changed. Societies have changed. People have changed. But God's Word remains the same.

  -FB

- Alas, often applications are made which can scarcely be called interpretations! All the Bible is *for* us, but it is not all *about* us…Interpretation is *dispensational* and *prophetic.* Application is *moral* and *practical.*

-Herbert Lockyer
(APB, pg. 21)

Nothing New Under The Sun

I was saved out of a cult that spoke of God, prayed in the name of Jesus, and encouraged strong families, pious living, and promoted a light that appeared attractive, but what was behind it was an anti-Christ spirit. Once the real light of Jesus caused the false light to dissipate, one is faced with the darkness of deception that is over the souls of people who have come under the seductive covering of a cult or this present world.

When I became a believer, I wanted to make sure I was never deceived again by a false light. However, I began to realize that the world is wrapped up in so many lies that if one does not choose to love the truth and cry out to God for discernment and protection, they can be taken with the great delusion that is sweeping many into a quasi-religious environment that will end in judgement and destruction.

We clearly live in perilous times. I am not just talking about the wickedness of the world; but the condition of what we know as the visible church. We can't be casual about believing and possessing the right God, lazy about rightly dividing His Word, complacent about establishing the ways of righteousness in our lives, and just getting by in our spiritual walk if we are going to survive the times that we live in.

The reality is the truth of Jesus, His redemption, and His promises have been under attack since His miraculous conception. Whether it was Satan, the world with its cohorts and ways, man-made religion with its dead-letter oppression, and etc., Christianity has been targeted by subtle lies, repackaged heresies, worldly anti-God philosophies, and waves of persecution.

When I first became a Christian, I learned about **Gnostism** where a few elites will be saved by spiritual enlightenment while the rest are left in darkness. It separated the body from the soul, stating that since you sin in your body, the soul has no part in its wickedness. Part of the gnostic belief includes **Docetism**, which includes the belief that Jesus was not fully human, but only appeared to be human.

The Apostle John dealt with this heresy in his first epistle. This heresy is not gone, and it is once again being resurrected and is becoming a popular tide that those who seek "greater knowledge" are being taken into the waters of judgment.

I learned each generation had their own struggles with heresy. For example, during Charles Finney's time, he had to contend with **Universalism**; for Spurgeon, it was **Higher Criticism**, and for Smith Wigglesworth it was **Christian Science**. The lies have been repackaged to present a more subtle lie according to the digression of societies. Each generation has been conditioned by the last assault against truth to accept a more subtle form of each lie or to embrace a more blatant lie.

I heard about Universalism early in my Christian walk where everyone will be saved, but it has now turned into **Universal Reconciliation** where everyone will be reconciled back to God. The way to life is narrow and does not embrace the concept of masses being saved. Only one person can enter through the narrow gate at a time. The Bible is clear that the masses may be invited and many are called to follow Jesus into a new life, but few will enter in. The idea of the masses being saved is another false gospel.

I was made aware of **critical thinking** that came down through the colleges, taking the absolutes out of God's Word. Today that critical thinking has been rendered into theories such as **critical race**

theory that is driving people into an insane reality that has no limit to its depths of destruction.

I was taught the core of the religion of **Humanism** in school. It is called "**evolution**." Man has evolved from a beast and was not formed in the image of God. To the humanist, there is no God. Man is his own god in control of his own destiny, but there is not much hope for mankind because only the fittest will survive in the end.

The philosophy of humanism was that the vulnerable should be sacrificed and will be because they have no means to fight off that which is stronger. Is it no wonder our children, unborn and born are being blatantly sacrificed, along with the push to euthanize the elderly and those who fall into the classification of being "useless" since they can't add anything of "value" to our society. Like before, the helpless are proving to be the greatest victims of our time.

With humanism came the big push of **psychology** being the solution to the conflicts of the soul and relationships. Sin was removed from the equation as self was esteemed instead of denied. The fault of deviation or iniquity was transposed on others or one's poor financial status or standing as a means to excuse it away.

I had a brush with **agnostics** who did not deny there was a God, but questioned everything about God and His Word. For almost a half of a century of being a Christian I have met my share of scoffers, ever ready to negate the authority of God's Word.

In Christianity, there are also many false lights and ways. I was introduced to **Positive Confession** where the right words can take God down to the mat where He will have to agree to bring a matter about according to the promise used on Him and not His perfect will and plan. This heresy was opposite of true faith and was a means of witchcraft to control God and a way to get around truly trusting God. The sad truth is that these different heretical teachings roll through Christendom without much opposition from those who had the loudest pulpits.

Each wave gained momentum, swallowing more and more of the soul of this country and silencing the authority of the Word and the testimony of the true Church. Each tidal wave of delusion has taken a greater number of people with it, while leaving a spiritual vacuum behind that has often been filled with greater lies.

The next inroad came from **Hinduism**, that of Eastern spirituality. It promoted many of the **New Age** practices that are found in the church: Yoga, contemplative prayer, mind science, mantras, the Christ within or Christ consciousness, reincarnation, vegetarianism, and planetary stewardship. The goal was to turn 5½ billion minds from a multitude of "cultural ignorance" to a unified mind. In order to do this, they realized they had to alter one's worldview about everything.

To bring everyone down to the same perverted page, they had to influence mediums that would condition people, education that would indoctrinate them, and social unrest through pitting people against each other by using race, religion, and financial status so that in the end each culture in chaos would be willing to give up all autonomy to have some type of peace. They had to gain footholds into the political arena to bring about social change by embracing such philosophies as **socialism**, **collective salvation,** and **climate change** which promoted redistribution of goods and greater oppression of the masses.

They had to redefine religious emphasis and practices by promoting different "gospels" such as the **social gospel** that would emphasize people sacrificing all they had for the good of mankind leaving everyone at the same level of poverty. This was clearly to stop God's people from declaring the great hope because of the sacrifice of Christ on behalf of mankind. In the end, all religions could meet at the altars of good deeds, spirituality, and mystical experiences in the name of unity while sacrificing any absolutes of truth and true religion as set forth in the Word of God.

This was to create, "**Oneness**" where everything shares in the same essence. It became about unity of collective divinity. Its message had not really changed as it declares, "nature is God, we are God, the energy of the universe is God."

Where has this brought us? We are now living in what is called the age of **Re-enchantment** which finds its springboard in the Age of Aquarius. This age has man doing everything to conjure up the spiritual, the supernatural, and the demonic. This however has led to the latest pursuit and that is **transhumanism**.

Man will be somewhat human, but will be labeled a machine because of chips and nano particles being implanted in him with such means as the mask, Covid 19 tests and "vaccinations", and the chem-trails. This transhuman will be controlled by the elite through such means as 5G satellites. They will be programed to do their bidding and if they fail to do so, they will be destroyed.

Meanwhile mankind is losing all distinction. Secular science has convinced him that he came from a beast, and that his sexual preference has to do with a gene. However, even science can't agree with or close the door to the latest insane trend: Now people can choose their gender and even if they want to be anything other than human such as a cat or dog, they can classify themselves as such.

The main key to the insanity and abomination of transhumanism is God will be programed out of man's conscience. As he becomes more machine, he loses his identity as a soul. This creation is Satan's creation to rid this world of any image of God, and a manifestation of man's ultimate defiance in this abominable recreation, that is nothing more than a mutation, will prove to be an utter failure in the end. However, it will prove to be the worst nightmare to mankind who has not even begun to wake up to its hellish implications.

As I see what is happening, I am becoming more aware of what Jesus stated in Matthew 24:22, "And except those days should be shortened, there should no flesh be saved: but for the elect's sake those days shall be shortened."

I know the meek will inherit the earth and that the saved will be spared from the wrath of God. However, what we are witnessing is not God's wrath, but the unveiling of the face of evil that is beyond description.

As believers we must stand by faith, withstand with truth, and continue to stand on His promises until His great deliverance comes. Meanwhile, let us not lose faith as we continue to look up with expectant hope, knowing HE IS COMING!

(If you would like to know more about the above subjects, Carl Teichrib wrote an exceptional book exposing all of its tenacles called, *GAME OF GODS.*)

+———•━━•——+

- Either we submit to the authority of Scripture, or we don't. Partial submission is total rebellion.

  -Michael Boldea Jr.
  (EJ, pg. 103)

- Beware of half-truths, you may wind up with the wrong half.

  -FB

- Missionary Jonathan Goforth took exception towards "higher criticism" and "modernism" being taught in the colleges. He deemed it "a lowering of standards of truth." Like those who stand for truth today, he was called "intolerant!" He made this statement, "Intolerant!" If you saw one undermining the foundation of a structure you, and others with you, had given the best of their lives to build, would it be intolerant to use every ounce of strength in combating the wrecker?" (TK, pg. 149).

- The New Testament is not written to prove that Jesus Christ was the Son of God, but written for those who believe He is. There are no problems in the New Testament.

  -Oswald Chambers
  (CWC, pg. 26)

- The Word of God cleanses, purges, and separates us. However, for it to do this we must believe it, apply it, and obey it. As you can see, it does a complete work. In its cleansing, it will separate us from the defiled. In its purging, it will prepare us for the life that we are called to. In its separation, His Word will distinguish us through identification to the One who is holy.

  -RJK

- Nobody ever outgrows Scripture. The book widens and deepens with our years.

  -Charles Spurgeon

- No dictator, government or ideology can stand against God's Word. When we obediently pay the price to proclaim it, God is faithful to bring forth eternal fruit through His Word.

  -Cole Richard
  President of The Voice of the Martyrs
  January 2024 (Magazine)

- Don't be comforted by the world's lies because you feel uncomfortable by the Bible's truth.

  -FB

- We will not believe more than we know, and we will not live higher than our beliefs. The many fronts of Christians' compromise in this generation can be directly traced to biblical illiteracy in the pews and the absence of biblical preaching and teaching in our homes and churches.

-Harbingers Daily
Genesis Series

- It begs the questions if we are unshakeable, if we cannot be deceived, if none can wander off the path into the open maw of the wolves, why are there so many warnings throughout the Bible about being vigilant and about how to identify those with nefarious intent?

-Michael Boldea Jr.
(EJ, pg. 10)

- Truth always becomes the greatest enemy of wickedness, while righteousness shakes the fragile worlds of those who advocate evil.

-RJK

- Everyone loves the promises of the Bible, but ignore the warnings. We have to meet the conditions in order to receive the promise.

-FB

- There is widespread ignorance of God's Word in the evangelical church. Even worse is the eagerness to follow the world in contemptuous disregard of what the Bible unmistakably teaches.

-Dave Hunt
The Berean Call, July 2023

- It is true that truth can be very shocking to our fragile realities, but it is the only virtue that will set us free to face what is shocking. Truth is a two-edged sword. The initial situation when the sword penetrates our reality will shock us, but the second swipe will reveal the hope of Jesus, bringing sanity and comfort back into our lives.

-RJK

- There is no such thing as new truth; error might be old or new, but truth is as old as the universe.

-Frederick Douglass

- The only thing that keeps me stable and settled in these days of uncertainty is the absolute dependability of God's Word.

-FB

- When a man's heart is right with God the mysterious utterances of the Bible are spirit and life to him. Spiritual truth is discernible only to a pure heart, not to a keen intellect. It is not a question of profundity of intellect, but of purity of heart.

-Oswald Chambers
(CWC, pg. 231)

- Think of the Bible as a gold testing kit. You take the nugget of shiny stuff and rub it up against the Bible. The Bible will tell you whether it's real or not, and if it's not real because the Bible told you it's not, then if you treasure that piece of rock that isn't real as though it were, that's on you.

-Michael Boldea Jr.
(EJ, pg. 20)

- The Word of God tells us that God seeks those who are seeking Him with their whole heart. In man's fallen state we know that he has no inclination to seek God. The reality is few of us seek FOR Him. Granted, we may seek knowledge ABOUT Him, we may seek some FORM OF RELIGION to connect with Him, and we may seek OUT THOSE who are considered experts in their religious field to answer our questions about God, but FEW seek Him.

-RJK

- Ignorance of the Bible is the root of all error. Knowledge of the Bible is the best antidote against modern heresies.

-J.C. Ryle

- The Word of God is always most precious to the man who most lives upon it.

-Charles Spurgeon

- There is a world of difference between knowing the Word of God and knowing the God of the Word.

-Leonard Ravenhill

- Many people are faithful to their own beliefs, but not to the truth.

-RJK

- The Bible is real. Just don't let a liar teach it to you.

-FB

- When we do not allow the entirety of Scripture to speak to us, guide us, and instruct us, our spiritual growth will be stunted at best and inexistent at worse. We remain in this same spiritual state in perpetuity because we refuse to be fed by the whole of God's word and only nibble on the bits we like.

-Michael Boldea Jr.
(EJ, pg. 22)

- A lie can catch a ride with anybody, but the truth will walk alone.

-FB

- The words of Jesus will eventually bring us to some very defining crossroads in our spiritual lives. We must choose how we are going to respond to them. Some of His words will comfort us, while some will feed our spirit. In some cases, His words will challenge us to think beyond the norm, but at other times, they will actually insult us. They will rip at the very fiber of our being. They will tear up the ground of our hearts and cause our understanding to become confused, uncertain, and fearful.

  -RJK

- Dust on your Bible could lead to dirt in your life.

  -FB

- Even so, we will bicker, question, and sow doubt, we will twist words and take phrases out of context; we will reinterpret the interpretations of long-dead men just to get a different outcome than what is clearly written within the pages of Scriptures.

  -Michael Boldea Jr.
  (EJ, pg. 34)

Mysticism

I have wrestled with what mysticism is. Some of the people whose Christian writings have inspired and challenged me have been labeled as being mystics. Hence enters the challenge to understand if the title is truly applicable to the authors in question. Admittedly, after reading some of their material, I have felt left behind as some of them have seemed to enter another dimension. Whether it is revelation that points to the author exploring greater heights or depths in God that were really too great to speak of as in the case of Paul's revelation of the third heaven, or actual mysticism where it becomes a spiritual experience that in the end proves to be unscriptural, disagreeable to the spirits of sound Christians, and lacking reason, logic, and common-sense must be properly discerned.

The problem is that mysticism operates in the realm of imagination where emotions are taken for a ride of euphoric proportions while affections are taken captive. In such a mental environment, even a lie becomes more real than truth and supersedes any scriptural challenge. Any time such a reality becomes more real than truth, it is because seduction is in operation. What people end up with is a good fable wrapped up in sentiment and foolish notions but will not stand when tested.

This brings us to what mysticism is. In the February 2023 issue of *The Berean Call,* "mysticism" is defined as the process of turning from the objective truth of God's Word to the subjective realm of the imagination, feelings, and emotions. The obscurity of biblical doctrine, and the theological concept of it is called **pantheism** or **panentheism** which believes God is everything, and God is in everything.

It is a process of taking the truth of God's Word and distorting it so badly that it becomes foolish when brought to the light or properly challenged. People who operate in mysticism profess to have a direct intercourse with the Spirit of God, but the fruit of it is doctrinal confusion that proves to be nothing more than a scheme to deceive humanity. In some cases, it is subtle, but in others it is outright blasphemy.

Muslims even have their form of mysticism. It is called **Sufism**. This is the belief and practice in which Muslims seek to find the truth of divine love and knowledge by way of a direct personal experience with Allah. Such a pursuit and practice will simply throw them into the throes of experimental and subjective beliefs and practices that opens them up to such manifestations as barking and howling. Does this behavior sound familiar? The Laughing Revival. The Muslims who practice Sufism reject the rules of Sharia and have no problem coexisting with other religions.

The real fruit that gives such mysticism away is arrogance. It will not be humbled, challenged, and tested. Behind it is a great fear that it may be proven wrong, which means the individual has bought a lie. Even Christians can sometimes take pride in the idea that they would never fall for any type of seduction, but that is where subtility comes in, and Jesus was clear that if it were possible even the elect would be deceived. As Scripture warns, when we think we are solidly standing because something looks, feels, or seems right to our way of thinking, we are probably close to falling flat on our faces in utter failure, despair, and destruction.

When I encounter the label of mysticism, I always look for evidence of humility and the willingness to be wrong. However, being wrong to a saint is not based on man's idea; rather the faithfulness of God to bring conviction of the Spirit and scriptural backing that the Spirit and truth is missing in a matter. True humility will always concede when such conviction is present and the matter brought to the light.

- The Word of God is clear that the way of the Christian life is hard. It is the way of the cross (death), the oven of afflictions (suffering), and the fiery tests of faith (preparation) in order to ensure depth, growth, and victory.

-RJK

- The Gospel is meant to change the sinner. Not for the sinner to change the Gospel to suit their sin.

-FB

- Rather than denying self, "Christian psychology," thinking it can improve God's infallible and all-sufficient Word with the theories of atheistic anti-Christians, coddles rebellious Self with the offer of "self-esteem, self-love, self-acceptance, self-image, self-improvement, self-assertion," and all the other selfisms, ad nauseam.

-Dave Hunt
The Berean Call, July 2023

(Note: If someone discusses something *ad nauseam*, they talk about it so much that it becomes a point of being nauseous.)

- Truth does not mind being questioned. A lie does not like being challenged.

-FB

- Let me state the only place we will always win any argument, always establish we are right about our conclusions, and be able to maintain the serenity about our reality is in the courtroom of our own minds; otherwise, we are going to be challenged in every other arena of life. We are going to find ourselves in conflict with others over opinions and theories. We are going to be agitated and offended by people who insist on their reality or take on something as right, leaving us wrong. We are going to wrestle over minor details while at times missing the major issue of a matter. We are going to find ourselves wounded and bruised when we fail to stand on the Rock of God's truth and move away from it in order to defend our own personal pinnacles or small mounds of truth.

-RJK

- Many within these growing ranks are demanding that the Church interpret and apply Scripture in the context of changing values and contemporary culture in order to properly understand the intended meaning of the text. The notion that the Word of God should be interpreted according to the shifting humanistic value system, or molded to fit the sensitivities of modern society is a grievous affront to God, and portends calamitous consequences.

-David Rosenthal
Zion's Fire
July/August 2022

- People often claim to hunger for truth but rarely like the taste when it's served.

-FB

- Emotions must line up to the Word of God before people can perceive spiritual truths and properly receive from God. Once the inclination is towards God, the heart fixed, the will set, the intellect giving way to the right mentality, and the emotions in line with God's Word, then the strength to seek after God will be tempered in order to be brought into a place of meekness before God by His Spirit.

-RJK

- We've come to a time when men build an entire theology around the defense of their sin, rather than the defense of the Word of God.

-Narrow Path
(FB)

- Most Christians tend to hold on to the belief in the authority of God's Word, but functionally they bail out on it. That's because they don't really believe in the *sufficiency* of Scripture. That's unfortunate. It's also senseless. Why? Because anyone who claims to believe in the authority of God's Word but denies its sufficiency means he doesn't believe it has all the answers that it claims.

-T.A. McMahon
The Berean Call, June 2023

- Biblical Christianity is unpopular. Popular Christianity is not Biblical. Don't fall for non-biblical ideas by people who don't want to "offend" people. Read the Bible.

-FB

- If people can change the biblical concept of Hell to make it better fit the culture of the day, then they can change the doctrine of Heaven or any other doctrine they don't like on the same basis. When this happens the concept of an inerrant, infallible Word of God as the measuring rod for life is meaningless.

-Marvin Rosenthal
Zion Fire
July/August 2022

- I choose to believe what the Word has declared about God. I maintain that all that is said in the Word of God is "amen, so be it on earth, for it is already so in heaven."

-RJK

- Let nothing be said about anyone unless it passes through the three sieves: Is it true? Is it kind? Is it necessary?

-Amy Carmichael

- Once you put forward the idea that your feelings superseded the Word of God and that the dogma, creed, and theology of a church body must change to fit your interpretation, we're not going to find common ground, and there is nothing further that we must debate.

-Michael Boldea Jr.
(EJ, pg. 37)

- We tend to think the opposite of war is peace. In a very limited sense, that is correct. However, peace is much more than the absence of conflict and war. It is the presence of God and His truth. If we are not walking with God in His truth, we cannot have peace with Him. Spending eternity without peace with God is far worse than the sufferings of war in this world.

-Josh Davis
Prophetic Observer
November 2023

- Follow the Word—not the herd.

-FB

- I've experienced His Presence in the deepest darkest hell that men can create…I have tested the promises of the Bible, and believe me, you can count on them.

-Corrie ten Boom

- You won't become a saint by studying your Bible; you'll become a saint by living it.

-Leonard Ravenhill

- Whatever men believe that is antithetical to Scripture is the crack that the enemy can exploit in their lives. He will use that one thing as a wedge, and a fulcrum to tear at your peace, your conviction, your steadfastness, and your commitment to the truth.

-Micheal Boldea Jr.
(EJ, pg. 15)

- Before you use the Bible for a weapon, first use it as a mirror.

  -FB

- Truth has to be absolute, eternal and unchanging or it is not the truth.

  -Opah Reddin

- Beware of studying doctrine, precept, or experiences apart from the Lord Jesus. Jesus, who is the soul of all. Doctrine without Christ will be nothing better than an empty tomb. Doctrine with Christ is a glorious high throne, with the King sitting on it.

  -Charles Spurgeon

- The Bible is the antidote to lies and deception. The truth of Scripture acts as a shield and a protective covering over your heart so that anything not of God will not be able to germinate and take root but be rejected outright.

  -Michael Boldea Jr.
  (EJ, pg. 14)

- When I got saved, I lost my worldly friends and when I began to really study the Bible, I lost all my "Christian" friends.

  -FB

- How well you know your Bible is not a luxury, nor is it an option. The Days of Deception are upon us and they will increase. Without His Word embedded in your heart and mind, you will not survive the coming storm.

  -Jack Hibbs

- When your eyes close for the last time in death, and never again read the Word of God in Scripture, you will open them to the Word of God in the flesh, that same Jesus the Bible whom you have known for so long, standing before you to take you forever to His eternal home.

-Geoff Thomas

- If you read the Word of God, you would see that God never sent prophets and preachers to tell His people how to get rich, He sent them to tell His people to get right before it's too late

-FB

Holy Spirit

The Transformer

It is important for servants of God to understand who changes lives. It is the Holy Spirit who must convict man of his sin and reveal his lost state. Once the lost soul accepts Jesus' invitation to come and partake of the living water of His Spirit, then man receives the gift of life as he is born again of the Spirit of God and the water of His Word. Once the Spirit resides within, He begins the work of sanctification which revives and renews the spirit and transforms the mind.

William Henry Brett became known by some as the "Apostle to the Indians of Guiana." He spent almost 40 years in the jungles and swamps of South America laboring among the Caribs, Waraoons, Arawaks tribes, and the migratory Acawioos.

The Caribs were fierce and cannibals, and the Waraoons appeared savage in their nakedness but were strong since their homes were in the trees and they swung among them with strong ropes. The Arawaks were violent people and dealt in much witchcraft and poisons. The Acawoios had no real homes and wandered through the woods with their deadly blow-pipes to secure food.

Brett was gifted in language, which was an asset since he had to learn four Indian languages, none of which were in a written form.

He had to endure various challenges with creatures that walked on all fours, slithered, and hid in river beds. Beside surviving bouts of malaria, he waded through swamps bare foot, endured insects that made one's existence miserable, and canoe trips that were often dangerous.

He was ever compelled by his burden for the people. Every great burden comes from the Spirit. He is the One who leads through troubled waters to bring followers of Jesus into places where He begins to do the work of preparation. He is the power and the anointing upon the message of salvation and hope. Brett knew that the heavenly power of the Gospel would deliver these souls from the tyranny of the immemorial superstitions and make them Christians.

Missionary work takes ordinary people and causes them to become part of the extraordinary. These stout heroes of the faith will admit that in and of themselves they had nothing to offer, but their calling opened the door in which the God of the universe did the impossible by snatching lost souls from the grave darkness of paganism, changing their lives by His Spirit, and placing them in the eternal hope of heaven.

Brett would testify of this fact. He watched God transform lives by turning savages into Christians. In the center of Brett's labors more than 5,000 souls were identified with their faith through water baptism.

Brett did pass his work on to a younger fellow missionary after 40 years of laboring in the jungles and swamps. He retired in England but did visit the Indian missions that were established. In 1878 he made his last trip to his former mission field and passed away in 1886 at the age of 66, leaving an incredible legacy and witness behind. (AMH, pgs. 231-246)

- Being born again of the Spirit is an unmistakable work of God, as mysterious as the wind. Beware of the tendency to water down the supernatural in religion.

  -Oswald Chambers
  (CWC, pg. 15)

- The Holy Spirit 1st brings the presence of Jesus, 2nd produces the likeness of Jesus, 3rd works the power of Jesus.

  -FB

- Throughout Scripture, *oil* is an eloquent symbol of the fullness of the Holy Spirit, who alone is responsible for the out-shining of Christian character. In Him is an inexhaustible supply of power and illumination.

  -Herbert Lockyer
  (APB, pg. 109)

- But here is the heart of Jesus, the mission of the Spirit is to show me a new exhibit of God's power—His power of infinite stooping. The divine majesty has ceased to dwell in the heavens; it has begun to bend downwards. It has refused to admit any longer that it is outside the world of suffering; if it be infinite, it must include the cross as well as the crown.

  -George Matheson
  (VS, pg. 73)

When I Think on Things Above

When I think about believers being the trees of God, it is obvious that they will stand tall because of righteousness. The life of Christ in them will reach heavenward ensuring their right standing before God.

When I think of the rivers of water, I know the water points to the unending flow of the Spirit from the throne of God. He is that

77

presence within the believer that flows upward, opening up each of us to the endless treasures of heaven. He is the presence around us that enfolds us into the protection and ways of God as He guides us to the treasures of truth. He is the presence that flows from above that connects with the water from within and merges with the water around us, totally immersing us with and into a new, powerful, abundant, and fruitful life.

When I think of things above, I can't help but realize that my mind will be lifted above this world, my praise will take flight on the wings of hope, and my worship will enter into the sweet chambers of communion with God.

Prayer: Lord, I thank You for the means of feeding my mind with Your Word, disciplining my body with godliness, and nourishing my soul with the ways of righteousness. I praise You for providing an abundant life through the presence and work of Your Spirit. Amen.

- I don't want the world to define God for me. I want the Holy Spirit to reveal God to me.

  -A. W. Tozer

- (In relationship to the indwelling Spirit of God) The ark of Thy presence was once shut in to keep out the flood, but now it is open to take in the flood itself.

  -George Matheson
  (VS, pg. 52)

- By His resurrection, Jesus Christ has power to impart to us the Holy Spirit, which means a totally new life. The Holy Ghost is the Deity in proceeding power Who applies the Atonement of the Son of God in our experience. Jesus Christ laid all the emphasis on the coming of the Holy Spirit.

-Oswald Chambers
(CWC, pg. 148)

Complete Surrender

A controversial truth is Jesus' Lordship. Jesus being "Lord" is not a doctrine but a reality for He is Lord of all. "Lord" means owner or possessor of that which belongs to Him. To be Lord of all points to Him being Adonai. Obedience to Jesus as Lord is not a work to obtain salvation, but a natural response of one who is saved and understands that as Jesus' servant, they are now in service to His household.

Ownership is about rights when it comes to authority in relationship to a Lord's household and possessions, whether it is the affairs, the goods, or the servants of the household, the owner has total autonomy over all of it.

The Bible is clear that as Christians we have been bought with a price (1 Corinthians 6:20; 7:23). Jesus completed the transaction for us on the cross. It is called *redemption*. And we must believe in our hearts God raised Jesus from the dead and confess Him as, "Lord" to be saved (Romans 10:9-10).

It is based on His Lordship that Jesus will recognize us as to whether we truly are His servants. And, what is the main responsibility of the servants of Jesus? It is the same as His when He was here on earth: to do the will of the Father. To do the will of another requires neglecting our will in preference to carry out the will of the other party in a right spirit and with a right attitude.

Whether one tries to debate this from a legal, moral, or ethical standpoint, the Bible makes it clear that we are born into slavery to sin and because of what Jesus did on the cross, we now have the liberty to choose who we will serve. We can continue to be a slave to sin or choose to become a servant to Jesus, but we can't serve two masters at the same time.

According to 1 Corinthians 12:3, we are told that no one can say Jesus is Lord except by the Holy Spirit. It is not a matter of calling Jesus Lord, it is a matter of recognizing Him AS Lord. Only the Holy Spirit can give us a revelation of Jesus being Lord, our Lord, and revealing those areas in our life that we have not yet surrendered to our Lord to ensure honorable service in His household.

J. Gregory Mantle points out the goal of the Holy Spirit's work on the inner man, "Only He can enthrone Jesus in the yielded heart and enable you to sanctify Christ as Lord."

The inner work the Holy Spirit does is called sanctification and as Mantle pointed out, enthroning Jesus in our heart is just the beginning. He goes on to say, "He will constantly discover new territory which He covets for the King. He will enable you to apply the principle of absolute surrender as you yield more and more completely to His guidance." (COS, pg. 128)

We must give up our right to self in order to surrender all to the Holy Spirit. We must ensure He has free range in our life to do as He will so in the end we will have the mark of Jesus' ownership on our souls, true servitude that is clearly expressed in our outer life, and identification in the spirit to the Kingdom of God.

─────────── • ◄══ • ─────────

- We must possess our souls in patience no matter what the environment. If we do possess them, we can be ensured of the working of the Spirit upon them. He will have the freedom to convict us if we are becoming complacent towards His ways, renew us if we are becoming insensitive to His gentle leading, and quicken us to the lack of quality our life is taking on if we are failing to walk in agreement with Him in sweet communion.

-RJK

- Before Calvary the Holy Spirit came upon certain individuals for prophecy and mighty miracles, but He never came to abide until Pentecost.

-David Webber
Prophetic Observer
September 2023

- Christian life and character in its beginning, middle, and end, is the Spirit's work.

-Professor James Denney
(COS, pg. 139)

Are You Thirsty Yet?

One of Jesus' cries on the cross was, "I thirst." J. Gregory Mantle points this out "Thirst is one of the most intense appetites of our nature. Only those who are accustomed to a scarcity of water know the suffering which intense thirst causes." (COS, pg. 139)

There are different types of thirst. There is a thirst for knowledge, a thirst for adventure, and a thirst for excitement, etc. All of these pursuits can become intense and even obsessive but how many of us have experienced the thirst that comes out of having no water to drink?

We mask real thirst in our day with all kinds of lousy substitutes keeping many from recognizing they are really dehydrated and their body is suffering from it. They do not realize the repercussions of it until later after the body begins to rebel or break down in some way.

Jesus experienced the intensity of physical thirst on the cross so we would not have to experience the same intensity that will come from spiritual thirst. The intensity I am talking about is judgment that is leveled at those who are void of the spiritual waters of the Holy Spirit that quenches the soul and revives the spirit. He is the Rivers of Living Water that brings eternal life to those who partake of this life-giving source by faith.

The tragedy when it comes to spiritual thirst is we often don't recognize our precarious position until it is too late. I have heard of stories where people died of physical thirst and they found water on them. Obviously, these people were holding onto the water until that moment came when they needed it the most and they would use it to pull themselves out of the grips of death. However, they did not recognize that there was a point their body could not be revived by any amount of water and that when death claimed them, they had no means to reverse the dying condition they were in.

The advice I have heard is when you are in a dire situation such as being lost and short on water, that you must not hold back the water to preserve your life; rather, you must drink it as your body needs it to prolong your life. This is true for the spiritual water of the soul.

We must drink the spiritual water knowing that 1) Jesus invited us to partake of His water to bring forth eternal life, 2) water becomes useless and stagnant if it is not being used, and 3) we need to be filled up daily to maintain our spiritual life. The question is how do I know I am spiritually dehydrated? Here are some clues. First of all, water refreshes a thirsty soul.

To have a thirsty soul, points to having a contrite or humble attitude towards God. It is out of *contrition* I see my need is desperate and out of humility I can rightfully ask for my need to be met and receive it. If you do not see the need for water and feel and know the desperation of having it missing, you will not be humbled by the fact that without God's intervention you will die in your miserable state. It is only the living water of the Spirit that can refresh the soul and revive the spirit.

Secondly, if you are partaking of the Living Water your soul is at peace, and your spirit is at rest. There is nothing that creates *restlessness* like dissatisfaction that something is missing. It makes your soul restless and your spirit lean.

Thirdly, the living water is *abundant* and is able to satisfy your soul. If satisfaction is missing, you are not partaking of the water, allowing you to experience the abundance of the life you have been given.

Another characteristic of a powerful river with moving water is that it carves out masterpieces in the terrain. The Holy Spirit is *masterful* in changing the terrain of our inner man. The Spirit is bringing forth a masterpiece that will reflect the image of Christ. As believers we must be honest enough about whether we are reflecting Jesus.

We are reminded that the Holy Spirit's work is to sanctify us and that entails enthroning Christ as the center of our life. However, for this sanctification to take place, we must drink the water by faith and assimilate it in obedience so we can apprehend the life we have in Jesus.

- The Lord is bringing us forth through His Spirit. We are being sanctified unto obedience. We have been begotten unto a living hope by His resurrection. Our faith is clearly alive. Our future has already been set before us. Our hope is sure as it rests upon the One who could not be held back from fulfilling the plan of salvation, even by the grip of death and the silent hopelessness of a grave.

-RJK

- Salvation is God's greatest gift to the world, the baptism in the Holy Spirit is God's greatest gift to the Church.

  -Pastor Donnie Swaggert

- If we seek the baptism of the Holy Ghost in order that God may make us great servants of His, we shall never receive anything. God baptizes us with the Holy Ghost that He may be All in all.

  -Oswald Chambers

  (CWC, pg. 572)

Prayer: Lord, thank You for giving me a spirit and soul that can always receive more of Your Spirit, Word, and wisdom. Lord, touch each area to overflow with Your Living Water, always enlarging me to receive more from Your throne. Amen.

Filing A Missing Person's Report

Through the years I have visited different churches. I have always hoped to find one particular Person every time I visit a new church. When I have encountered Him at different churches and unexpected times, He has enfolded me with such love and peace. I have a great sense of awe and feel the freedom to truly worship the God of heaven.

I know when He is present, I am assured of truth being lifted up, hearts touched, lives changed, and the salvation and healing of souls. I know that His presence brings anointing to the pastor, power to the message, revival to the troubled spirit, and revelation to the seeking heart.

When I fail to encounter Him in churches, there is no real life to interact with, no real point of agreement to meet at, and no real protection from the enemy of our souls, for He alone is what ensures discernment. The Word of God is rendered lifeless and ineffective, and without this Person present there is no revelation of Jesus to be found that can enlarge the soul, transform the mind, and seal the believer to their inheritance.

In his book, *The Epistle of Jude An Uncompromising Message for a Compromised Generation,* Michael Boldea Jr. points out that the enemy desires to leave the children of God powerless and rudderless comes down to separating them from the Word of God or the power of God. He points out one guides, sets the course and determines the destination while the other one gives strength to endure and provides the required energy to reach it. He goes on to say that a Christian without the guidance, presence, and power of God will falter along the way, flail about in their spiritual life, grow weary, and lose confidence. (EJ, pg. 81)

We know the Word of God guides, but the Holy Spirit empowers us. He is the hand on the rudder, the Word, who will bring us to our destination. He is the wind that moves us through the troubled waters of this world. He is the One who must be present to bring forth life to the Word, prepare the eyes of faith to see, enlarge the mind to be reasoned with by God's Word, and the heart to receive what is true. Bodea describes the tragedy of missing ingredients in today's church as "raising a generation of spiritual cripples who are fully convinced they are marathon runners for Jesus." (EJ, pg. 88)

Today when I walk into churches, I realize the one Person who needs to be there is often missing. Without the One the other One, His name is Jesus, will never be magnified in a way that will bring salvation, healing, and liberty. In fact, Jesus' name is simply tacked on. He is no longer that which is being pursued, but as Boldea puts it, "a means to an end." (EJ, pg. 81)

Sadly, in many churches no one seems to notice that this Person, the Holy Spirit is missing. It is business as usual. Pastors spew out lifeless words that reveals their personal spiritual vacuum, leaving the sheep empty. There are sheep that are becoming hungrier and more desperate but do not know where to go. They know something is missing, but they have never really been introduced or encountered the presence of this Person to know what is missing.

It is clear that since many churches have substituted so much of the world's philosophies, ways, and methods with the work of the Person of the Holy Spirit, they see no need for Him. And, since many have become self-sufficient in their religious circles, no one is concerned enough, discerning enough, or in a place of authority to file a "missing person report" to warn those who are seeking the fullness of God to beware that He is nowhere to be found in any of the activities.

I want to encourage those who know something is missing to consult the Word of God. It has provided all the necessary descriptions as to who is missing, the way to discern if He is missing, even why He is missing, and where He can be found.

If the Holy Spirit is missing, it is time to file a "missing person's report" to warn others, and seek the place where He can be once again encountered. It is time He is taken out of the lost and found bin of religious history and notions and put back into the column as being found moving once again in the midst of God's people, bringing life to the Word, magnifying Jesus in greater revelation, convicting lost souls of sin, righteousness and judgment, and reviving the spirit of those who have lost their way in the maze of religious nonsense.

Prayer

The Big Challenge

One of the big challenges in my life concerns my prayer life. I spent the initial years of my Christian life in confusion about what prayer was all about. I learned some people religiously pray. Others selfishly pray, while there are those who use prayer as an option. Finally, you have those who pray without ceasing.

When you consider prayer, it is actually a privilege wrought by Jesus on the cross. But few know how to use this privilege in the right way. For most who religiously pray, it is not treated as a privilege, but a duty. In some cases, this duty can be very repetitious, proving to be lifeless.

When it comes to those who selfishly pray, these people pray amiss for they ask for things to heap upon their flesh or for their way to be done. For those who treat prayer as an option, they only pray in times of crises, and often become angry when God fails to perform according to their wishes.

What does it mean to pray in a manner that will catch God's attention? Prayer is not about getting God to perform; rather, it is a means to seek God's will in a situation. The Bible tells us that if we pray according to God's will, He will hear us. Jesus clearly did not seek His own will in prayer, but the Father's will.

Prayer is also about communion. It is a doorway into the place of fellowship with God. What communion teaches us is that prayer is communication with God. Communication is not just a matter of speaking but of hearing.

Today there is a lot of talking going on in the world, but there is not much communication. We often speak to propagate our personal reality, not to confront a matter to ensure truth and integrity. Therefore, there is much propaganda, but little truth being expounded.

For some, prayer is a tool to use when they want something from God, but it is not a "tool" but a means for God to shape our attitude towards Him as we seek His face and His will in ALL matters pertaining to life and godliness.

Prayer: Lord, we must be tamed by Your Spirit, disciplined by Your Word, and brought into line with Your character to know the majesty of Your power and life. Amen.

- A Church on its knees is more powerful than an army on its feet.
  -FB

- Prayer girds human weakness with divine strength, turns human folly into heavenly wisdom and gives to troubled mouths the peace of God. We know not what prayer can do.
  -Charles Spurgeon

Prayer: Lord, we are blessed by Your death. We will truly experience true liberty as we hide in Your death and burial in order to experience resurrection of a new way of life. Amen.

- For God to reveal His Son's glory to Christians means calling them aside from normalcy, apart from the world in prayer, and to a place that requires them to step outside of the box of ordinary living to consider the heights of that which is eternal and heavenly.

  -RJK

- Every grain shall produce a crown; and every tear shall bring forth a pearl; and every minute in pains or prayers, an age of joy and glory.

  -Joseph Alliene
  (TK. pg. 38)

Prayer: Lord in the midst of oppression, You are the great deliverer. May I have the fear to trust You, the faith to believe You, the preparation to obey You, and the desperation to cling to You. Lord, I know I have need of such things for I need Your deliverance to be my constant reality. Amen.

- If a Christian does not pray, he becomes a worrier. If he does pray, he becomes a warrior.

  -FB

- In the Bible when Job had everything, he prayed. When he had nothing, he still prayed. Prayer isn't about your circumstances, it's about who God is.

  -Daily Inspired

Effective Prayer

What does it take to hit the target when it comes to God? So much of the effectiveness of the Christian life comes down to the heart.

89

The right heart looks beyond in expectation, reaches up with child-like faith, and like the woman with the issue of blood manages to touch the "hem" of God. This heart is known as a pure heart. After all, those who are pure in heart shall see God.

"Purity" points to perfection or what we consider to be spiritual "maturity." We are to be child-like towards God as far as trust, but spiritually maturing when it comes to our walk. Our walk should be manifesting the life, attitude, and ways of Christ.

The heart is considered both the ground in which truth must be established and the altar in which everything must be offered to be purged by the fires of God. What comes from such a heart is that of integrity and a sweet savor and incense (prayer) that reaches the very throne of God.

The Christian faith has and always will be a matter of the heart. So many who start out on the Christian walk lose heart because their heart has not been established on the immovable Rock. So many become overwhelmed by the darkness because their heart has not been purified to confidently stand in darkness.

The final reason some people become hopeless in this world is because they have no vision of the world beyond. They perceive there is nothing past this world that is of significance. They wallow in self-pity as they swallow tears of bitterness while mourning the passing of dreams, time, and opportunities.

May we never give up on what God has established in our hearts as being true. May we never lose heart towards Him or cease to seek Him in prayer. May we be convicted enough to look up towards the only answer we have, take courage in who He is and stand on His promises and keep our focus on Jesus. He will never steer any of us in a wrong way.

Prayer: Lord, save me from my self-sufficiency. Help me to guard my heart, maintain my ways, and be vigorous in my devotion to the ways of righteousness. Give me the means to possess my spiritual inheritance so that You can be glorified. Remind me of who You are so I can be generous and valiant in my walk. Lord, You are my shepherd. Lead me in the paths of righteousness so I can experience Your complete salvation. Amen.

- Prayer is definite talk to God, around which God puts an atmosphere, and we get answers back.

-Oswald Chambers
(CWC, pg. 171)

- The wonderful thing about praying is that you leave a world of not being able to do something and enter God's realm where everything is possible.

-Corrie Ten Boom

Prayer: Lord, You have done everything on my behalf so I can live. However, before I can discover this life, I must be proven and humbled. I embrace the humbling process for without it I will remain stiff-necked towards Your authority, self-sufficient in regard to Your blessings, and a fool in my ignorance of You. I need to be humbled so you can be exalted in my life. It is when You are exalted that I will discover true, satisfying life. Amen.

- Prayer is communication. Communication is more about listening so one can respond properly to what is being communicated from the other party. How we need to hear what the Spirit is saying!

-RJK

- Don't worry. God is never blind to your tears, never deaf to your prayers, and never silent to your pain. He sees, He hears, and He will deliver you.

-FB

- There must be an enlargement of soul before any remarkable success on others; and a great diligence in prayer and strict watchfulness over my own soul previous to any remarkable and habitual enlargement in ministry; and deep humiliation must precede both.

-Philip Doddridge
(TK, pg. 74)

Prayer: Lord, You have given much, but we so often withhold our best from You. You gave Your best, but we only give that which costs us nothing. You call us to Yourself, while we keep our heart aloof from You. You show mercy, and we show ingratitude. You show grace, and we show contempt. Oh Lord, I choose to love and serve You, but save me from my sinful disposition and wicked ways so I can walk in the ways of righteousness and blessings. Amen.

- Prayer is often an interruption to personal ambition, and no man who is busy has time to pray. What will suffer is the life of God in him, which is nourished not by food but by prayer.

Oswald Chambers
(CWC, pg. 608)

- Speak with God in the morning before you speak with the world; and speak with God at night, after you have been with the world.

-J. C. Ryle

A Place of Protection

Man is always looking for some place to hide from the wicked enemies of their soul. We know that in reality there is no place for man to hide in this world except God. He is the One who is able to hide things in plain sight.

The Scottish Covenanters discovered this special defense many times due to the great persecution of a man known as "bloody Claverhouse." This despot had a diabolic hatred and murderous persecution towards the saints who refused to denounced Jesus as their king.

One day the Scottish Covenanters were meeting in the shelter of a hollow in the mountain when the sentries announced that the dragoons of Claverhouse were upon them. There was no place to run or hide so the devoted pastor said, "O Lord, the wolf is at hand. Thy defenseless sheep will be slain, apart from thy swift interposition by those who delight in shedding their blood. Wilt thou not, at this very moment, protect them by throwing Thy cloak around them, and hiding them in Thy lap from the fury of the oppressors?"

In an instant the prayer was answered. A thick mist fell upon the congregation and hid them from their cruel oppressors who went galloping past and did not see one of God's faithful, but defenseless children. (COS, pgs. 127-128)

The following stanza followed the story.

Fear Him ye saints, and you will then
Have nothing else to fear;
Make you His service your delight,
He'll make your wants His care.

- Many of our troubles come from much time on our hands and not enough times on our knees.

  -FB

- We generally look upon prayer as a means of getting things for ourselves, whereas the Bible idea of prayer is that God's holiness and God's purpose and God's wise order may be brought about, irrespective of who comes or who goes.

  -Oswald Chambers
  (CWC, pg. 608)

Prayer: Lord, there are so many struggles with the "ifs" and "whys" of life. However, there is one truth that remains constant, and that is You. Help me believe You about forgiveness when the "ifs" of my past life haunt me, and trust You when the "whys" of my present life mock me, and when the hallow echo of the "when's" and "where's" of a matter can't change the future. Amen.

- The most important people today are the men and women of prayer, not those who talk about prayer, nor those who say they believe in prayer, but those who take time to pray.

  -Vesta Mangum

- When a man is at his wits' end, it is not a cowardly thing to pray, it is the only way to get in touch with Reality. As long as we are self-sufficient and complacent, we don't need to ask God for anything, we don't want Him; it is only when we know we are powerless that we are prepared to listen to Jesus Christ and to what He says.

  -Oswald Chambers
  (CWC, pg. 609)

Prayer: Lord, I want to bind Your commandments to my heart so I will not sin against You. I want them around my neck so they can discipline and guide me. I want them bound to my hands so that my service will be pure and acceptable to You. God, thank You for Your commandments. Amen.

- It is not so true that "prayer changes things" as that prayer changes *me,* and then I change things; consequently, we must not ask God to do what He has created us to do.

-Oswald Chambers
(CWC, pg. 609)

- When I pray, I talk to God, but when I read the Bible, God talks to me.

-FB

The Right Position of Learning

Andrew Fraser was dying of "quick consumption," but he wanted to share so much with the young man, **H. A Ironside** who had a call to preach. The Irish man lived in a tent with his faithful companion, the Bible behind Ironside's parents' home.

Fraser could barely speak because his lungs were almost gone, but he invited Ironside to sit down and talk with him about the Word of God. The dying man opened his Bible and went from passage to passage sharing the revelation that he had received from his years of studying it.

Tears began to run down Ironside's face and that is when he asked, "Where did you get these things? Could you tell me where I could find a book that would open them up to me?" Ironside then asked if he had learned these things in some seminary or college? Ironside stated that he would never forget the dying man's answer.

"My dear young man, I learned these things on my knees on the mud floor of a little sod cottage in the north of Ireland. There with my open Bible before me, I used to kneel for hours at a time, and ask the Spirit of God to reveal Christ to my soul and to open the Word to my heart, and He taught me more on my knees on that mud floor than I ever could have learned in all the seminaries or colleges in the world."

Ironside went on to say that we do not stay long enough in the presence of God. From all appearances, "meditation" has become a lost art in our day. How many really chew on the Word like a cow chews her cud? He goes on to say, "It has been well said that it is a great thing when the mouth and the foot agree when we feed on the Word and walk in the power of the truth." (GE, (E) pgs. 86-88)

Prayer: Lord, the Christian life is a cut above this world. Therefore, I have no reason for living, thinking, and acting like the world. Give me a vision and heart to rise above the world so that I can walk in Your perfect ways. Amen.

- Negligence in prayer withers the inner man. Nothing can be a substitute for it, and to even Christian work. Many are so preoccupied with the work that they allow little time for prayer. Hence, they cannot cast out demons. Prayer enables us first to overcome the enemy and outwardly to deal with him.

  -Watchman Nee

- Prayers don't have to be long and eloquent. They need only come from a sincere and humble heart.

  -FB

Prayer: May God so fill us today with the heart of Christ that we may glow with divine fire of holy desire.

-A. B. Simpson

- We cannot pray in love and live in hate and still think we are worshipping God.

-FB

Prayer: Lord, we lose our way because we forget that You are not only our starting place, You are our point of finish. The journey between the starting place and the point of finish is all about discovering You in greater ways. True to Your promise, keep my feet on this narrow path that will lead me to You. Amen.

- To pray "thy will be done," I must be willing if the answer requires it that my will, will be undone.

-Elisabeth Elliot

Prayer: Lord, You are holy and it is on the ground of holiness that You are able to meet with and commune with Your people. Forgive us for thinking that if You love us, You would meet us in the pigpens of the world. Amen.

- The strongest men are not found in the gym. They are found on their knees in the presence of God.

-FB

Light To See By

What light are you walking by? What we see will determine what type of light we are walking by. Seeing in many cases has to do with understanding. The physical eyes must not just see something, they must be able to distinguish what they are seeing. They must understand it to identify what they are looking at, define what they are observing and properly describe it so others can know what they are looking at or for.

The physical eyes are what we trust in the most, but they are the most unreliable. They are not trained to discern what is, take note of details, or have an unbiased or reliable account of something because much of what affects one's understanding is the type of emotional impact it leaves on them. For the most part details are consumed by strong impressions and the confusion or uncertainty.

Through the years I have met blind people who see more clearly when it comes to the unseen realm. I remember one blind person who died, but was brought back, and what she saw was incredible colors. What was amazing is that she knew what each color was even though she had never seen color before.

How about blind Christian song-writer, **Fanny Crosby**, whose faith allowed her to see spiritual truths that became songs we sing today. She was content to know that the first face she would see was Jesus Himself.

Faith gives us the eyes to see, but so many times it is in prayer that the heavenly is unveiled to us through faith. I can't tell you how many people have received greater revelation of Jesus and His Word on their knees in humility as they sought in prayer to know Him and see Him.

Even though physically blind, **George Matheson** saw plenty in his life when it came to spiritual truths and principles. At 18 months old his mother was told that her son had inflammation of the eyes that would eventually rob him of his sight. The dark curtain completely came over his eyes at age 18, but the darkness of this world did not stop him from discovering the light of the next one.

He was a pastor of a church and wrote poems that were made into hymns and books that are considered prized classics. Without physical sight he could not read the Word, but he was able to memorize his sermons and quote Scriptures, as well as the hymns. His hands always lifted up in need and surrender when speaking from the pulpit, while putting aside the activities of the mind to hear the Scripture that the Lord wanted him to share with the congregation.

For many of us, we seek that secret place of communion with God, but for Matheson, he had discovered that sweet chamber in the darkness that had enfolded him. He was not blinded by or tempted to succumb to the world's light or vain activities. Even though he needed assistance, God provided it through his two sisters. In a sense, he was allotted a freedom few of us know. Did he feel the loss of his eyesight was a great cost or did he see the blessedness of it?

Prayer became an integral part of his life. A man who tries to function without prayer is a man who has failed to discover that he is utterly helpless regardless of whether or not he has all of his faculties. As far as Matheson was concerned, he dared not enter into any place of communion or the pulpit without first bowing in the awesome presence of his Almighty God to see what He wanted to say.

Darkness creates its own silence. For Matheson that silence became his sanctuary where he could meditate on the beauty of His Lord. He knew there was a great vastness in darkness, but he also had discovered that God's presence is greater.

Eleven years before his death at 66 in 1906, he discovered a valuable truth that even brought him higher in his spiritual life. Even though such truths are before us and we hear them and read them, we can skim over them, searching for some other nugget that catches our attention. For Matheson it was "seeing" that in the spiritual realm, descent must precede ascent.

This truth came from Ephesians 4:10. Nothing can come higher unless it is willing to go lower in the terms of humility. Matheson had been brought down low by physical blindness only to be brought higher by seeing the light of God's truth. He always had to descend in great need to reach greater heights to receive that which would enrich the soul and satisfy the spirit.

Matheson knew that death was the gate to higher work and purer joys. His life had been planted in darkness in order to refine him and yield greater fruit. He had grown in grace and in knowledge of His Lord.

It was said of Matheson by author Lillian Harvey, "This dear man who had traveled the road of descent all of his life had found death but an ascent into the presence of his beloved Savior." (TK, pgs. 121-133)

Worship and Communion

The Secret to Worship

Is there a secret to true worship? Yes and no! There is no secret to true worship, but it is somewhat hidden to those who seek their own concept of worship. Our level of worship is determined by our relationship with our Creator, the One who is worthy of all worship.

We will not worship something lower than ourselves because worship requires us to exalt what we are considering to be worthy of honor. We will not be in awe of something that we can understand or compete with, only that which is shrouded in a bit of mystery that causes us to be overwhelmed at times by the immensity of its ability and power. We can't worship that which we neither love nor fear.

Love is the platform of adoration, while fear is what creates an attitude of reverence that can tremble before that which is holy and produce awe that comes out of humility. Although man worships creation, there is nothing loftier than God in the heavens. When man tries to worship man, he finds that the pinnacles beneath him have no means to maintain such arrogant heights. When man worships intelligence, talents, and abilities, he soon discovers all of it is profane, corrupt, and limited.

The Father seeks true worshippers because He is worthy. We are to worship in Spirit to ensure love and purity in our adoration, and in truth to ensure the right attitude in worship. We must understand our worship of God is determined by our faith towards Him. When it comes to our perception about His eternal qualities, that are somewhat understandable, we must recognize they belong to an unseen dimension and are mysterious because they are eternal and work according to the sovereignty of God.

* We must behold the Son in greater measure to close any gap in our relationship with God. After all Jesus is the bridge that connects us to our life in Him, our worship towards Him, and our service because of who He is.

-RJK

* There is a place in your heart called a throne. Someone always occupies that place. The rival claimants are Christ and Self. Which of these is on the throne?

-J. Gregory Mantle
(COS, pg. 123)

* Without private worship, public worship is just a performance.

-FB

* Many people have become familiar with their own concepts about Jesus, but few know Him. This familiarity has caused many to accept their perception of Him as final or complete. The demotion of Christ in people's way of thinking has taken the fascination out

of discovering the depths and heights of God. It has taken away the awe, fear, and wisdom to pursue Him in humility. It has made people casual, redefining righteousness as they adjust their perception to what is tolerable and comfortable. This compromise has defiled the place of worship, opening people up to embrace the substitutes of dead or fleshly worship.

-RJK

- Intensity of communion is not in feelings or emotions or in special places, but in quiet, fixed, confident centering of God.

-Oswald Chambers
(CWC, pg. 9)

- Seeking God should be our main priority each new day and in each new challenge to ensure the continuation of a satisfying life. Knowing His heart should be our desire. Gaining His perspective should be our goal. Communing with Him should serve as our bread. Worshipping Him should be our breath, doing His will should be our meat, and loving Him should be our heartbeat. After all, this privilege to seek out and find God was wrought on the cross by Jesus. Such a search will end in peace. One must keep in mind that it is a privilege to pursue after God as well as a point of grace, and this privilege must not be taken for granted or abused.

-RJK

- When one begins with the wrong worldview, worship is directed to creation instead of the Creator, and the consequences are dire. On the other hand, when one begins with the proper worldview, worship is directed to the Creator God, and fear, guilt and dread of the future melts away.

-Josh Davis
Prophetic Observer
January 2024

- Christ fell into the ground in death, and now has become the firstfruits of them that slept, and we worship with adoring gratitude for all that this means to us.

-H.A. Ironside
(GE (G) pg. 150)

- Lowliness in attitude points to the state of humility. We must not think highly of what we know or can do. Humility occurs at the lowest points of failure, the lowest places of brokenness and repentance, and the darkest places of desperation. The only height humility dares seek is when it looks up where praises of the Lord catch the currents of the Spirit to be brought to high places of awe and worship.

-RJK

- Worship is an act of love given back to Him who first loved us. It is beautiful, but our models of worship are not equivalent to who He is: "To whom then will you liken God? Or what likeness will your compare to Him?

-Carl Teichrib
(GG, pg. 244)

- Communion is about partaking of Jesus' life, becoming identified in His work of redemption on the cross, sharing in His sufferings, being part of His work, and being associated with His glory. In John 6, we are invited to partake of His body (bread from heaven) and of His blood (the covenant) in order to live. To partake of Him in this text means to *believe on* Him as to the words He spoke, to *believe* Him because of who He is, and to *believe in* Him because of what He did on the cross for us. Such belief points to totally assimilating every aspect of His Word, person, and work as being truth that must be applied to our daily walk to ensure life.

-RJK

- The purpose of God in redeeming men was not to save them from hell only, but to save them to worship.

-A. W. Tozer
(WOG, pg. 38)

- We must prepare our high places and secret places to worship God in Spirit and truth. God is jealous, and will not accept divided worship, service, or commitment from us. Everything in our lives must be dedicated to Him. Our minds must perceive His truth, our hearts must see Him in His glory, and our ears must hear His voice.

-RJK

- The expression of our lips must correspond with our communion with God. It is easy to say good and true things without troubling to live up to them; consequently the Christian talker is more likely to be a hypocrite than any other kind of worker.

-Oswald Chambers
(CWC, pg. 9)

- Worship is about who God is. Praise is about what God has done. Let us not sit silent and miserable when in the valley of despair

-FB

- Fear without love remains fear. However, love that walks in a proper attitude of fear will express itself in wisdom, honor, awe, and worship.

                                                                     -RJK

- Consider who we profess to worship, and we shall not hurry into his presence as men turn to a fire. Moses, the man of God was warned to put off his shoes from off his feet when God only revealed himself in a bush; how should we prepare ourselves when we come to him who reveals himself in Christ Jesus his dear Son?

                                                          -Charles Spurgeon

- You cannot exalt someone who is not greater than you. The problem is most men bring God down to their understanding, causing them to worship their concepts or emotions about Him, rather than who He is.

                                                                     -RJK

Hallelujah

How many times have you heard the word, "Hallelujah?" I must point out it is also spelled "Alleluia" in Revelation 19:1-6. When I hear it, depending on the context of it my spirit is set free to rejoice or my soul is brought down to a place of reverence where I can hardly speak the word without being overwhelmed by the majesty of it.

The meaning of the word is "Praise ye the Lord." The Hebrew use of this word is an adoring exclamation that means, "Praise ye Jah!" "Jah" is the primitive word for the English word "Jehovah" or the Hebrew word, "Yahweh." Therefore, when you read, "praise ye the Lord," you are declaring "Hallelujah."

To declare, "Hallelujah" must not be done in a casual and light way. It is not to be used like some mantra or a point of repetition. It is to be used as an exclamation mark or as a whisper of the heart that softly floats up to the throne of God in wonderment. For example, when it comes to God dealing with a sinner or sin in the case of revelation, it is to show your agreement with God in how He is handling the matter. You are acknowledging that His way, regardless of how a bit abrasive it may seem to one's understanding, is the wise, righteous, and necessary way to ensure His will, His plan, and the righteous order of His kingdom.

When you study this adoring exclamation in Scripture, you will realize it has the ability to take you into great heights of praise or to bring you down to a place of humble worship. It creates the panorama of emotions because it acknowledges the infinite character, the great work, and the righteous ways of God. Regardless of how God's ways are expressed, it calls for one to humble oneself, sometimes in utter brokenness before the Lord, in willing acceptance, adoration, and worship to give Him praise, if not for the circumstances, then for who He is. It is for this reason praise is biblically considered one of the acceptable, spiritual sacrifices in the church age.

Let's consider some of the situations that called for God's people to declare, "Hallelujah." Psalm 106:1, 48 praises the Lord for His goodness and His steadfast love, and Psalm 117 speaks of praising him for His faithfulness that endures forever. Psalm 135:1, 21 speaks of praising the One who dwells in Jerusalem, while Psalm 146:1, 10 praises Him because He will reign forever. Psalm 148:1, 14 talks about praising the One on High who has exalted the horn (authority-points to Christ) of His people

In Psalm 147:1, 20 we are told that it is pleasant to praise the Lord for He has established His people among those who know nothing of Him. In Psalm 111:1 we see where we must praise the Lord with all of our heart. Psalm 112:1 praises God because true happiness comes out of fearing Him and being devoted to keep His commandments.

In Revelation we see this exclamation mark going up and forth for various reasons. In 19:1-2 it acknowledges that salvation, glory, honor, and power belong to God and that His judgements towards the whore are righteous and just. We see in 19:4 that it became part of the smoke that represents holiness rising up towards the Lord, and is mingled with the worship of those around His throne.

In Revelation 19:5-6 we see those around the throne, whether great or small being commanded to praise the Lord. We are told that John then heard a voice of a great multitude as it if it was a voice of many waters and of mighty thunderings, saying, "Alleluia: for the Lord God omnipotent reigneth."

Revelation 19:7 tells us to be glad, rejoice, and give honor to Him, for the marriage of the Lamb is come. In Revelation 19:9, John was told to write, "Blessed are they which are called unto this marriage supper of the Lamb." After that proclamation comes Our Lord on a white horse and He is called "Faithful" and "True."

The Lord's eyes were a flame of fire and He wore many crowns on His head. He was clothed with a vesture dipped in blood, and His name is "The Word of God." Out of His mouth went a sharp sword and His judgment was set forth in fierceness and wrath. On His vesture and thigh was the name, the KING OF KINGS AND THE LORD OF LORDS."

In the best of time, "Hallelujah" can be missing, but in the humblest of times is when this declaration can be set free with the wings of thankfulness. In the worst of times, this special exclamation mark will lift the spirit. In challenging times, it will encourage the soul to reach higher in praise. In times of worship, it can lead one up to the very throne of God.

When was the last time the exclamation mark of heaven took flight from your heart? Perhaps the situation wasn't great and maybe the times were trying, but you looked above it all into the vastness of the heavens and realized your Lord still sits on the throne. And, that regardless of the tribulation and despair on earth, all is well with your soul because you know the Creator of heaven and earth, you know the one and only true God who deserves all praise because of who HE IS! Hallelujah, amen.

Sacrifice

The Simplest and Earnest

What will the godly say about you? As believers we can't get caught up with what the world thinks of us, the religious person says about us, or how the carnal-minded Christian judges us. In God's kingdom we must be cringing beggars, to the world we will be considered foolish, to the religious a fanatic, to the curious a spectacle, and to the poor in spirit a breath of fresh air.

The truth is if your focus is Christ, the opinions, judgments, and accusations will not matter. After all, if you are about the Father's business, you have only one goal in mind and that is to faithfully finish the course set before you while carrying the torch of God as high as you can while running through the spiritual darkness of the age.

It was said of the Scottish missionary, **Frederick Stanley Arnot** that he was a forlorn man, existing day from day, almost homeless and often possessing only the basic necessities of life. In some situations, he even seemed a bit eccentric because he would refuse certain conveniences that might make him soft or lackadaisical, even preparing himself for the rigors of mission life. In the end Arnot proved to be a remarkable man, the simplest and most earnest man, for he had one desire and that was to do God's service. This was all about him being as near to his Master as he could be.

Arnot was born in 1858. Perhaps his calling and inspiration to travel to Central Africa, where he would later be referred to as "the pioneer of Garenganze," had to do with the fact that his family were the neighbors of the family of David Livingstone. The great pioneer missionary and adventurer was not only Arnot's hero but he may have sparked that fire in him to follow in his footsteps. In fact, as a boy he studied the artifacts and maps of David Livingstone as he most likely began to plot his own path.

Landing in Africa in 1881 just two months before his 23rd birthday, Arnot disappeared into the interior and was not heard from for seven years. It was during that time that Arnot matched Dr. Livingstone's exploits as an explorer, covering the broad strip of central Africa that was made up of Angola, the southern Congo, and Zambia. His travels took him through the hostile kingdom of Botswana, across the Kalahari Desert, and the watersheds of both the Zambezi and Congo Rivers, finally ending up on the Angolan coast. It was there that he would settle down for two years in which he built a small clinic, a church, a school and a small orphanage by faith without any regular funding.

Needless to say, Arnot's experiences were many. He faced many obstacles that included political unrest, dangerous beasts, and challenging terrain. He clearly became acquainted with his vast mission field that had not been reached even by Livingstone.

In 1888, he returned to England for a year. He found his exploits had gone before him and the Royal Geographical Society had him present a paper and named him a Fellow of the Society. Due to his now popular reputation, he was able to recruit thirteen young men to join his work, and in 1889, he returned with not only the young men but nis newly wedded wife, Harriet Jane Fisher.

Arnot's goal was to settle in Msidi's kingdom at Garenganze, but ill health stopped him. He set out to work at a mission in Angola.

Although his Open Brethren belief kept him from getting involved with the political unrest along with denouncing the corruption brought on by European greed, he still was quite disturbed.

Any unrest brings its own suffering as people are often caught in the middle of it and greed has a way of corrupting and sacrificing that which is innocent and pure. All Arnot could do was remain true to his calling.

In 1892 he returned home to England with his family, but Africa had his heart and he returned to his beloved mission field, and after more years of service he died on May 14, 1914 at the age of 56.

Arnot showed boldness and courage in his many exploits. Like Livingstone before him, no doubt he became a hero to young adventurers. He achieved much but it was the quality of his character that caused him to stand tall and persevere in his work for Christ in the face of loneliness, sickness, danger, and disappointment.

His heart was to bring the life changing message to those who were held captive by pagan beliefs and walking in such dark practices as trafficking and sacrificing children. He became a parent to many children who were cast aside by cultures and became one of the "saviors" of Africa who prepared the way for others to follow in his steps.

When we follow the steps of the Savior of the world, there is one thing that becomes obvious, we must present our bodies, our lives as a living sacrifice to keep our hearts true, our service viable, and our focus steadfast towards glory, towards eternity. (AMH, pgs. 141-157)

- As we can see, sin will usually cost others before the offender will taste the bitterness of its consequences. This can be seen in the fact that it cost God dearly. In His holiness, God could not overlook, downplay, or tolerate our sin. He had to provide the means by which our sin would be properly dealt with. We know the story. He provided the ultimate sacrifice, His Son, Jesus Christ.

-RJK

- Those who are willing to risk everything and gain nothing are probably on the side of truth.

-Flat Horizons

- (In regard to Jesus.) His first cry tore the silence. His second cry tore the veil. His final cry will tear open the sky.

-Watchman Ezekiel
(FB)

- The Holy Spirit is a gift, remission of sins is a gift, eternal life is a gift, on the ground of the Cross of our Lord and Saviour Jesus Christ. Ignore that, and life is a wayless wilderness, where all our ideals fade and falter, leaving us only a grey, uncertain outlook, gathering to an eternal night.

-Oswald Chambers
(CWC, pg. 30)

- Sadly, uncleanness always contaminates those who partake of it or come into agreement with it. This is why holiness calls for separation, brokenness, and sacrifice. A person must separate to be purified, broken to receive, and their life offered up as a sacrifice to become pliable to ensure reconciliation to God and restoration of what is pure and acceptable.

-RJK

The Manifestations of Sacrifices

When you consider the five sacrifices in Leviticus 1-6, you begin to realize all of them pointed to Jesus. The priests were forever standing before God, offering up sacrifices, and maintaining the service of the tabernacle. There was no rest for the priests, even on the Sabbath.

Sacrifices had to be offered up to remind people of their sin. However, Jesus changed that. He offered up the ultimate sacrifice, and then He sat down on the right hand of the Father. Today, as the High Priest, He continues to make intercession for His people

In the reality of these sacrifices was the need for man to keep God at the center. Sin has a way of dulling man towards God, as well as causing man to forget. The sacrifices of fire were a way to remind people that the purpose for their existence was to know, love, and serve God. They had to keep Him a constant reality. Even though sacrifices were made for man's atonement, the priest's main activity was to keep God ever before him and the people in thought, practice, and duty.

We also see man's responsibility. He must rest at times in order to learn how to enjoy God. He had to afflict his soul at other times to maintain his life in righteousness and to prepare for personal growth. He must also feast to learn how to celebrate the gift of life. However, all of this was to keep man aware of the One, Jesus Christ who is the giver and essence of real life.

We are to offer our bodies as a living sacrifice as we pour out our life before God while maintaining the fires on the altar of our heart.

- When life is not a bed or roses, remember who wore the thorns.
  -Church Sign

- Morality may keep you out of prison, but only the blood of Christ can keep you out of hell.

  -Michael Boldea Jr.
  (EJ, pg. 99)

- The cross of Christ stands unique and alone; we are never called upon to carry His Cross. Our cross is something that comes only with the peculiar relationship of a disciple to Jesus Christ; it is the evidence that we have denied the right to ourselves.

  -Oswald Chambers
  (CWC, pg. 16)

- The animal sacrifices made atonement for sin. This means the shed blood covered the sins. However, God provided a sacrifice that would take away our sins, satisfy the Law, and reconcile man back to Him. This sacrifice came by way of Jesus Christ, the Lamb of God, who took away the sin of the world.

  -RJK

- It is by obedience that we take up the cross, not by singing about the cross. By taking the cross we are obeying, and when we obey, we carry the cross.

  -A. W. Tozer
  (WOG, pg. 58)

- When Jesus cried out, "It is Finished," righteousness was perfected, divine justice was satisfied, blood was shed, redemption was paid, sins were forgiven, reconciliation was achieved, death was conquered and salvation was secured.

  -FB

Opening the Way

Has the veil over your soul been ripped asunder so that you can see into the glory of the inner sanctuary? On the night Jesus became sin on the cross to pay the price for our sins, Hebrews 10:19-20 states, "Having therefore, brethren, boldness to enter into the holiest by the blood of Jesus, By a new and living way, which he hath consecrated for us, through the veil, that is to say, his flesh."

Once Jesus paid the price for our sins by offering His body, the great veil between the Most Holy Place and the Holy Place was ripped in half. This may not sound like a big deal, but this curtain was a thick, massive curtain that was 60 feet long and 30 feet high. (Note: According to the Jewish historian, Josephus, Herod had the veil raised to about 60' high.) It had the thickness of the palm of the hand (about 4 inches thick) and was wrought in 72 squares that were firmly joined together, and it needed many priests at a time to manipulate this veil.

It is clear that no mere convulsion of nature in her agony could have torn that curtain. An earthquake could have not rent it nor did the shattering of the rocky tombs tear it; only the hand of God could have ripped it in half, opening the way for every seeking heart to come into the inner sanctuaries of service and communion.

We are told in 2 Corinthians 3 and 4 that there is a dark veil over our hearts and it takes Christ to take it away so that we can see, not only into the inner sanctuaries of service and worship, but we can see Jesus in His glory, the Spirit in His Work, and the Father in His love.

Has the veil been torn away from your gross heart for you to see into the glory of the next age to come and receive its gifts and promises?

- All heaven is interested in the Cross of Christ, all hell terribly afraid of it, while men are the only beings who more or less ignore its meaning.

  -Oswald Chambers
  (CWC, pg. 130)

- God prepared the offering of His Son. His Son prepared the offering of His life. It was also the Jewish priest who designated that Jesus needed to die so many could possibly live. It was the Roman government that offered Him on the altar of the cross. It was God who laid the sin of the world upon Him as He was slain before the foundation of the world.

  -RJK

- Deliverance ministry won't cast out bad character, lack of self-discipline and commitment problems. You're gonna have to crucify that.

  -FB

- The cross of Jesus Christ is a revelation; our cross is an experience. What the Cross was to Our Lord such also in measure was it to be to those who followed Him. The cross is the pain involved in doing the will of God.

  -Oswald Chambers
  (CWC, pg. 16)

- ...there was such perverseness in Israel that the heathen world wondered at it. But the marvel is that the eye of God looked upon His people in the light that streamed from His own grace, across the blood of the sacrificial offerings presented in their behalf, and on to the atoning death of His well-beloved Son.

  -Herbert Lockyer
  (APB, pg. 32)

- As the servant Jesus took on a body, as the Son He became a Lamb, as a sacrifice He became our redeemer.

-RJK

The Qeren

According to a seven-part series in the periodical, *News From Israel,* the word "qeren" is a Hebrew word that is used in four different ways. It is used in relationship to a sacrifice that could be offered on the altar in the sanctuary where the blood would be poured out. It points to a horn of oil that was carried to anoint kings and it was also used in context of victory. This victory would be made known when the horns were blown to alert the people of Israel about the victory that had been secured. We see the horns blowing in the case of the collapse of Jericho.

The first three usages of the word "qeren" points to the fourth meaning which is a culmination of the three usages in the sacrifice of Jesus Christ. In Hanna's prayer in 1 Samuel 2:10, she requested this about the King of Israel, Jesus, "to exalt the horn of his anointed." The horn points to authority and anointing to the oil of the Holy Spirit. Jesus was anointed and given power to carry out His mission as the Lamb of God, the promised Prophet and Messiah. He was God's sacrifice that was offered upon the cross by mankind.

Jesus willingly offered up His life and His blood was shed for our sins so that we could become kings and priests in His kingdom. When He rose again, He proved victory over death. "Qeren" is clearly the complete work of redemption wrought in, through and by Jesus' great sacrifice.

In essence, Jesus Christ is our "qeren," and one day the last trump will sound and He will come for His church. Meanwhile, we must become an extension of His work. We must present our bodies as a living sacrifice, come under the anointing of the Holy Spirit, proclaim the Gospel, and be prepared to meet Him face to face when that last trump sounds.

Christian Living

Striving for the Unobtainable

We all desire to be perfect, but we live in an imperfect world, possess a natural bent (due to Adam) towards the undesirable, and reside in dying bodies. We constantly taste the bitterness of loss, the despair of suffering, the disillusionment of disappointments and broken dreams, and the hopelessness of ever finding and securing paradise in this world.

We desire perfection, but it eludes us at every turn. We want things right only to see them go miserably wrong. It was only in misery did I begin to consider what it would mean to find the joy and peace I so desired. In my plight I later discovered there was perfection and it came in the form of Jesus Christ. There is life, but it came from outside of me from heaven. There was hope but not in what I could see or obtain; rather, it was in the unseen. It was by faith I received not only eternal life, but abundant life that proved to be satisfying even in a dark, dying world.

Christianity is a life. It is the life of Christ in us, and His life is eternal. Therefore, the one aspect of His life is that it is ongoing. It is meant to change, enlarge, and bring purpose to every believer.

Life that remains stagnant in a believer becomes unbearable. Life that lacks challenge becomes aimless. Life that is never enlarged by learning lessons becomes spiritually small and dull. Life that is not disciplined becomes useless.

Clearly, the life of Christ must be experienced and lived out in every arena of our lives. It is meant to make us into new creations that become living expressions of our Lord and Savior.

———•———

- Most Christians today acknowledge Jesus with their mouth then walk out the door and deny Him with their lifestyle. We must examine ourselves according to Scripture.

  -FB

- The Bible does not say we are the elite, but the elected.

  J. Haley

- Our faith is in a Person Who is not deceived in anything He says or in the way He looks at things. Christianity is personal, passionate devotion to Jesus Christ as God manifest in the flesh.
  -Oswald Chambers
  (CWC, pg. 37)

- When I am real with my struggle, God is real with my victory.
  -Stacy J. Sanchez

Prayer: Lord, Your will should be my desire, worshipping You my agenda, and bringing honor and glory to You my goal. However, to ensure Your place in my life, I must dwell in Your presence. Lord, hear my heart's cry, and bring me into those secret places of communion with You. Amen.

- Christianity is not a message of morality that leads to forgiveness. It's a message of forgiveness that leads to morality.

  -FB

- Clearly, the Christian life must be walked out in order to take on the likeness of Christ. As we walk this life out, it will be worked in us by the Spirit, worked through us as we come into submission to Jesus' Lordship, and worked out of us through obedience to the Word.

  -RJK

- But the moment we serve for notoriety and reward we rob our service of its bloom and fragrance.

  -J. Gregory Mantle
  (COS, pgs. 104-105)

- *"And this is life eternal, that they might know thee the only true God, and Jesus Christ, whom thou hast sent" John 17:3.* What does this world have to offer that is greater than that? In spite of knowing this, however, many professing Christians today who still live for what this world has to offer cannot honestly answer the question, "When is enough, enough?" Is it not enough to know the only true God, and Jesus Christ? And yet, there still remains professing Christians who, "down deep," think that they somehow deserve to experience "abundant life" with one foot still in the world and the other foot in religion. Such will suffer from dissatisfaction, confusion, half-heartedness, lack of purpose, and a divided heart. Their faith will be weak, their "light" dim, their "salt" tasteless, their "fruit" blemished, and their lifestyle hypocritical. *"But godliness with contentment is great gain" 1 Timothy 6:6.*

  -J. Haley

- Christianity is beyond coming to church. It is the ability to represent Christ wherever you are.

  -FB

- Christian liberty is freedom from sin, not freedom to sin.

  -A.W. Tozer

- Don't be a hearer only, but become a disciple. Experience is never your guide; experience is the doorway for you to know the Author of the experience.

  -Oswald Chambers
  (CWC, pg. 20)

- Refresh your soul. Run to the feet of Jesus instead of to the comforts of this world and let Jesus become your everything.

  -FB

Others May, You Cannot

Most of you are probably well acquainted with the following inspired classic writing, but it's a good reminder for all of us who know Whom we have Believed, know Who we belong to, and know Whom we are living for: "Others May, You Cannot"

***

If God has called you to be really like Jesus, He will draw you into a life of crucifixion and humility, and put upon you such demands of obedience, that you will not be able to follow other people, or measure yourself by other Christians, and in many ways, He will seem to let other good people do things which He will not let you do.

Other Christians and ministers who seem very religious and useful, may push themselves, pull wires, and work schemes to carry out their plans, but you cannot do it; and if you attempt it, you will meet with such failure and rebuke from the Lord as to make you sorely penitent.

Others may boast of themselves, of their work, of their success, of their writings, but the Holy Spirit will not allow you to do any such thing, and if you begin it, He will lead you into some deep mortification that will make you despise yourself and all your good works.

Others may be allowed to succeed in making money, or may have a legacy left to them, but it is likely God will keep you poor, because He wants you to have something far better than gold, namely, a helpless dependence on Him, that He may have the privilege of supplying your needs day by day out of an unseen treasury.

The Lord may let others be honored and put forward, and keep you hidden in obscurity, because He wants you to produce some choice, fragrant fruit for His coming glory, which can only be produced in the shade. He may let others be great, but keep you small. He may let others do a work for Him and get the credit for it, but He will make you work and toil on without knowing how much you are doing; and then to make your work still more precious, He may let others get the credit for the work which you have done, and thus make your reward ten times greater when Jesus comes.

The Holy Spirit will put a strict watch over you, with a jealous love, and will rebuke you for little words and feelings, or for wasting your time, which other Christians never seem distressed over. So make up your mind that God is an infinite Sovereign, and has a right to do as He pleases with His own. He may not explain to you a thousand things which puzzle your reason in His dealings with you, but if you absolutely sell yourself to be His love slave, He will wrap you up in a jealous love, and bestow upon you many blessings which come only to those who are in the inner circle.

Settle it forever, then, that you are to deal directly with the Holy Spirit, and that He is to have the privilege of tying your tongue, or chaining your hand, or closing your eyes, in ways that He does not seem to use with others. Now when you are so possessed with the loving God that you are, in your secret heart, pleased and delighted over this peculiar, personal, private, jealous guardianship and management of the Holy Spirit over your life, you will have found the vestibule of Heaven.

-G. D. Watson
Living Words

- A Christian should be a striking likeness of Jesus Christ. You have read lives of Christ beautifully and eloquently written, but the best life of Christ is His living biography written out in the words and actions of His people.

-Charles Spurgeon

- Don't be afraid of being outnumbered. Eagles fly alone. Pigeons flock together.

-FB

- In our day, we have degraded Christianity to be a kind of soft vaccine against hell and sin. We gather people, stick them with a religious needle, and say, "If you just accept Jesus, you will not go to hell, you will go to heaven when you die. Keep living as well as you can, and when you die, you'll go to heaven. Many are preaching what I refer to as a kind of lifeboat salvation, and even the songs today reflect that idea.

-A. W. Tozer
(WOG, pg. 38)

- Humility is not thinking less of yourself but rather, thinking of yourself less.

-FB

- We must allow His timing to trump our plans. And we won't always know why. *Why* is for Him to figure out. It's beyond our control.

-Todd Nettleton
(WFF, pg. 20)

- Get at the knowledge of God for yourself, be a continuous learner, and the truth will open on the right hand and on the left until you find there is not a problem in human life that Jesus Christ cannot deal with.

-Oswald Chambers
(CWC, pg. 20)

- The desire of Christians should be to see this heavenly life come forth in them and reproduce itself in others. Reproduction is the very reason we are here in this present world. It is not about us living life, but discovering it for ourselves and letting it come forth through the hopeless darkness of the age we live in.

-RJK

American Christianity

We sleep, we eat,
We go to work,
Show up on Sunday,
Clap hands, say "Amen,"
And leave emotionally filled
But spiritually empty.

We are more in love with the experience
Rather than Jesus Himself.
We have reduced Christianity
  To goosebumps and butterflies.

-FB

- Christians must learn how to walk by faith, run with patience, and stand according to godly character. Believers are in a battle, but it is not to gain territory, but to maintain the territory that has already been committed to God.

-RJK

- ...Christian liberty is not license to live after the flesh, but it is liberty to glorify God.

-H. A. Ironside
(GE, (G) pg. 185)

- That is what the psalmist was talking about when he said, "He restoreth my soul" (Psalms 23:3). Souls are restored in proportion as they place their thoughts and affections on the things of God and resign themselves to do His will. For the time being, at least, we can take ourselves into that blessed realm where we can ". . . mount up with wings as eagles; . . . run and not be weary; . . . walk, and not faint" (Isaiah 40:31).

-Howard E. Kershner
(DPS, pg. 31)

- We must be courageously obedient. It is not a question of whether you want to be obedient or not. It is a matter of whether you will be obedient or be blind. The obedient Christians will be the seeing Christian.

-A. W. Tozer
(WOG, pg. 58)

- Kindness is more than words and deeds. It is a character quality deep within one's soul.

  -FB

- Read your New Testament again and you will agree that mediocrity in the Christian life is not the highest that Jesus offers. Certainly God is not honored by our arrested spiritual development—our permanent halfway spiritual condition.

  -A. W. Tozer
  (WFF, pg. 47)

- The supreme test of a Christian is that he has the Spirit of Jesus Christ in his actual life.

  -Oswald Chambers
  (CWC, pg. 25)

- The challenging call to each believer does not have to do with us fulfilling some destiny on earth, our real call is to discipleship so we will be trained to fulfill our high calling on earth.

  -RJK

Prayer: Lord, You have given us the sword to use against the wolf, the rod to use against the hireling, and the Spirit to expose their wicked agendas. Help me to learn how to use Your arsenal in the fight against all that affronts Your truth. Amen.

It is Not Over Until...

It will only be from the point of meeting Jesus in His unhindered glory, that completion will come to my life and the work that has been set before me. It will be from the point of His glory that true worship and praise will rightfully lift Him up in His majesty and greatness. It will be from such a perspective that the endless volumes that have been written about Him and His redemption will finally stand completed, for He is the Alpha and Omega.

Up until then, there is always greater territory to seek in regards to His infinite character and ways. There are always greater revelations to be unveiled to the seeking heart. There is always that need to seek out and find Jesus in the midst of His Word, as well as in the fiery ovens of faith, and in the trials of spiritual growth.

- The Christian who says, "Well I'm not as bad as THEY are," will rarely be looking to be as good as Jesus is.

-FB

- Unlovely harshness is meetness for the inheritance of perdition. Cherish the character that would be at home in heaven.

-Richard Glover
(APB, pg. 152)

- Being servants in the kingdom of God requires constant preparation. The idea that things are given to us without proper preparation to receive, possess, and take necessary responsibility for it is immature and foolish. However, many of the self-serving and indulging younger generations have this attitude that everything is owed them. They believe they do not need to develop character or responsibility to be entrusted with any matters of life and property.

-RJK

- Just as there is no such thing as passive income, there's no such thing as passive Christianity.

-Michael Boldea Jr.
(EJ, pg. 41)

- Legalism is obeying man's rules that God never made, obedience is following Christ to please Him.

  -FB

- Belonging to a visible church does not necessarily include membership in the true Christ. People may be religious yet not regenerated, baptized yet never washed in the blood of Christ; professors yet not possessors.

  -Herbert Lockyer
  (APB, pg. 207)

- The strongest people are not those who show strength in front of us, but those who win battles we know nothing about.

  -Jonathan Harnisch

- Christianity does not "progress" with the times. If it did, it would be a false religion. Do not be deceived into thinking there is a progressive form of Christianity. It does not exist because the truth never changes. God's Word is the same yesterday, today, and forever—Amen.

  -FB

- Today, discipleship is greatly missing. People are being made converts to a certain way of thinking, while they are being made followers of other teachers or schools of thought. As a result, Christianity has ceased to be a way of living. Such a life can only come out of love for the Master, devotion to His ways, obedience to His instruction, and wisdom in applying His examples to our walk.

  -RJK

- If cracks exist in a foundation, they can be exploited over time. If there are cracks in your spiritual foundation, the enemy is patient enough and wily enough to hammer at them until they grow and stretch, and your spiritual house becomes something other than the place of peace, joy, and intimacy with God that it should be.

-Michael Boldea
(EJ, pg. 15)

- Love is the true economist,
    Her weights and measures pass in heaven;
What others lavish on the feast
    She to the Lord Himself hath given.

(COS, pg. 110)

- Good develops in the process of overcoming evil. Living in a sinful world men develop character when they choose to be righteous.

-Howard E. Kershner
(DPS, pg. 36)

- A man is only joyful when he fulfils the design of God's creation of him, and that is a joy that can never be quenched.

-Oswald Chambers
(CWC, pg. 486)

- As believers, we are all called to stand for truth. Truth will place us on the Rock of ages. On the Rock we will endure the tidal waves of destruction. These waves will take out the sand castles of wishful thinking, but they will have no power to move the Rock from its eternal foundation.

-RJK

- If we are not God's *wheat* then we must be Satan's *tares.*

-Herbert Lockyer
(APB, pg. 207)

- There's a thin line between confidence and arrogance. It's called humility. Confidence smiles. Arrogance smirks.

  -FB

- Professional Christianity is a religion of possessions that are devoted to God; the religion of Jesus Christ is a religion of personal relationship to God and has nothing to do with possessions.

  -Oswald Chambers
  (CWC, pg. 8)

- Many people suffer an identity crisis. New converts to the Christian faith must be aware of what has defined them, and what will redefine them. Clearly, the world initially gives us our identity. Our parents give us our name, society determines our function, friends put pressure on us to fit in, and religion can put a burden on us as far as how we must conform. However, none of these exercises cause us to find our true place in Christ.

  -RJK

GO, the First Two
Letters of the Gospel

God had His tabernacle in the wilderness and now He has temples that are not made by the hands of man that are designed, built and established by Him. These temples are believers. Therefore, wherever we go the presence of God is in us and hopefully leading us.

Jesus made it clear that He did not have a place to lay His head, but He also declared that His body was a temple and as long as He was in the will of His Father, He could rest anywhere, whether in a bouncing wave-tossed vessel, in the gardens of the world, or in the wilderness, the Father's will would be His sweet pillow.

A Frenchman born of Huguenot parents by the name of **M. (Francois) Coillard** along with his wife traveled in a vortekker, which was a type of wagon as missionaries in the Barotseland, which is a vast region to the north between the Limpopo and Zambezi rivers in Africa. Coillard already had been part of building up a strong native Church among the valleys of "Switzerland of South Africa," but the call of wider horizons was already upon his heart as he thought about the tribes to the north.

He had built a nice home for his wife and himself after doing pioneer work in South Africa for 20 years when he lifted up his eyes upon virgin territory. His mission to expand the harvest was ordained by the Church of Basutoland. However, every inroad into the fallow field of dark and hard hearts always brought new and different challenges with it.

Under false pretense, Coillard had been invited by a ruthless king to come to his area, but the king was not interested in the Gospel; rather, he wanted to benefit from trade and Western technology. This king caused much hardship, exerted extreme cruelties and grave oppression upon the missionary and his wife and their small group, but in spite of it Coillard courageously pressed forward as he steadfastly preached the Gospel and fought against the horrors of the slave trade and pagan life.

Dark hearts may oppress, but during such oppression, the light of Christ will continue to shine forth and eventually break through. Due to Coillard's steadfastness, a successful mission was developed in the area. In 1895, he suffered a severe illness that forced him to return to Europe for recovery. However, in 1899, he returned to his beloved Africa where he continued the work until he entered glory in 1904. (AMH, pgs. 129-140)

There are two things I know for sure about serving the Lord. I have never read any part in the Bible where we are told to stop when it comes to carrying out our commission regardless of the hardships, because the first two letters in the word "Gospel" spells "go."

The second fact that there is no retirement plan, except past this world, shows me that my work will never be completed here. I must always press on until I cross the finish line into the glory of the promised new age.

- …our belief is that the problems of this world arise because men separate themselves from God. Those who abide in the shadow of the Almighty, keep His Commandments and seek to do His will go through life with shining faces and are spared the tragedy and suffering that afflicts all who refuse or neglect to be reconciled to Him.

  -Howard E. Kershner
  (DPS, pg. 157)

- There is the citadel--the spirit; there is the city--the soul; there are the walls--the body, with its five gates of access. You cannot keep the wonderful little kingdom, for while you are watching at one gate, the sleepless enemy will come in at another. "Except the Lord keep the city, the watchman waketh but in vain"

  -J. Gregory Mantle
  (COS, pg. 123)

- We are only what we are in the dark; all the rest is reputation. What God looks at is what we are in the dark—the imaginations of our minds; the thoughts of our heart; the habits of our bodies; these are the things that mark us in God's sight.

  -Oswald Chamber

- We, as believers, must possess our souls in patience to come into the place of blessed communion with our God. We must take possession of our souls daily by giving way to the working of the Spirit, the disciplines of God's Word, and the wisdom, righteousness, sanctification, and redemption found in the life, examples, and work of Jesus.

  -RJK

- At the end of life, what really matters is not what we bought but what we built; not what we got but what we shared; not our competence but our character, and not our success, but our significance. Live a life that matters. Live a life of love.

  -Author Unknown

Prayer: Lord, Your will should be my desire, worshipping You my agenda, and bringing honor and glory to You my goal. However, to ensure Your place in my life, I must dwell in Your presence. Lord, hear my heart's cry, and bring me into those secret places of communion with You. Amen.

- Some people need guidance, need a reminder of hope. In your words and actions, you can become the map to Christ. You become the road, you become the sign, you become the model. This requires us to have integrity in all areas of life. This requires humility—being honest without taking pride in it and understanding it is by God's mercy you can accomplish anything.

  -K. P. Yohannan
  K.P.'s Corner
  Rejoice Periodical
  October 2023

- The Lord has many sons and daughters, but few disciples. "And he said to them all, If any man will come after me, let him deny himself, and take up his cross daily, and follow me." (Luke 9:23) The big word is "IF."

-J. Haley

Meekness

What is meekness? In our society, the meaning of "meekness" points to weakness. We associate it to people who appear to be good doormats because they never stand up for what is right to that which is wrong, and against that which is unjust and dishonorable. In the Bible, meekness is an interesting term. It simply points to strength being under control. Clearly, such strength is not unruly, unyielding, undisciplined, or unmanageable. It does not hide behind some veneer of discipline; rather, it gives way to that which is allowed to channel it in a productive way. For the Christian, it simply means that their strength is yielded to the authority of heaven, disciplined by the Spirit, managed by the hand of God, and ruled by the Lord of lords.

- One of the frightening realities for me is that the Christianity being presented today is not the Christianity of the Bible. The Christianity of today has no prize that must be gained through loss, no depth in which to delve to discover treasures, no heights in which to ascend to gain a heavenly perspective, no personal growth in which to aspire too, no challenge in which to forge character, and no battle in which one is seasoned to endure to the end.

-RJK

- CHARACTER is how you treat someone who can do nothing for you.

-FB

- As believers, we must produce fruit. In fact, if the life of Christ is in us and the Holy Spirit is freely moving through us, there is no way we cannot help but produce heavenly fruit. There is also no way that those who are hungry and thirsty would reject it.

-RJK

Prayer: Lord, it is easy to design our own yoke, but pride will dictate that it must be immense, self will call for it to bring distinction to us, and the world will require it to be ornate with the things of the present age. In the end, it will simply bury me. Lord, replace Your yoke for my yoke. Amen.

Opportunities

It is natural for even Christians to become a bit lazy or casual towards life when it is filled with the daily drudgery of simply trying to live in the midst of the nominal, lifeless activities of the world. However, there are always opportunities to stir oneself up to avoid settling for the usual, while reaching for the extraordinary that will lift one to the heights of excellence. After all, the devil uses the ordinary to trip us up to fall into a pit where we end up with a restless spirit and a dissatisfied soul.

There is story about a London man named Thomas Britton who lived over 300 years ago. He had a coal business that was in a London stable. He never could really get above the daily grind of his status, yet he had a great love for music and because of his devotion for it, he gained great attainment in this difficult art. As a result, for nearly forty years he conducted well-attended concerts from the loft over the stable. One person who attended more than once was Handel. (DPS, pg. 39)

We can let the daily grime of this present world set our attitudes and moods, but we have been given opportunities from heaven to reach above the present status that will lift us above the drudgery of it all, and reach excellent heights that can prove to be steps of opportunities that lead us up the staircase of heavenly inspiration.

The key in reaching such heights is that our focus must be heavenward, our conviction must be sure, our devotion unwavering, and our love for the Lord fervent.

◆——————◦◦◀◉▶◦◦——————◆

- In my youth we were very poor but not discouraged or hopeless. Poverty is not tragedy; lack of character and hope is tragedy. . . Tragedy is separation from God and the disintegration of human character that accompanies it.

-Howard E. Kershner
(DPS, pg. 121)

- To spiritually overcome the wickedness that has taken center stage in this nation, we must choose the ways of righteousness. But we must remember that there is nothing nominal, complacent, or indifferent about righteousness when it comes to sin. It is wise enough to see that to be silent when evil reigns is suicidal, to be complacent when wickedness tears at the moral fiber of what is right is to sign a death warrant, and to lay down when righteousness demands you to stand against the tidal wave of injustice is to prove that one is not courageous or worthy to know or experience the goodness that will naturally flow from what is right, just, and honorable.

-RJK

- But Christianity is not a religion, a creed, a set of doctrines; it is a life. The Person of Christ is inextricably interwoven with His teaching. That teaching always centers in Him Who is the Way, the Truth and the Life. It is absolutely impossible to separate the

138

teaching of Jesus Christ from Jesus Christ Himself. Real Christianity is, in short, "Christ in you."

-J. Gregory Mantle
(COS, pg. 167)

- We are not called to be like other Christians, we are called to be like Christ.

-FB

- Herbert Spencer said people were trained to think like pagans six days a week and like Christians the remaining day; consequently, in the actual things of life we decide as pagans, not as Christians at all.

-Oswald Chambers
(CWC, pg. 39)

- Genuine Christian devotion is grounded by disciplines that keep it sharp when challenged by compromise, steadfast when shaken by uncertainties, and enduring when faith is being tested by the dark cloud of unbelief.

-RJK

- When you're hanging by a thread, make sure it is the hem of His garment.

-Church Sign

Is It the Correct Spelling

How do you spell the word "Christian?" It depends on how you approach it. Is it simply a word, a concept, an idea, a philosophy, a theological doctrine, or is it something even more than all of these descriptions put together?

I have had to ask myself this question. I call myself a Christian, but am I a Christian in word only or is it some concept that I have formulated in my mind, and because I think I understand it, I assume that makes me a Christian according to my way of thinking?

Perhaps I have an idea as to what being a Christian means, but an idea of something does not make it a reality. I could be hiding behind a great philosophy about being a Christian, but philosophies have a tendency to change with different generations. Maybe I have become religious enough by trying to reform my outer person to live up to some theological understanding of being a Christian, but that often ends up proving to be a burdensome duty that lacks heart.

I did find a very interesting presentation of the word **CHRIST** I-A-N on Facebook. "If I take out **Christ** in my life:

I

A-m

N-othing."

What makes us a Christian is the presence of the life of Christ in us due to being born again of the Spirit of God. There are many different Jesus's being offered, but there is only one Christ who identifies us to the kingdom of God. There are many ways being offered to heaven, but there is only ONE WAY that leads to heaven (John 14:6). Many are calling themselves a Christian but they do not have the Christ of the Bible; therefore, it is a lifeless word that gives them a false foundation.

Some have packaged the word "Christian" within the nice confines of a concept that creates a blinding smugness, an idea that lacks truth, a philosophy that has no stable foundation, or a doctrine that has no life, but once again the true Jesus, along with His life and Spirit, is missing. Such a person is a non-Christian for the Christ of the Bible is missing; therefore, they are left in a state of nothingness.

We may spell the word "Christian" right, but like so many words that lack the right intent or spirit it remains a word without any real substance to back it up. It is a word taken out of context, leaving people either deluded or standing on shifting ground as to their real eternal destination.

The Apostle Paul tells us in 2 Corinthians 13:5 to examine ourselves and see if we are in the faith, and what determines if we are in the faith is Jesus Christ. We need to make sure that when we stand before God on the day of reckoning, we must not be standing with nothing to offer or show, revealing we are nothing before God because Christ has always been missing from the word "Christian" in our life.

Faith And Grace

Often Overlooked
But Not Forgotten

There are a lot of stories about the men who served on the mission fields, but what about the women? Their names are mentioned, but their feats and sacrifices are rarely mentioned outside of the man's adventures. Is their contribution to the kingdom of heaven unimportant; is their sacrifice insignificant to God that there is no need to mention them except as a side note?

In Jesus' day they served Jesus and one woman's action of anointing Jesus for His burial serves as a memorial to us today. They were mentioned as co-laborers with Paul in Romans 16 and he even called one his mother, implying she was his "spiritual" mother.

They ministered alongside their husbands like Priscilla did Aquilla, prophesied like Philip's daughters, and like Lydia, started home churches. There are points where the man or men were instructed to adhere to a woman such as in the case of Abraham being told by God to do as his wife Sarah said, Balak seeking out the judge Deborah, priests seeking out the prophetess Huldah during the reign of King Josiah, and Paul instructed those of Rome to assist

Phoebe. In the case of Peter's wife, she not only ministered with her husband, but legend has it she died beside him on a cross.

In my studies of missionaries, women played a big role in the mission field. In fact, the women who served tirelessly as missionaries are double compared to men. Many of them are like Paul was in his service before the Lord; they were or remained single after the death of their spouse. It is said of Hudson Taylor that he preferred women in the mission field because he didn't have to contend with egos like he did with the men.

In God's economy He is not interested in our gender but in our heart. He is not caught up with some criteria as to those who do the work; rather, He is looking for those who will willingly and wholehearted do it. Women must count the cost as well when serving God. The cost might be a "normal" life, their husband's life, their children's lives, and it might just cost them their lives as well. There are stories where both men and women have buried their spouses and children in the ground of the mission fields as they sprinkled the small parcel of land with their tears.

The truth is there have always been both men and women of great faith laboring in the mission fields of the world. They have adhered to their great calling as ambassadors of Christ and their commission to share the Gospel and disciple those among them. They have lived their faith, walked in their faith, and died in their faith. Their footprints may have been wiped out by the winds of time, but their witness remains as being vital in the furtherance of the kingdom of God.

In some cases, the woman continued the ministry of their loved ones after their death. Consider the sister of Nate Saint, one of the five martyrs in 1955 in Ecuador. **Rachel Saint** went among the very native people who killed her brother and the other four missionaries to minister to them in 1958. She remained among them until her death in 1994 at the age of 80. She not only poured into these people for 36 years, but her body was buried there among them

***

Evelyn Constance (Harris) Brand is another missionary that continued to minister among the people of India after her husband, Jesse's death. They had married in 1913 and he passed away from blackwater fever at the age of 44 after laboring among the people for 22 years. In spite of the missionary board having great concerns for Evelyn's (Evie) welfare, she could not leave her husband, his vision, and her love for the people behind.

She went on to reach untouched areas of India with the Gospel. She officially retired at 70 from the missionary organization but she was not done. In 1968 at the age of 89 there were 33 people including herself manning sixteen stations under some challenging conditions in an area that missionaries avoided, but her husband had declared a burden for before his death. It was in her 95th year that she finally entered glory to see her precious Jesus and Jesse. She was affectionately known as "Granny Brand" and her epitaph read, "Trust and Triumph."

***

Another woman who carried on the work of her husband was **Mary Bosanquet Fletcher**. Her husband John was called the Apostle of Madeley. John was born in 1729 into a noble household in Switzerland. Even though he was born into means, he felt called to identify with the less fortunate, and as a result became one of the saintliest and humblest of men. He was greatly educated and could have chosen any parish, but felt called to the poorest of parishes and perceived he could not properly care for and support a wife. However, if he was to marry, he would choose Mary Bosanquet. (TK, pgs. 45-65)

Mary Bosanquet suffered different hardships. She so loved and was thoroughly committed to her Jesus that she was kicked out of her house by her father who would not tolerate such a strong, unbending devotion. She could have found relief by marrying a well-to-do farmer, but she did not feel that was her calling.

She went from riches to rags because of her faith, but embraced each stripping of possessions and pride with such confidence that her Lord would meet her, and because of her attitude she would become richer in faith for it. It was not until she was completely bankrupted at 42, that the 52-year-old John Fletcher realized that regardless of his small means, he had a parsonage and enough to get by. They had not seen each other for 15 years, and it would mark a quarter of a century of knowing about each other and waiting before the Lord on the matter of such a union that a proposal of marriage was finally given and quickly accepted.

After 14 months of married life, John wrote to Charles Wesley, "I was afraid to say much of the matter, for new married people do not, at first, know each other. But having now lived fourteen months in my new state, I can tell you that Providence has reserved a prize for me, and that my wife is far better to me than the Church to Christ; so that if the parallel fails, it will be on my side." (TK, pg. 61)

John and Mary would spend only three years, nine months and two days together before he graduated to glory. Mary went from writing how her cup was overflowing in her union with John down to that dreadful moment of his departure. However, she knew who to cling to, for her Lord would never leave or forsake her.

Due to her process, Mary was a prepared vessel to minister with him. John had told his wife that when she married him, she must marry his parish as well. For the next thirty years after his death, she labored among those of the parish in various ways and prove to be a shepherdess in her own way. She was allowed to live in their home they had shared for a very small sum of rent, and was active in picking the vicars with great success. She had a disciplined life where she stopped seven times a day to pray but she never wrote about her daily routine because her life was being consumed by her search for what was eternal.

Mary would experience another great loss when her daughter that she had adopted when she was in her twenties was taken from her as well. Each experience, no matter how deep, caused her hunger for more of God to increase. Her dairy writings revealed that her deep longing for God never grew old or ceased. No doubt this was the source of her victorious life as a saint of the Most High.

***

Rosalind Goforth was married to Jonathan Goforth, a missionary, who proved in his commitment as well as his work in different mission fields, whether it was the slums of Toronto or in the great vastness of China, that he was thoroughly sold-out to Jesus.

Many missionaries had to do pioneer work, blazing trails into the unknown. Such ventures proved to be more challenging because the unseen enemy lurks in attitudes, suspicious cultures, tough terrain, and diseases. The losses can prove to be great. For the Goforth's, they lost five children as well as valuable possessions in a fire and flood. They had to endure conflict within the country such as the Boxer Rebellion. It took them ten years before they could enter the region that they perceived they were called to.

During this time Goforth was reading about great revivals happening in Wales. He so desired to see God move among the Chinese in like manner. In fact, at reaching his 45th milepost, a strange restlessness began to prevail in his soul after reading in the Bible about doing greater works. The restlessness produced an intense burning. He asked himself if the promise of "greater works" could be fulfilled in his life, and did not God promise it in His Word?

He humbly bowed before the Lord, knowing all great works begin on the knees. The fruits that followed confirmed Goforth's trust towards God and His promises. There was revival and it was said by one who attended his meetings, "The cross burns like a living fire in the heart of every address." (TK, pgs. 135-151)

He would not stay in one centralized area but he ended up traveling throughout China leaving behind fruits unto eternal life. This brings us to his wife Rosalind, Rose for short. It is said of her that she was undaunted and that her story had many humorous sidelights as she kept pace with her husband.

She was born May 6th, 1864 in London. She joined seven brothers and four sisters. Rose had inherited her father's artistic talent, but she was also strong-willed, which created its own challenge when it came to her mother disciplining the imperious and passionate twelfth child.

They moved to Canada when she was three, and at age eleven she attended a revival where she took Jesus Christ as her Lord and Master. She would, with all earnestness, commit her life to the Lord. Like most people Rose was refined in her faith in fiery ovens. She started out pursuing her life in the world to only find restlessness in her soul. She went through the school of suffering when her father passed away and she was taken ill with inflammatory rheumatism where her life hung in the balance, but through it all her faith would not waver. She told the Lord if she was to marry, He would have to lead one to her who was wholly given up to Him and to His service, for she wanted no other.

Jonathan had been engaged to another woman but she could not reconcile their denominational differences and had broken it off. He had come to conduct a meeting where Rose was asked to be an organist. She was introduced to a "shabby fellow" who was identified as the city missionary by the name of Jonathan Goforth. However, his shabbiness was overshadowed by the wonderful challenge in his eyes and after looking at his well-read bible, she said to herself, "That is the man I would like to marry!"

Before they married, Jonathan had her promise that she would always allow him to put His Lord and His work first, even before her.

She would be quickly tested when he came to her and asked her if she would not mind receiving an engagement ring due to material on China that needed to be printed and distributed.

Rose knew she had the same calling as her husband. Nothing came easy, but God had begun a deep work to temper this strong-willed missionary to Himself. Through it all He was not only directing her steps, but He was teaching her, oftentimes through her husband's examples, ways, and messages. She learned how to rightly evaluate things, especially after experiencing diverse losses.

She realized that even though her husband was out front that the Gospel message had to be her message to walk out and share. She learned that all belonged to God and that the best must be offered to Him first regardless of the cost. Rose learned the practical and acceptable way may not be the right way and that she must trust and obey God no matter how little sense something made or how dangerous it appeared to avoid the greater loss that can come with disobedience.

She discovered that the safest place is the place of ordained duty and that losing one's temper can be costly. She found out that she must make time for personal communion with the Lord regardless of the demands, and that proper submission ensures right standing.

Rose spent almost 50 years with her husband before he went on to glory. It was after his death that she wrote about his experiences in China. Probably what summarized her life was her own autobiography, entitled, *Climbing.* So much of what we learn comes from climbing out of pits of failure, up steep mountains with ropes of faith, stepping over personal rights, facing losses, and walking through fiery furnaces to once again see God's design, purpose, and His work. Regardless of the challenging terrain this world and dark souls present, as believers we must ever ascend to the heights of excellence to discover the abiding care of our God and witness His moves that reveal His greatness. (TK, pgs. 153-175)

***

Have you ever heard of a woman named **Kate Lee**? There is nothing about her name that would imply anything out of the ordinary, but that happens to be the case for most names. They are often based on the most common names around a child's birth. However, Kate Lee may have had an ordinary name, but she had an extra ordinary way of calming the beast in people.

Was it her light touch? Perhaps her delicate fame, or maybe it was her blue eyes that seemed to speak volumes. But, what could her eyes say to defuse drunks and derelicts who may have been bent on destruction?

Harold Begbie, an author and journalist described what she possessed that would defuse the beast in man, "She loved the worst people in the world...She smiled and waited, waited at the prison door, waited in the pit of abomination, waited at the hard heart. And while she waited, she prayed quietly and calmly; and while she prayed, so great was the love of God in her heart, she smiled. There is no hope for the world until the love that was in Kate Lee is in us. I never looked into a human face so full of the love of God, so shinning with love of humanity, as the face of this 'Angel Adjutant.'"

It was her older sister Lucy that not only led Kate to the place where she would experience salvation but also to her life-time calling in the Salvation Army. She was born in 1872, a frail child who also proved to be a shy one. Both made her an unlikely candidate to work among those who lived on the streets, fought at the drop of a pin, and whose works proved they preferred darkness.

She enlisted full-time with the Army when she was 17 and would labor in it for 31 years. It became evident that she was not an orator; rather, that as a good soldier she was up early, seeking out and praying for the souls who had accepted the invitation to come to Jesus the night before, to not fall back into the temptation or their old ways. She would seek out such individuals to either tap them on the arm to remind them of their new commitment, pray for them if the temptation was upon them, and greet them to encourage them.

Paul talked about how God's love both constrained and compelled him. It constrained him in his responses to ensure he did right and compelled him in his ministry to go whatever distance he needed to go to reach heirs of salvation. Paul knew that the constraint pointed to the crucified life, the cross, but the life it produced was compelled by the love of God. The crucified life is the life that has the freedom to risk all out of love.

We have no idea of the sacrifice Kate offered to God. To some, her great sacrifice might have been in remaining single in her service to God. No doubt in it she came to know the great companionship of the Lord Himself. Perhaps it was the time she spent on her knees or walking the streets of human despair or entering into dark places where storms raged in the souls of men. However, nothing would deter her because she had made and reaffirmed her covenant with the Lord with all of her heart.

Love animated this frail young woman's life. Her love for God made her consecration to Him a light burden when it came to serving others. His love in her made the yoke for souls easy because the Lord is the one who carries the heaviest part.

Her covenant to the Lord became her anchor, prayer her sustaining substance, intercession her choice weapon, and love the cords to draw and confirm her concern and commitment to the forgotten, the untouchables, and the downcast.

In the end, the love of God caused this angel assistant to exhaust her own life's energies for the worst of humanity and die penniless but happy, knowing that what was before her was far more glorious.

It was obvious that in life Kate Lee had run the race, in love she stayed the course, and in prayer she fought a good fight. She was not interested in being recognized, but on the day her body was carried to its final resting place, the streets were lined with thousands, which proved that heaven's trophies are touched lives, changed hearts, and saved souls, and it was all because the love of God was shed abroad in the heart of one "angel adjutant." (TK, pgs. 176-187)

***

Missionaries in general can get a bad rap due to the abuses of a few "unloving" missionaries who put heavy chains of religious oppression on those who are already in bondage to superstition, idols, and shamans; or, whether they get put down by the intolerant world for offering those who are in such dark spiritual captivity the way out of it to walk in newness of life. After all, the god of this world, Satan does not want his captive souls to be set free. In spite of the abuses and the criticism, missionaries have left witnesses behind to confirm God's power to save and change lives.

In 1820, seventeen missionaries sailed for the Hawaiian Islands. A missionary by the name of Mr. Bishop, evangelized around the main island of Hawaii. One of his early converts was **Queen Kapiolani**. She was one of the most noted of all the female chiefs of Hawaii and ruled over large possessions in the southern part of the Big Island.

Kapiolani devoted herself to Jehovah God and became committed to bring Christ to her people. Her remarkable faith turned her people to the true and living God but not without first facing down demonic influences and powers.

She confronted the sins of their reckless and intemperate lifestyle, and led the way by dismissing all of her husbands but one. With a firm hand on the reins, she uprooted idolatrous notions and customs which included infanticide, murder, drunkenness, and robbery without being concerned about the possible repercussions to herself.

However, there was one goddess that held the people in such grips. It was the terrible and grim Pele who had her dwelling-place within the crater of the burning volcano. This goddess had priests and prophets, both male and female, that kept the people stirred up with fear.

Kapiolani saw clearly that the power this fire goddess had, had to be broken. She resolved to challenge the power of this goddess at her own stronghold. She would face off with her on the very floor of the crater of Kilauea.

The queen broke two tabus in the crater by eating the ohelo berry that was only for Pele to eat and coming to the Halemanmau itself, "House of Everlasting Burning" and casting fragments of lava defiantly towards the seething cauldron. Having desecrated Pele's holy of holies, Kapiolani spoke these words, "My God is Jehovah. He it was who kindled these fires. I do not fear Pele. Should I perish by her wrath, then you may fear her power. But if Jehovah saves me while I am breaking her tabus, then you must fear and love Him. The gods of Hawaii are vain."

The queen's actions and words lead to many including Pele's priests and prophets turning to Jehovah God. In fact, there was a follower of Pele who came to wrought great destruction among those who were seeking after the true God. This man brought terror to people's hearts, but he also was conquered by the Gospel of love and peace and likewise became a follower of Jesus Christ.

Mr. Bishop ended up preaching to assemblages that numbered upwards to 10,000 persons. Many of them were chiefs and chieftainesses who followed Kapiolani's example and declared their faith in Jesus Christ. (AMH, pgs. 349-361)

Who can God use? Anyone who is open and available.

———————————

- In our praying we draw on our memories, on our past experiences, on our present desires. We only learn to draw on the grace of God by pureness, by knowledge, by long-suffering. How many of us have to learn that temperance is knowledge?

-Oswald Chambers
(CWC, pg. 41)

- Any concept of grace that makes us feel more comfortable sinning is NOT Biblical grace.

-FB

- Childlike faith silences logic, puts reason on hold, and allows us to securely land on the work and promises of God.

-RJK

- Signs, wonders, and miracles do not establish FAITH...only the WORD OF GOD does. Search God out in His Word...not in experiences!

-J. Haley

- When we see the faith maligned, distorted, misrepresented, and denatured, we're not told to sit idly by and watch it happen. On the contrary, we are told we must contend earnestly for the faith, meaning we should put up a fight.

-Michael Boldea
(EJ, pg. 8)

- Care more for a grain of faith than a ton of excitement.

-Charles Spurgeon

Prayer: Lord, it takes faith to persevere in prayer, the confidence of faith to wait, the assurance of faith to stand, and the steadfastness of faith to move forward in our spiritual walk. Lord, thank You for giving us the measure of faith to take the next step of obedience to finish the course. Amen.

Are You Examining Yourself

"Examine yourselves whether ye be in the faith; prove your own selves. Know ye not your own selves, how that Jesus Christ is in You, except ye be reprobates" (2 Corinthians 13:5). Faith towards God is a topic that can never be exhausted no matter how many books are written on the subject. However, Andrew Murray summarized the walk of faith in this manner, "The life of faith is a life of obedience."

When I examine my spiritual life, I cannot help but examine my faith. Every mountain I climb requires me to exercise the sturdy cords of my belief. Every challenging wave that I encounter on the ocean of life tests the steadfastness of my confidence towards my Creator. Every storm I have had to endure exposes the source of my faith. Every time I encounter calm waters, the sharpness of my faith is tried.

It is at such times I must question my faith. Will I maintain the balance in my life because my faith is directed and found in the character of God, or will I find it running amuck in the midst of the encroaching darkness of the world. I must always test my loyalty, point of confidence, and place of assurance and rest to maintain my ways before the Lord.

Prayer: Lord, I know my faith is what I must keep to stay on course. Help me to remember to look up and not down or around me. I do not want circumstances, challenges, or situations to take my eyes off of You and put them on the shifting sands of the world. Amen.

- Wrapped in humanity, God's gift of grace through His Son, Jesus Christ, pierced the darkness to bring us light and life! One day – I believe very soon – this same Jesus will return to establish a kingdom of righteousness on the earth. What a glorious day that will be!

  -David Rosenthal
  Zion's Fire
  September-October 2023

- Trust the past to God's mercy, the present to God's love and the future to God's providence.

  -Augustine

- To have right standing with God, I first must simply believe a matter concerning God before He can count my standing and attitude **for** righteousness. It is because of faith God can reckon a matter as being acceptable which establishes us **in** righteousness before Him. Once that faith turns into actions of obedience, then He can count it **as** being righteous.

  -RJK

- Men abuse the grace of God because they've been taught there are no consequences to doing so. In their minds, they serve a one-dimensional God incapable of anything other than love.

  -Michael Boldea Jr.
  (EJ, pg. 17)

- Faith in God is a terrific venture in the dark; I have to believe that God is good in spite of all that contradicts it in my experience. It is not easy to say that God is love when everything that happens actually gives the lie to it.

  -Oswald Chambers
  (CWC, pg. 82)

- Admire the grace which saves, the mercy which spares, the love which pardons thee.

  -Charles Spurgeon

Prayer: Lord, thank You for the measure and gift of faith. There is no way we could walk through or survive this present world without faith towards You. Your mercy made faith available to us, Your grace provided it, and Your love inspires and sustains it in our lives. Amen.

- If we are born again, we are reminded that the Gospel was preached to us, and that we have received it. This means we have received it by faith into our hearts. We also stand by it, in it, and for it. This means we stand on the hope of the Gospel, which is the power of God unto salvation. We stand in the power of the Gospel, which ensures our ongoing deliverance, and we stand for the truth of the Gospel, which serves as the promise of life for others.

  -RJK

- There is a gentle peace that surrounds you when your faith becomes stronger than your fear.

  -FB

- All fear and corroding care are evidence of the lack of faith in the sovereignty and sufficiency of God. Because of His care and provision all anxiety is superfluous.

  -Herbert Lockyer
  (APB, pg. 150)

- Two thousand years ago, shortly after the death, burial and resurrection of Christ, the enemy was hard at work in attempting to pervert and twist the grace of God into licentiousness...In layman's terms, it's insisting that grace is a license to sin rather than an impetus to abstain from it.

-Michael Boldea Jr.
(EJ, pgs. 23, 39)

- The Christian faith means that the historic Cross of Christ is the pinhole in actual history through which we get a view of the purpose of God all through. Jesus Christ is "the Lamb slain from the foundation of the world."

-Oswald Chambers
(CWC, pg. 235)

- Whether it be godly character—we can't have it unless we are in the flow of God's grace for only God can show us favor in our needs and provide us with them. We must allow grace to flow down to us in our despair, and let grace reign in us during the testing of our faith to avoid being the most miserable creatures on earth.

-RJK

- Were it not for His grace, the darkness and depravity of this evil world would overwhelm us, and the sting of death would hold us captive to its power.

-David Rosenthal

Prayer: Lord, thank You for being the anchor that never moves, the Rock that remains standing, and providing the mooring lines of Your grace that can't be broken by the crashing waves of this world. Amen.

A Matter of Forgiveness

How do we find grace? We first must seek mercy according to Hebrews 4:16. God shows mercy when He forgives us, but mercy is a matter of grace because we can't earn it nor do we deserve it.

According to H. A. Ironside, there are three distinct ways in which forgiveness has been presented in Scripture. There is *eternal forgiveness* where a believers stand justified before God regardless of past sins. They will never be brought up again before the great Judge.

The second type of forgiveness is *restorative forgiveness* of the Father. God can't look at sin, but once sin, past or present, has been confessed and forgiven, the path of reconciliation has been opened that will end in restoration of our relationship with the Father.

The third aspect of forgiveness is called *governmental forgiveness*. Our sins result in paying consequences. Government reminds us there are laws that govern us, consequences when broken, and litigation when legal matters must be resolved in light of a just court. Once the transgressions are confessed, there are times when the great Judge will absolve one from all consequences and bring complete healing and restoration of what was lost. This points to governmental forgiveness. (GE, (E) pgs. 58-59)

Regardless of the forgiveness we encounter along the way, it is a matter of God's grace. The Judge of the universe desires to show us mercy by forgiving us and in doing so, shows us His incredible grace.

- It was not the salvation of individual men and women like you and me that was being finished (on the cross), but the whole human race was put on the basis of Redemption. Redemption is not going to be finished: it is finished. Believing does not make a man redeemed; believing enables him to realize that he is redeemed.

-Oswald Chambers
(CWC, pg. 235)

- When grace becomes an excuse to live in sin, you are no longer under grace but under deception.

-FB

- It's gotten to the point that so-called pastors of Christian churches no longer identify as Christian but as spiritual. Even the cornerstones of the faith, such as Jesus being the only begotten Son of God who lived, and died, and rose again, are being called into question, and dispensations are being handed out telling people they don't have to believe that to be the case to go to heaven.

-Michael Boldea Jr.
(EJ, pg. 43)

- God is the essence of all salvation. To look to any other source for deliverance is foolish. Faith towards God is the choice of the will, trust is the preference of the wisdom of the intellect, and assurance is the place where all undisciplined emotions have landed on the path of righteousness.

-RJK

Prayer: Lord, Your Word tells me that my faith must be towards You. To rely on any other source is a form of spiritual suicide. I choose to trust You. Amen.

- If your faith in God doesn't propel you into active obedience, is it really faith?

  -Stacy L. Sanchez

- God is always preparing us as His people so that He can grace us with His presence, honor us with His acceptance, and refresh us with His promises. The real key in preparation is by faith we must allow God to prepare us.

  -RJK

Prayer: Lord, Your amazing grace overwhelms me at times. To know Your grace is humbling, to experience Your grace is sweet to the soul, and to walk in it is to discover the real virtue and disciplined life of a saint. Thank You for Your wondrous grace. Amen.

- God will continue to show His grace through kindness in ages to come, and why does He need to show such riches even in eternity? It is because that is who He is? His love is everlasting--always there, His grace continues to flow--always active, His holiness ever transparent, and His light always present.

  -RJK

- Growth in grace—achieving sonship to God is something which one must do for himself alone. There is not something for nothing in that realm. In the spiritual world socialism is revealed as the stark skeleton it is. Perhaps that is the reason why Marxists are so anti-religious. They can grovel in the earth but they cannot aspire to heaven.

  -Howard E. Kershner
  (DPS, pg. 96)

- Faith is praising God in the storm, trusting God in the valley, following Him no matter what.

  -FB

- As Christians we have been given the means to be upright through simple faith in the Lord Jesus. Faith establishes us before God in right standing, confirms itself with a right attitude, and expresses itself in godly conduct.

  -RJK

Prayer: Oh Lord, make my heart child-like so that I can hear and see in order to understand and perceive your pure, simple truths. Help me, Lord, to have the faith of a child so I can trust you without reservation. Help me become pure, for the pure in heart shall see you. Amen.

- Faith serves as those eyes that can see afar off in light of eternal hope. It is the muscle that allows us to walk in expectation of seeing the fulfillment of glorious promises. It is the eternal virtue of optimism that causes us to be a stranger and a pilgrim in this world, while being an ardent citizen of the next one to come. Oh, to have faith like Abraham, confidence like Moses, assurance like David, and boldness like Paul would be to know the liberty that faith brings to each step, allowing us to advance in this present, dark world towards our final destination.

  -RJK

- It is the grace of God working in the soul that makes the believer delight in holiness, in righteousness, in obedience to the will of God, for real joy is found in the service of the Lord Jesus Christ.

  -H. A. Ironside
  (GE, (G) pg. 180)

- Faith is living without scheming. It is obeying God no matter what happens.

  -FB

- Faith never considers the obstacles. As Christians it is time to climb down from pinnacles of greatness, jump off of molehills of self-importance, and quit trying to catch, capture, or ride the high waves of personal accomplishments and euphoric sensationalism, and out of child-like faith respond to Jesus' beckoning, "Follow Me."

  -RJK

- Pray big, worry small, trust God, love one another. Laugh more, stress less. Have faith, rejoice and be grateful.

  -FB

Prayer: Lord, by Your grace You put the desire in me to look up from a point of humility for I need to look into Your lovely face to see the glory and riches of heaven in Your eyes of love. Lord, never let me settle for the fading revelations of yesterday when it comes to You, the decaying crumbs of past experiences, and unrealistic molehills of silly, fleshly notions about my life in You. Amen.

- Worry is like a rocking chair; it keeps you moving but doesn't get you anywhere.

  -FB

- What gives us confidence is the fact that God is dealing with His people today, not according to their righteousness, but according to His divine grace—so that His plan for Israel and the world will be fulfilled.

-Fredi Winkler
News From Israel
December 2022

- When each of us recognizes that all we have must be first submitted to the Spirit in order to realize the best God has for us, we begin to comprehend how God's grace works.

-RJK

- No one hates grace as much as the man who is trying to save himself by his own efforts.

-H. A. Ironside
(GE, (G) pg. 172)

Prayer: Lord, there will be no reason why we failed to produce heavenly fruit, except we chose to not believe, cutting off all connections to heaven. Forgive me for the weeds of unbelief. Help my roots of faith to reach deep and wide into the fertile ground of Your Spirit and truth. Amen.

Hope

A Living Hope

What makes a person risk it all for the sake of Christ? We know they are often compelled by love for their Lord, a vision for the lost, a sense of destiny, a faith that can't be deterred, and a destination that speaks of indescribable glory.

However, there is something else that is behind the compelling sense to lose all this life has to offer in light of gaining a greater life, and that is a living hope. So much of hope is based on that which is lifeless, useless, and temporary. It wishes for things that have no real value, tries to put some type of meaning on that which is useless, and settles for glimpses, crumbs, and bits of scraps along the way to keep it pursuing that which has nothing to offer.

Alexander Mackay, a Scottish missionary to Uganda had a living hope that would not allow him to back away from the constant affronts that Satan made against him to stop any of his progression to bring the light of the Gospel to this dark region. Whether it was the offering up of missionaries or the persecution and death of new converts, Mackay was steadfast in his mission to bring the light of Christ to a dark land of hard-hearted Pharaohs, and an oppressed people who lived in great darkness in an untamed terrain that magnified their paganism and hardships.

Regardless of the tyranny he lived under, the constant threats against his well-being and life, he forged ahead to bring contrast through his engineering skills, with the Gospel, and with godly examples. His goal was to both improve the people's lives on a physical basis in order to gain their trust so when the opportunity presented itself, he could offer them the life-changing bread from heaven, Jesus Christ.

Mackay faced much adversity from many directions in the mission field, but he never forgot the hope behind his high calling. He tirelessly worked in and around this mission field from 1876 to 1890 until his death from a severe strain of malarial fever at the age of 41.

Mackay left a powerful legacy behind him. Due to him forging ahead as an engineer in an unforgiving landscape, he was known as the "second David Livingstone" and it is because of his sincere heart and selfless works for the people that he was called, "the Hero of Uganda." (AMH, pgs. 93-109)

- To love Jesus' appearing means we are living for it. We desire it because Jesus is the Master we have chosen to love. We prepare for it because He is worthy to receive the best. We look forward to it because it serves as our blessed hope and expectation. Such hope will determine the direction of our pursuit and focus.

-RJK

- Christians are people of hope. We long for the day when the kingdom of God will be fully revealed, when Jesus will return in glory, and when death itself will be conquered. This is our hope, the hope of Christians past and present.

Stewart E. Kelly
(GG, pg. 539)

- Sometimes we feel hemmed in. The cards are stacked against us. Try as we will we cannot win. Every means of escape from an intolerable situation seems blocked. But we are wrong. One way is never blocked—the escape upward.

-Howard E. Kershner
(DPS, pg. 30)

- The beauty about being the children of the light is that we know our identity is not attached to the present world of darkness. Our Christian life is a vocation that defines our responsibility, a high calling that distinguishes us, a way of walking that leads us, and a way of living that will bring satisfaction and contentment to our very souls.

-RJK

- My hope is not in this coming year but in the One who is coming back.

-FB

Where Is Your Hope?

How do you know if you possess real hope. There are different types of hope, but there is only one hope that will hold you in sorrow, comfort you in despair and lift you up and out of depression.

Hope is not a mental process, a sentiment based on wishful thinking, or fantasy that dances on the edges of our greatest expectations. There is nothing substantial or sure about hope because it is based on the unknown, unseen, and the unobtainable. Granted, our imaginations can cause hope to rise up on some possible sentiment, our intellect can convince us that something unseen is so, even though it may not be, and our reasoning about something sets us up to fall into a pit that reveals that we harbored false hope about many things.

A noted English preacher by the name of **Dr. Joseph Parker** discovered the basis of real hope for every man, woman, and child. There was a time he put too much stock in the modern theories concerning religion of his day that would prove to be profane. As he got caught up with the latest presentations surrounding the philosophies purported in books, he began to lose his grip intellectually upon the great fundamental doctrine of salvation alone through the atoning work of the Lord Jesus Christ on the cross.

However, he found out how substantial these ideas were when his precious wife passed away. All that he knew could not give him comfort, and all that had caught his reason couldn't silence the emotions that were consuming him. All of the world's philosophies proved lifeless because they could not address his broken heart.

It was at the moment of great darkness, the light of Christ's great act of love and sacrifice on the cross began to part the darkness. Parker began to remember that great work of redemption done on his behalf and he put his foot on that point of great hope in order to firmly stand on it.

Parker summarized his experience in this way, "I stand there today, and I shall die resting upon that blessed glorious truth of salvation alone through the precious blood of Christ." (GE, (E) pgs. 55-56)

▪ Christianity is all about relationship with God. We begin this journey as a lost sinner seeking hope. Once we receive God's provision, our hope takes on the face of faith and obedience. In faith we begin to walk towards this hope as we obey His Word.

-RJK

- Persecution may devastate the faithful, but it does not destroy hope.

-Carl Teichrib
(GG, pg. 254

- I must constantly remind myself that I am just passing through this world and that my citizenship is not here, my future is not based on the present age, my hope is not founded in the temporary, and my expectation is not dependent on the unpredictable seasons of this present age.

-RJK

- There is not much hope for the scorner and the fool, but there is every hope for the simple one.

-A. W. Tozer
(WOG, pg. 115)

- Keep in mind that the word *hope* in the Bible does not mean "hope so," like a child hoping for a doll or a bike at Christmas. The word carries with it "assurance for the future." The believer's hope is, of course, the return of Jesus Christ for His church.

-Warren W. Wiersbe
(WBC, (NT) pg. 590)

Wisdom

The Will of God

How important is it to do the will of God? Is it optional or is it something that identifies you to His kingdom as being part of it? In one of the most sobering Scriptures in Matthew 7:21-23 the prerequisite to be recognized by Jesus as being His true servant is to do the will of the Father. Any service outside of His will is a matter of iniquity and will be considered unclean to Him.

God's will is wrapped up in His sovereignty and power to bring it about according to His ways and timing. The Apostle Paul talks about doing God's will in light of wisdom in Ephesians 5:17. We need wisdom from above to understand the will of God, discretion to discern the will of God, and insight in how to properly walk it out in our lives.

In fact, Paul points out in Ephesians 5:15-17 that we need to be wise in three areas. We are first told to be wise in our **conduct**, then wise about **redeeming time**, and to be wise about **God's will**. If you are a fool, God's wisdom will be far from you. If you are silly, God's wisdom will set you up to play the fool. If you are arrogant, you will be proven to be a fool. If you are self-sufficient, you will be found to be a deluded fool.

We must understand the will of God. In spite of the American presentation of Christianity, it becomes clear as you study the will of God in His Word, if you are not in His will and doing His will, you will not enter His kingdom.

There is what I call the **general** will of God which is in His Word, the **collective** will of God which has to do with His Church, and the **personal** will of God in relationship to one's life.

His will also works within three arenas: His **permissive** will where He allows one to do their own will but due to what these people are sowing in their rebellious ways, they will reap consequences. There is His **providential** will where He is using circumstances to line one up to His **perfect** will. His perfect will allows Him to have His way in a person's life

It is clear that in His **permissive** will man is not interested or seeking it. In His **providential** will man is ready to submit to it because nothing else makes sense, and in His **perfect** will man needs to accept what it is, and be willing to prove its integrity by walking it out.

The main fruit that God's will is being adhered to is that He will be glorified in the end. None will be able to share in His glory because it will be obvious that the results speak of His perfection.

One godly man described God's "perfect" will as an impartial love of the will of God. It is love that causes us to seek, know, and prefer His will over all others, including ourselves.

In his book, *The Counterfeit Christ And Other Sermons,* J. Gregory Mantle talks about how it is one thing to get into the will of God and another thing to stand there. Satan will do all he can to dislodge us from this place. Sadly, many who step outside of God's will because of Satan's attacks, will never get back into the "garden" of God's will again. (See pgs. 151-161.)

Mantle goes on to explain that once we have truly yielded to a life in the will of God, all strategy of the enemy is employed to drive us from our citadel. It is clear that what we have to do is stand in the evil day, and having done all continue to stand.

People think that God's will is a place of immunity from the wiles of Satan, but instead it makes us even more so a target. What brings one consolation is that one is actually in the will of God and will not dread facing Him.

Once we continue to stand according to His will, we will find ourselves standing complete in the will of God. In the center of God's will there is no debate as to what is right. At this stage one's will has been made **suppliant**, ready to do God's will, while doing His bidding which presents the opportunity to please Him. It is quick to say, "Not my will but Your will be done."

It is a **submitted** will that becomes a **surrendered** will that will endure all things for the glory of God in order to become an **identified** will that will share in His sufferings. It is at this point it becomes an **exultant** will that will cause us to press towards experiencing the fullness of the glory attached to doing God's will.

Mantle summarized God's will in this way, "To antagonize God's will is destruction. To surrender to it, accepting His plan and program for the life, is to get on board the train and to be able to sing at all times and under all circumstances:

'Ill that He blesses is my good,
And unblest good is ill;
And all is right that seems most wrong,
If it be His sweet will.'"

* Too many times we think that if we are thinking right or understand a matter that we have it right and there is nothing more we need to consider. However, wisdom is knowledge put into practice. Oswald Chambers made this statement, "Never get

off on the intellectual line, "think proper thoughts. *Live proper lives!* And you will think proper thoughts." (CWC, pg. 19)

- If we had never known ugliness, would we appreciate beauty? If the world were all roses, without weeds and thistles, would it captivate us? Could we really enjoy a beautiful sunshiny day, if we had never been wet and cold from battling tempests?
  -Howard E. Kershner
  (DPS, pg. 36)

- Words fill my breath. In a sense they are an intricate part of my life. I think about them, ponder their use, and strive to enlarge my vocabulary. I want to challenge minds, encourage hearts, and edify souls with them. I want my words to count as being true and trustworthy, inspired by the Spirit and filled with life. I want them to be laced with grace, salted by truth, dipped in the sweetness of heavenly wisdom, and anointed by the oil of heaven.
  -RJK

- The past is a place of learning not a place of living.
  -Thoughts Wander

- While no child needs to be taught how to be outraged or entertained, children must be taught how to occupy their leisure. That has always been the case…but is especially vital in a day and age in which children—indeed, all Americans—are constantly bombarded by different forms of entertainment totally at odds with genuine leisure.
  -The Berean Call, July 2023

- God's truths must become wisdom in order to become life. Wisdom is knowledge put into practice; therefore, life must be experienced to gain wisdom.

  -RJK

- The richest wealth is Wisdom.
  The strongest weapon is Patience.
  The best security is Faith.
  The greatest tonic is Laughter,
      And surprisingly, ALL ARE FREE.

  -FB

- Human wisdom has given us poetry, art, and religions. The wisdom of God is all-embracing, the key to every door, the secret to all mysteries, but men cannot always find it.

  -A. W. Tozer
  (WOG, pg. 66)

- Mere fleshly wisdom can never find food in the Word. All truth is revelation.

  -Herbert Lockyer
  (APB, pg. 45)

- Many Christians are journeying through life carrying more baggage than they should be…these believers are paying a price for carrying too much weight. Maybe your extra bag is un-forgiveness; you're carrying a grudge that's making your bag too heavy.

  -Todd Nettleton
  (WFF, pg.12)

- Be careful what you tell people. A friend today could be an enemy tomorrow.

  -FB

- You will not find true wisdom among the opinionated dogmatic, bigoted, and experts of the age.

  -RJK

- Take care of your body as if you were going to live forever; and take care of your soul as if you were going to die tomorrow.

  -St. Augustine

Who Does God Use?

There is often a misunderstanding about who God uses. Many in American churches perceive that a real minister of God looks a certain way, must be confirmed by having degrees, and must be of a particular gender. However, where have such notions come from because God is clear in His Word that His vessels and instruments will not meet the requirements of the world.

In 1 Corinthians 1:19-28 a list as to who God uses would prove that those the world overlooks, mocks, and casts aside are the ones God ordains. The reason for God using the unlikely, the overlooked, the downcast, and the poor is because He does not have to deal with the competition that comes from the arrogant, the "experts" of the age, those with degrees, and those whose knowledge is, in their minds, their savior.

The truth of it is that God's wisdom may sound foolish, appear simple, offend the expert, and receive a mocking sneer from the sceptic of the age, but in the end, it will prove to be pure. God's wisdom is not complicated, but it is beyond the comprehension of the "religious elite." It is not some intellectual enlightenment, but a spiritual revelation that will bring such clarity to those with a child-like faith that it will cause those that the world looks at with disdain to look wise in the end.

Many people are seeking God's wisdom but they are looking for it in the wrong places. There are those who desire it, but settle for the perverted crumbs of foolishness of the world.

We are told that God will not give or share His glory with man. It is for this reason that he chooses servants who are realistic about their status before Him and to keep them from the temptation of falling into the net of trusting their own abilities.

God's ways may seem foolish to those "enlightened" by this age and its god, Satan, but in the end such individuals will find they played the fool, and the bad joke will be on them, and they will know the darkness of hell, the taste of hopelessness, and hear the mocking of demons as their cries and screams in hell go unheeded.

- Wisdom is a loving spirit and will not tolerate blasphemy. The Spirit of the Lord fills the world. To fear the Lord is the root of all wisdom. Reverence flows from divine wisdom.

  -A. W. Tozer
  (WOG, pgs. 56-57)

- Life humbles you as you age. You realize how much time you've wasted on nonsense.

  -FB

- A wise man fills his brain before emptying his mouth.
  -African Proverb

- Wisdom will enable believers to stand in three ways. They will be able to stand on it, for its truths are eternal. Believers will be able to stand with it, for it is an eternal cornerstone that will ensure support. Finally, believers will be able to stand in it for it serves as a pillar that holds up the eternal, as it confirms what is real.

-RJK

- Skill, training, understanding, and character cannot be bequeathed or purchased. They require the concentrated effort of those who would acquire them.

-Howard E. Kershner
(DPS, pg. 151)

- Until Jesus satisfies your heart, no person or thing ever will.

-FB

- The best way to get riches, is out of doubt to set them lowest in one's desire.

-Joseph Alleine
(TK. Pg. 27)

- It is absurd to tell a man he must believe this and that; in the meantime, he can't! Skepticism is produced by telling men what to believe…Our Lord's word "believe" does not refer to an intellectual act, but to a moral act.

-Oswald Chambers
(CWC, pg. 25)

- Great minds discuss ideas; average minds discuss events; small minds discuss people.

-FB

- True leadership in the kingdom of God never comes from heights of arrogance but from depths of humility.

-RJK

- What we know is a drop, what we don't know is an ocean.
  -Isaac Newton

- Selfishness will blind us, and as we put self on the cross, our eyes will be opened. Wisdom poured into our life will create an attitude of selflessness.
  -A. W. Tozer
  (WOG, pg. 58)

- Gossip dies when it hits a wise person's ears.
  -FB

- Christian beware of thinking lightly of sin. Take heed in case you fall little by little.
  -C. H. Spurgeon

- There is tremendous good in asking questions. It can signal a search for Wisdom. But in the post-modern context wherein questions are an end to themselves, a masquerade for knowledge – a justification for the abandonment of truth – then the only thing left is absurdity and despair.
  -Carl Teichrib
  (GG, pg. 98)

- (In light of the *Wisdom of Solomon, 1:4):* Wisdom, according to this ancient wisdom, will not enter into a malicious soul, but is poured out upon a man who is pure and will not come upon any person subject to sin. The inner heart and the outer body both have to be clean.
  -A. W. Tozer
  (WOG, pg. 25)

Prayer: Lord, it is foolishness to cling to my take on things, stupid to insist on it, and suicidal if You give it to me. Help me to cease from foolishness, flee the stupid ways of self, and bow out of committing spiritual suicide over nothing more than the vanity of the world. Amen.

- Sometimes you have to eat your words, chew your ego, swallow your pride and accept that you are wrong. That's not giving up—that's growing up!

  -FB

- Wisdom and power cannot be separated from the cross. If we do not obey, we blind ourselves, and we become dependent upon our own intellect, which will be in no way sufficient to teach others.

  -A. W. Tozer
  (WOG, pg. 58)

Consecration

Pouring Out One's Life

What does it mean to consecrate your life? There are a couple of ways to describe this act, 1) it is setting something apart for God to use, and for the believer that points to their bodies and lives. And 2) it is offering all up to God so that He will be glorified in the end.

The one way in which consecration happens for a Christian is called discipleship. To consecrate oneself, they must first deny self to any right to their own life, pick up the cross to mortify the old and then follow Jesus into a new life that will be identified as possessing a holy disposition, being righteous in attitude, and godly in conduct.

For missionaries who have a true calling, they must consecrate themselves first before embarking on the mission field. They will have to deny self of all their former life to gain the new life. The old must be poured out so that the saint can become an open vessel where the Lord's life can be poured through them into others. It is a life that will eventually be consumed by the burden of their calling, as they partake of the divine, become part of the miraculous, and end up becoming a walking, living witness to dying souls.

These people are acquainted with grief that becomes part of their identification in Jesus' suffering, coming face to face with the adversary of souls, surviving extreme dangers, witnessing the miraculous, and sometimes they are offered up on the altars of the world to pagan idols.

For many missionaries of the past, their deeds are unknown but for those who have left a written witness behind, we can peek into their lives, adventures, challenges, and impact, knowing there are many such stories that may never be known here, but they are written in the annuals of heaven. In the following summaries you will see the immensity of the mission fields these stout-hearted individuals were entrusted with.

Mr. **John Horden** along with his wife in 1851 began to serve among the Indians and Eskimos in Canada in a region that comprised 2,250,000 square miles, known as Moose Factory, a settlement of Hudson Bay Company.

Horden immersed himself in the harvest field, traveling through the region on foot, by dogsled, canoe, and any other mode that would advance his mission. He endured hardships that included 100 degree temperatures in the summer and 50 degrees below zero in the winter. His linguistic abilities helped him master the Cree Indian language and he accomplished two literary feats, which included a book on the grammar of the Cree language and a complete translation of the New Testament in Cree.

The New Testament was completed on his deathbed in 1893 at age 65 years old, which marked the end of his 42 years of service on earth to the Lord. When Horden passed from this world to the next, more than one Indian had been educated and ordained for the work of the ministry. There were 26 native lay teachers, both Indian and Eskimo and they were busy ministering in various parts of the diocese. Thousands of individuals had been baptized, and showed peaceable and upright lives that they were not merely Christian in name only. (AMH, pgs. 179-193)

***

James Evans was known in a couple of ways. By the Indians he served he was known as "The Praying Master," but because of him spreading the Gospel among those he was called to, he was known as "The Apostle of the North." However, he simply considered himself a servant and soldier of the Cross.

Evans was trained for the grocery business and in 1822 had traveled to Canada to find better employment. However, it was there that he was born again and received a burden for the people. In 1828 he accepted a position to teach at a mission school for Indian children. He quickly picked up the Ojibwe and Cree languages and began teaching and sharing the Gospel with the Indians on the various circuits he traveled, ever seeking out new converts in the vast wilderness of Canada.

In 1840 he was appointed by the Wesleyan Methodist Missionary Society to the post at Norway House, Manitoba. This work allowed him to continue to travel far and wide to reach as many Indians as he could with the Gospel of Jesus Christ, which included not only Ojibwe and Cree, but the Blackfeet.

In 1846 after 24 years of service among the Indians of Canada, Evans finished his service. He had completed a speller for the Ojibwe Indians, as well as a hymnbook of Christians songs, the alphabet in the Cree language and publishing portions of the Bible in the Indian tongues. It was pointed out how complete his consecration was not only by the titles he held but by this statement, "James Evans demonstrated by word and by deed how one might live his life as a missionary of Christ." (AMH, pgs. 195-213)

***

When it comes to missionary work, a couple must be called together to a mission field before they can be sent forth. This requires them to first of all consecrate themselves individually to the Lord for His glory and then as a couple they must once again consecrate themselves for His work as a team.

Stephen and **Mary Riggs** were called to serve as missionaries to the Sioux peoples of the Dakota Tribe. They arrived at Traverse des Sioux in 1842 to embark on a remarkable adventure. Their consecration would show how the power of the Holy Spirit is the only One who can miraculously change the heathen life and culture through those who are faithful to the Lord's calling.

As in any case where missionaries are treading where the light has not penetrated hearts, there are many challenges and obstacles to overcome from lean times to dangerous times. This couple had few converts in their first 20 years of service but they had forsaken all to follow Jesus and it was His work and it would come forth in His time.

The Riggs did everything they could from running a school for Indian children to preaching on Sundays, to Stephen serving as military chaplain as well as visiting and encouraging other missionaries at other stations. They did finish a translation of the Bible in the Dakota language and Stephen completed nearly 50 literary works which included his personal biography, grammars and dictionaries of the Dakota language as well as the hymns.

Mary died in 1869 at the age of 56 never seeing the full fruits of their labors take hold but Stephen would go on to see incredible fruits in his 40 years of service to the Lord before his departure from this world. The Riggs' work was manifested in two ways: First, their six children would go on to do missionary work among the Indians and one even crossed oceans to share the Gospel among the native Chinese.

The second way was the great change that took place among the Indians themselves. Stephen noted that when they came there in 1837, they were surrounded by the whole Sioux nation that was in a state of ignorance and barbarism. However, in 1877, the majority of the Sioux had become both civilized and Christianized. Instead of hearing the once familiar sound of the war-whoop, the voice of praise and prayer could be heard on each Day of Rest from Indian cabins and their sanctuaries. (AMH, pgs. 215-230)

- Many of us are far too busy here and there on errands of minor importance, and allow a more solemn charge to escape us. We need more *concentration* as well as *consecration* – more *attention* with *intention.*

  -Herbert Lockyer
  (APB, pg. 41)

- Clearly, if we do not lose our present life, we will never find our promised life.

  -RJK

- Deliverance gets you out of Egypt, but discipleship gets Egypt out of you.

  -FB

The Places of Preparation

Present Christianity is often presented in a positive light. It seems that the looming shadows of loneliness, the twilights of uncertainty, the dark nights of testing, and long nights of struggle and despair are rarely mentioned. Yet, we see these very things in the life of our Lord and the saints that have gone before us.

Christianity is a lonely walk because each individual must live or walk out the life of Christ in them. Like Jesus, we must struggle alone in prayer through the night in preparation to bear our own cross. Like Jacob we must occasionally wrestle all through the night to receive a personal blessing. Like Elijah we will sometimes be driven out in the wilderness in fear and despair before we are brought to a place where we will hear the still small voice of His Spirit. As in the case of King David we will have many struggles in ourselves along with enemies and demons, but we will ultimately learn how to rest in who God is.

Most of Christianity is about preparation in order to truly consecrate ourselves to God. I can't count all the places of preparation the Lord has graciously and mercifully brought me too. At first, I questioned Him, but then I learned to trust Him. Once I could trust Him, I could look back to see how each place of preparation prepared me for the next place of revelation where He would entrust me with a tool of truth, service, or gift in which I could use in the work in the harvest field to further His kingdom.

We sell ourselves short when all we want is the positive side of religion and not the enduring side of preparation. We need to know that the positive side of religion will set us up to fail when the negative side of testing hits us without the preparation to stand and endure.

R.A. Torrey's conclusion of the Christianity of his day summarizes what is happening today. His conclusion was that Christians have just enough religion so they are miserable because they do not want to totally consecrate themselves to Christ in the fear that they might miss out on having some fun when it comes to the world.

It is obvious that surface religion might keep the conscience at bay, but it will never satisfy the soul or prevent a leanness from taking place in the spirit.

- God has already prepared the way. He's just preparing you.

-FB

- Let us think less and less of human commendation and approval; let us be possessed of a passionate desire to please our King, not only keeping His commands but anticipating the longings of His heart. This can only be accomplished by an entire and eternal consecration to Him.

  -J. Greogry Mantle
  (COS, pg.105)

- God wants full custody not just weekend visits.

  -FB

- Holiness is the opposite side of salvation.

  -Charles Spurgeon

- Jesus is not interested in big religious crowds. He already had one, and it crucified Him. He wants disciples.

  -Steven Lawson

Lordship

It is easy to make declarations about giving all to the Lord, but such claims are often made in the heat of zealous sentiment that is at its peak of self-sufficiency. However, within minutes or hours, the peak has suddenly been rendered into a molehill of reality at best as zealousness has waned and at worst a long valley of testing and challenges lies before the now former "zealot."

Real consecration entails coming to terms with the Lordship of Christ. We are all born into slavery but Jesus' redemption allows us to choose who we will serve. Servants in His household find themselves in different responsibilities depending on their relationship with Him. Some are entrusted with overseeing the affairs of the household, some carry out the duties of daily living, and some work in the harvest field.

One of the great battles this country fought was slavery. Slavery is a practice that has always been. The conquered become slaves, the vulnerable become indentured, the weak become obligated, and the poor are exploited. This is why slavery is a moral issue that often rides on or hides behind the shirttail of economic stability. The rich elite needs serfs, slaves or servants to do their bidding. Humanity in this case is a commodity that can be used, exploited, abused, and cast aside when used up.

Even though godly men fought against man owning man in this nation, they realized that they were bondservants to Christ. They knew that by serving the right master, they could reach their highest calling as a servant.

One such man was **Wendell Phillips** who was known as the "Boston Orator." He was a great orator and statesman of his time. One of the secrets behind his greatness was that he was incorruptible. When Phillips was asked by a friend shortly before his death whether there was any crisis in his life that explained his unfaltering devotion to His master, Jesus, Phillips shared about the pivotal point of time in his life.

He was 14 years old and he had heard Lyman Beecher preach on the Lordship of Jesus Christ. He told how he went to his room, locked the door and threw himself on the floor and cried out to the Lord. This is what he cried, "O God, I belong to Thee; take what is Thine own: I gladly recognize Thy ownership in me: I now take Thee as my Lord and Master." It was from that time on, Phillips admitted that he had never known a thing to be wrong without having an aversion to it; and he had never seen anything to be right without have an attraction to it.

J. Gregory Mantle added this bit of wisdom to the story of Phillips, "Many are perfectly ready to take life from Jesus Christ who hesitate to take *law* from Him. But there can be no real loyalty unless we make Him the Lord of our conduct as well as the Saviour of our soul." (COS, pgs. 120-121)

- True obedience is the refusal to **compromise** in any regard to our relationship with God regardless of the **consequences.**

-A. W. Tozer

- Holiness, obedience, sanctification are demands by God. It's not optional.

-FB

- By sin he (Adam) lost his beauty and fell short of the glory of God. Holiness is the recovery of the Divine likeness.

-J. Gregory Mantle
(COS), pg. 43)

Prayer: Lord, You have heard my heart cry. I want to offer You those gems that reflect Your fire, Your light, Your life, and Your glory. In order to have the passion of fire, fire must be put to my faith. In order to reflect Your light, I must walk in it. For Your glory to come forth, You must be unveiled in my life. Thank You Lord, for You will answer my prayers. Amen.

- Wearing a cross will not make you a disciple. Carrying your cross does!

-FB

SWALLOWED BY THE DARKNESS

The other day I took a journey,
Right from my office chair,
Searching for souls we fought for,
When we were "way back there."
Surely seeds we planted,

Had taken root and grown,
But from what I saw on Facebook,
It's as if they'd never known.
Face after face, and a few posts too,
Told me the story that God already knew.
The "windows of the soul" told the story,
Of love for the world, and rejection of glory.
Haunting and hollow, some blank with despair,
Belied the fake smiles and smirks I found there.
No mention of Jesus, or God's Word did I find,
But rather wrong choices, and perversion of mind.
This journey of mine was so short and quick,
But what I saw there made my heart sad, and sick.
Then the Spirit reminded me of what Jesus had said,
"Come follow Me, and let the dead bury the dead."

– J. Haley

Prayer: Lord, I do not want to miss You by tasting the bitterness of the soul caused by a leanness in the spirit, the dark garment of hopelessness, and the isolation of despair. Give me that great hunger and thirst for Your righteousness that will enable me to rise up out of the miry pits of this world and seek You with everything in me. Amen.

- The righteous carves his name upon the rock, but the wicked writes his remembrance in the sand.

  -Charles Spurgeon

- Consecrating natural gifts is popular but a snare... The only thing we can consecrate is our bodies. If we consecrate them to God, He takes them.

  -Oswald Chambers
  (CWC, pg. 29)

- Many have lost much for Him, but never did, never shall any lose by Him.

Joseph Alliene
(TK, pg. 27)

Being Made Unfit

When you talk to God's sold-out servants, you find one common thread that identifies them as to the fact that they had a decisive calling on their life that they could not ignore. That thread is that they never really fit into the environment of their times. It is clear that God makes His believers unfit in their time and generation in order to keep them separate as a means to consecrate them and make them fit for His kingdom and use.

This should not be a surprise since Abel was killed because he did not blend in with Cain's idea of sacrifice, Noah didn't fit in his wicked generation, nor did Abraham in the Promised Land of Canaan, Joseph when it came to his brothers, David in the political scene, Daniel in the decadent society, John the Baptist in the Levitical Priesthood, and Jesus in the religious scene. The truth for the servant of God is that being unfit does not just point to being a square peg that doesn't fit into some round hole designed by man's religion and the world's influence; rather, it points to the realization that there is no place in the world that they will ever fit in the scheme of things, and that it is God who has prepared their course and their place both in His church and kingdom for His glory.

+———————•➖•———————+

- What have I strength for, but to spend for God? What is a candle for but to be burned.

-Joseph Alleine
(TK, pg. 35)

Prayer: Lord, I want to be committed to You, and zealous against that which offends You. Give me Your disposition of obedience before You, Your hatred of sin, and a holy fear that will cause me to walk in sobriety. Amen.

- If we give ourselves over to meanness and to Satan, there is no end to the growth in devilishness; if we give ourselves over openly to God, there is no end to our development and growth in grace.

-Oswald Chambers
(CWC, pg. 167)

****

Once there lived another man within me,
   Child of earth and slave of Satan he;
But I nailed him to the Cross of Jesus,
   And that man is nothing now to me.

Now another man is living in me;
   And I count His blessed life as mine.
I have died with Him to all my own life,
   I have risen to all His life Divine.

Dr. A. B. Simpson

Judgment

Judgment Calls

We are making judgment calls all of the time. These calls are based on different criteria. Sadly, many judgment calls are based on feelings, feelings about how something makes a person feel personally or whether sentiment is aroused in them, passion is lit by some cause, or a sense of injustice takes seige of someone's conscious or sense of fair play.

The question is can we ride on the waves of judgments based on feelings or should other things of a more substantial measure be used to, not only test our present judgments, but our future ones? All judgments must be made in light of true justice which is based on truth and that which will prove honorable when tested according to the fruits it produces.

In his speech that was given at the 171st Commencement Ceremony held at Hillsdale College, May 13, 2023 and which was printed in the *Imprimis*, **Robert Barron**, the Bishop of the Diocese of Winona-Rochester Minnesota spoke on how truth is being cast aside. He shared two attitudes towards truth in relationship to that if all judgments are to be right and fair, they must be made in light of justice. He shared an interesting interaction between these two attitudes found in the writing of Plato called *Gorgias.*

In this writing an interaction takes place between Socrates and Polus, a student of Gorgias, a Greek sophist or teacher. Socrates approached the subject along these lines: if a rhetorician teaches a politician to do what is unjust, he does that man and his city more harm than good. Polus answers by means of an affront: "Wouldn't Socrates leap at the opportunity of having the power of life and death over others?"

Socrates rebuttal was along the line of true justice. His response was if someone is put to death unjustly, they are proving they have no power. He goes on to say that it is better to suffer wrongdoing than to do wrong oneself.

The other student of Gorgias, Callicles could no longer restrain himself from voicing his position which is the same that many hold today. The position is that what Socrates is calling "justice" is nothing but the constraints placed on the few strong by the many weak. It is a type of guilt-trip imposed by the powerless to limit the capacity of the powerful to get what they want.

This philosophy had a tight connection between Friedrich Nietzsche, a German philosopher and cultural critic who published intensively in the 1870s and 1880s. He is famous for uncompromising criticisms of traditional European morality and religion, as well as of conventional philosophical ideas and social and political pieties associated with modernity.

Let us consider what Socrates was saying. He was not defending a philosophy or a tradition; rather, he was advocating that true justice shows restraint in order to ensure it is true and fair. The truth is injustice ends in the corrosion of a soul who commits it, while damaging the moral structure of a person's character that must endure the terrible ways of injustice.

Injustice robs a society of hope because when injustice is not met with reasonable consequences, the door is opened wide for ongoing abuses against those who can't push it back or put a stop to it. In a sense, all of society finds itself being victimized by the lawlessness and growing appetites of a few elites who are nothing more than despots and tyrants who have no concern as to the destruction they leave behind.

Barron was presenting a case in his speech to the graduates in order to challenge them. He asked, "What kind of person will you be? Will you do whatever it takes to get what you want? Or will you accept even great suffering in order to do what is right? Everything else in your life will flow from your answer to that question."

Barron goes on to point out that when your foundation is the Bible, the real difference is not a matter of philosophy, where it is a question of "religion" vs. "secularism" but of idolatry and right worship. He goes on to point out that even in secularism they speak of the "higher good."

Scripturally we know that the "higher good" among humanity finds itself bowing before altars that may consist of man's best which is nothing more than filthy rags before God. Perhaps he does good deeds, but works that are not motivated by the right spirit and ordained by God are considered profane to Him.

Today America's great idol is money that is associated to control, power and status. However, this idol requires you to sell your soul. The more money people have the more unfaithful they become with it due to heaping it upon themselves. In addition, the smaller their world of selfishness becomes, the greater their point of fear and obsession becomes as they constantly wrestle with how they can hold onto it and maintain it.

Those who make the right decision based on what is right before God and honorable towards others, will be ensured justice in the end. They may feel like Elijah who stands against the 450 prophets of Baal but in the end, God did accept the prophet's offering by fire, while pronouncing judgment on the prophets of Baal.

In this world the righteous who stand for justice must be prepared to taste the bitterness of the world's injustice. They must remember the three major systems of the world were involved in the crucifixion of Jesus. Those of the religious system **unfairly** demanded He be crucified; those of the world **unwisely** went with a lie and chose a thief over Him as king; and the political system **unjustly** offered Him up on the cross to keep a veneer of peace with the religious system.

Meanwhile, regardless of what is going on around us, we must choose the narrow way of the cross and a life of discipleship. We must choose the fire that consumes and not vain activities of trying to get the attention of our idols. We must become identified with Christ in the world's rejection of Him if we are going to ultimately reign with Him. We must choose to worship the true God in heaven and not bow before the altars of the world in order to ensure we stand as just, do what is righteous, and prove what is godly in the end.

- There will not be a single excuse that will work on judgment day.
  -FB

- Eventually everything established by man will collapse in complete ruin. It will be judged by the Law of God, buried by the dust of vanity, lost in a maze of ineptness, marked by the ash of decay and death, and forgotten as the sands of time erase away all memories of its existence.

  -RJK

- A shrinking gospel? NO, it is a saving gospel, and while some say yes of the Good News, the history of humanity is soaked in the consequences of saying, "no thanks." Indeed, this is the *game of gods* – to say "no thanks" as we strive to save ourselves, either as individuals or in our communal towers of Babel. Without a personal Savior, there is no hope for personal salvation and ultimately no hope for the world.

-Carl Teichrib
(GG, pg. 547)

- The purpose of God is according to His grace, grace to those who could not earn it, who did not deserve anything but eternal judgment.

-H. A. Ironside
(GE, (E) pg. 27)

- Contrary to the myths you may have heard, you're gone, and there's no workaround once you're gone. It may comfort those left behind to light candles or pray for the souls of the dearly departed, but while you lived, you made choices, and your choices will have eternal consequences.

-Michael Boldea Jr.
(EJ, pg. 25)

- Hell is a terrible prison, and those who go there won't be eligible for parole.

-FB

No Recourse Available

A young lady committed a crime and she was sent to court. The punishment for the crime was life imprisonment. She shed tears for help, but there was no one available for help. When the case was called in court she started weeping.

Her family and friends who accompanied her started weeping but there was no hope. But something happened. Before the young lady could stand in the witness box a man stood up and the courtroom was silent. Everyone looked at Him. He was noble and gentle. He stood in the witness box and interceded on behalf of the woman.

The case was difficult, yet He used all His strength, energy, and resources to fight on behalf of the woman. After a long legal battle between the man and the accusers, the lady was set free. The lady fell before the man and asked "WHO ARE YOU?" The next day the lady deliberately committed another crime and was sent to the same court.

As soon as she entered the courtroom, she saw the man who interceded for her the previous day on the judgement seat. He was no longer a lawyer, but a judge. With smiles on her face the lady said "I have come again."

The man lifted his head and said 'yesterday I was a lawyer, so I fought for you, even when you were guilty. But today I am a judge and my judgement must be fair.' With tears in the lady's eyes she asked for the second time "WHO ARE YOU?" and the man replied

"YESTERDAY I WAS YOUR SAVIOUR. BUT NOW I AM YOUR JUDGE"

Today Christ Jesus is our lawyer and redeemer, but a day is coming when He will give a fair judgement to everyone as the ultimate Judge of all.

"JESUS IS COMING SOON, SO PREPARE TO MEET HIM".

-(FB)

- If we indulge in inordinate affection, anger, anxiety, God holds us responsible; but He also insists that we have to be passionately filled with the right emotions.

-Oswald Chambers
(CWC, pg. 114)

- The first time He (Christ) came to slay sin in men. The second time He will come to slay men in sin.

  -FB

- 5 minutes inside of eternity and we will wish that we had sacrificed more, wept more, loved more, grieved more, prayed more, sweated more and given more.

  -Leonard Ravenhill

- It's worth noting that every new addition to the human rights roster deconstructs the notion of the family and even the continuity of the human race. If God wasn't going to judge the nations, it's likely that we would have self-destructed all on our own without any assistance from Him.

  -Michael Boldea Jr.
  (EJ, pgs. 32-33)

- The greatest thought that has ever entered my mind is that one day I will have to stand before a holy God and give an account of my life.

  -Daniel Webster

- There is one thing which is worse than controversy and that is false doctrine, tolerated, allowed, and permitted without protest.

  -J. C. Riley

- Don't gamble with eternity. Hell has no exit doors. The moment we take our last breath, there will be no redoes. Seek the Lord while He may be found.

  -FB

Days of Noah

Lot lived in the wicked city of Sodom. Much like the days of Noah, the people of Sodom were busy giving in to their fleshly appetites. There seemed no boundaries to the people's evil except for the day that fire and brimstone rained down on the city and destroyed all the people, except for Lot and his wife and two daughters.

Jesus was clarifying that when He comes for the second time, wickedness will abound in the same way. People will be partying instead of repenting. They will be justifying grave wickedness, instead of wearing sackcloth to express the shame and disgrace for such ways. They will pursue every type of wicked imagination instead of being vexed over it and separating from it.

Jesus is assuring the hearers that just like in the days of Noah and Lot, judgment will also fall on the end of the last days. The challenge is the same as it was for Noah and Lot. When God instructs His people to leave all behind and seek the ark of His safety, they must not hesitate to flee the judgment that is coming. Then he makes this simple statement in Luke 17:32, "Remember Lot's wife." We must not hesitate or with longing turn back to look on what has been, or is being, judged.

Prayer: Lord, we are told to judge righteously. This means we discern according to Spirit, test according to Your Word, and consider all matters according to Your holy character. Amen.

- Do you understand how dangerous a thing it is to project your pettiness and vindictiveness onto God and assume that He is as spiteful as you are? Do you know the danger of speaking on behalf of God, for Him when He did not say what you say He said?

-Michael Boldea Jr.
(EJ, pg. 13)

- If men believe a false gospel, if they put their trust in something that is contrary to the Word of God, their loss will be not for time only but for eternity.

-H. A. Ironside
(GE, (G) pg. 27)

- Obedience to the Lord sometimes leads us along a painful path. Those who go against divine truth bring condemnation on their heads.

-Herbert Lockyer
(APB, pg. 41)

- Fear lest you should take counters of gold, or some common workings for grace. Oh, there is a world of counterfeit going. Multitudes perish by mistakes, and wait in hell, whilst they dream they were in heaven.

-Joseph Alleine
(TK, pg. 40)

- Quit worrying about what everybody thinks. When you come to the end of your life, you're not going to stand before people and give an account of your life. You are going to stand before God.

-FB

Injustice!

There is nothing that tears at the fiber of a society more than injustice. Even though man wants to do what he wants to do regardless of right and wrong, he will either become despondent or angry when injustice dares to touch his life or wake him to that which is inconvenient or uncomfortable. After all, there is no hope for right when wrong is sitting on any type of throne of tyranny. At such times prejudices will judge, indifference will wield judgments, cruelty will mock true justice, and injustice will swallow any attempts to bring out that which is right.

When it comes down to it, man has this inept philosophy that justice will in time win out but when he sees injustice in seats of judgment ruling with an iron fist, he begins to lose hope and this is what the enemy of our soul wants to happen. However, as believers we must take comfort in knowing that one day the Judge of all will execute justice, and injustice will no longer reign.

The issue of justice has always been debated. There are those who question who should execute justice in the first place. It all comes down to who establishes the standard and whether the judgment will ultimately prove beneficial in some way to the one who stands as judge.

Sadly, man can be bought, falsely persuaded, intimidated, and blatantly excuse himself as he stands on the side of injustice. He will turn a deaf ear to the cries of injustice, and he will heed bribes to avoid being counted among those who are foolish enough to seek justice in this world. He will become the oppressor without any real conviction pricking his conscience and he will prove to be an ardent tormentor and bully of those who seem weak and stupid to him because in his mind, he can without fear of consequences toy with them like a cat does a mouse. In the end, he will prove to be the greatest fool of all, but meanwhile, such a person becomes our test as Christians.

His judgments will be bitterness to our soul, his ways vexing to our spirits, and his indifference despairing to our resolve. However, as believers regardless of the injustice around us, we must be just in all we do.

The word "righteous" in the Hebrew is *tsdedqah* which means "justice." God is not only a God of justice but He loves to see righteousness and justice performed on earth. In the world where corruption is rampant at every level of society, the Lord continues to search out justice and loves those who uphold it.

May He find such justice in my life and your life. After all, justice is what the sinner secretly desires when injustice abounds. It is what the godless hopes for when injustice is in pursuit of his soul. It is the wisdom of justice that the foolish often long for when they foolishly fall into a trap. It is what the wicked will try to hide behind when caught in their brazen ways.

The truth is justice is a light that even the unjust can seek out when the world is spinning out of control due to the insanity of its time. We not only have that light in us, but we must guard and maintain it in our life to ensure it shines in the darkness of the age.

Prayer: Lord, when we hide in darkness to avoid judgment, it is because we refuse to see Your light. We know it will reveal all of our wicked ways and deeds. Lord, shine Your light upon me for I desire all wickedness to be exposed in my life, rooted out by Your fire, and swept away by the winds of Your Spirit. Amen.

- God did not spare the angels who sinned. He will not spare this generation just because it thinks He should.

  -Michael Boldea Jr.
  (EJ, pg. 126)

- When someone judges you, it isn't actually about you. It's about them and their own insecurities, limitations and needs.

  -FB

- Sin is measured in direct ratio to the grace it spurns.

  -Herbert Lockyer
  (APB, pg. 77)

- As a people, we are clearly reaping the misfortune of experiencing firsthand the consequences of what happens when a nation becomes complacent towards righteousness, ignores the responsibilities of righteousness, or compromises righteousness to live in peace with any form of wickedness. We now can see that in such a state of sin, foolishness replaces wisdom, folly mocks sobriety, insanity trumps reason, ignorance rejects truth, and lawlessness and rebellion rage against justice.

  -RJK

- When God offers men the truth and they deliberately turn away from it, they stand in danger of being delivered over judicially to that which is absolutely false.

  -H. A. Ironside
  (GE, (G) pg. 89)

- Stop trying to justify what you need to crucify.

  -FB

- Whatever excuses we come up with for sitting on the sidelines and allowing the enemy to do as he wills, however, will not suffice when we stand before the Almighty.

  -Michael Boldea Jr.
  (EJ, pg. 30)

- Never WORRY about who will be offended if you speak the TRUTH. Worry about who will be misled and destroyed if you don't.

  -FB

- The man who lives as if the truth were not true is as bad as the man who denies the truth. God judges a man by how he lives the truth, not by how he parrots the truth. So, there are two outstanding examples of a fool.

  -A. W. Tozer
  (WOG, pg. 108)

- Sinners, experiencing the patience, forbearance and long-suffering, hide in a false refuge if they believe that God will not execute His word regarding their ultimate doom, if they linger and die in their sin.

  -Hebert Lockyer
  (APB, pg. 75)

- God has sent us a strong delusion in our day. The Church has allowed delusions and feelings to drive their thoughts.

  -FB

- When it actually is an event of history, the irony of human folly became manifest: God destroys the pride of men by the very idols of their desires.

  -Herbert Lockyer
  (APB, pg. 77)

- There is anger which is human, and there is anger which is Divine. Human anger resents the *hurt*; Divine anger resents the *wrong*. Human anger is wounded in its *pride*; Divine anger is wounded in its *heart*. Human anger laments the injury to self; Divine anger laments the injury to God. Human anger cries out for revenge; Divine anger cries out for atonement.

  George Matheson
  (VS, pg. 20)

- There's not changing one's trajectory after they've breathed their last, no matter how many candles you light on their behalf. You can burn the world in the hope of lighting someone's way out of the pit, to no avail.

  -Michael Boldea
  (EJ, pgs. 25-26)

- God is shaking the fence of the earth so hard that people will be forced to fall on one side or the other.

  -FB

The World

Repackaging the Old

As we consider the days we live in, we must remember that all the systems of this present world or age, including the religious system, are being aligned to embrace a one-world leader who will use all of the systems to carry out his wicked agenda against God and His people. However, to bring about this one-world government, economic and religion system, people must be conditioned to embrace it.

It is important to remember Satan simply repackages lies after seducing and indoctrinating people into another reality. Like a cancer, his lies have slowly infiltrated the different systems, including Christian colleges, seminaries, universities, and organizations in each generation. This clever way has been to ebb away the absolutes of biblical truths with half-truths, propaganda, and false promises to bring society to the place where even the ardent religious are more concerned about social justice, than warning people to flee the just wrath of God that will come upon the face of the earth.

Christianity is being redefined without much concern or opposition from the Christian sector. Sadly, in this modern-day, quasi-religious state, humanity is much more willing to identify as spiritual rather than religious. This includes worship that emphasizes spirituality rather than the right spirit and truth. These individuals will settle for a vague notion of some "higher power" that will not insult any one person, rather than point to the only One who can bring healing, deliverance, salvation, and hope to a soul.

Christians who will not move from the truth of salvation are accused of being narrow-minded and exclusive in their beliefs. However, every believer knows one thing, this one-world religious system wants Christianity as a label, but minus the lordship, redemptive work, and the absolute truths of Christ. However, Christianity minus Christ EQUALS NOTHING.

Christ is the center, source and means of Christianity. He is the only way, and He alone is worthy of all worship for He is God Incarnate, Savior of our soul, and Lord of our life.

The line is being drawn as the great religious delusion of our day is taking people captive. They will either align to the real Jesus of the Bible or they will align with the anti-Christ and his system to keep their life and peace in this present age that stands doomed, but in the end, they will lose both.

We each must make sure we are on the right side of eternity-- that of the cross of redemption, and the winning side of heaven, and being on the side of Jesus who is the King of kings and Lord of lords and judge of all.

+———————•◄———►•———————+

- What is the world? The set of people with ambitions, religious or otherwise, that are not identified with the Lord Jesus Christ...When the world comes before us with its fascination and its power, it finds us dead to it, if we have agreed with God on His judgment about sin and the world.

-Oswald Chambers
(CWC, pg. 33)

Prayer: Lord, in our attempt to survive in this world, we often find ourselves becoming a victim of it. Please help me to separate the vain activities from that which would ensure my future with You. Help me to discern foolishness from necessity, and the good from the bad, the better from the best, and the excellent from that which has a false or temporary glory. Amen.

- World-kingdoms destitute of God must end in dust, and as we journey on to Christ's millennial reign the less enduring and the more worthless are the mere kingdoms of this world.

-Herbert Lockyer
(APB, pg. 94)

- We live at a time when the tongue of Satan (lies) has become the most common language in the world.

-FB

- We put a price tag on everything from a human standpoint, which is how our world works. We cannot, however, bring that over into our relationship with God. Our relationship with God must be based upon God's ways and not our ways.

-A. W. Tozer
(WOG, pg. 68)

- The world requires our souls, while Jesus gave up His life on our behalf. The world demands our all, while Jesus gave up His all so that He could become all in all to us. The world will sacrifice us, while Jesus became a sacrifice for us. The contrast is obvious, but sadly most people choose the world instead of Jesus. In the end, all they gain is emptiness and a foreboding sense of doom.

-RJK

- It's no accident that anything virtuous, moral, wholesome, or traditional is demonized to a degree heretofore unseen since perhaps the days of the apostles.

-Michael Boldea Jr.
(EJ, pg. 56)

- In a world full of trends, I want to remain a classic.

-FB

- God seems to have allowed us to live in a wicked, cruel world of many difficulties in order to develop within us the strength derived from overcoming the disagreeable conditions.

-Howard E. Kershner
(DPS, pg. 37)

Prayer: Lord, the more I deal in this lewd world, the more I long for You and heaven. The more I taste the purity of Your glory, encounter Your righteous ways, and taste Your goodness, the more I glory in my heavenly citizenship, knowing that Your Spirit gives me glimpses into that which is heavenly even now. Thank You. Amen.

- The Bible forever speaks of the vanity of this present world. Its glory is fading, its treasures temporary, its promises fleeting, and its end that of death.

-RJK

- Three ways to fail at everything in life:
  1) Complain about everything.

2) Blame others for your problems.
3) Never be grateful.

-FB

- I always cringe when I hear the word *unfair*. Nobody ever heard a holy man use the word, because the Christian does not know anything about fairness. He does not live in a world where people treat Christ fairly. Who treated the apostles justly? No one.

-A. W. Tozer
(WOG, pg. 94)

- Certainly a good conscience is a continual feast, and enough for a happy life: no man that warreth entangleth himself with the affairs of this life, that he may please Him Who hath chosen him to be a solider.

-Joseph Alleine
(TK, pg. 26

- We live in a world that has been turned upside down by sin. Granted, the Gospel can turn a person's world right side up, but meanwhile most people live in a world that has everything backwards. For example, the world lies in darkness; therefore, it thinks its form of light is real. It walks in perversion; therefore, it calls good evil and evil good. It justifies sin and rejects righteousness. It boasts of knowledge while mocking the wisdom of heaven. It prides itself on its foolishness while undermining justice. This is the harsh reality of the world we live in.

-RJK

- This present age is so flippant that if a man loves the Savior, he is a fanatic, and if he hates the powers of evil, he is a bigot.

-Charles Spurgeon

- See to it that you do not rest in a worldly religion: to give God your knee, while the world carries away your heart.

  -Joseph Alleine
  (TK, pg. 38)

- Those who study history recognize the pattern and know what's coming next. It can't happen all in one fell swoop; Rome wasn't built in a day, after all, but if you can manage to single out a particular class of individuals, isolate them, vilify them, demonize them, and dehumanize them, you can do pretty much anything to them, and no one will bat an eye.

  -Michael Boldea Jr.
  (EJ, pgs. 56-57)

- The death of any nation begins with its rejection of God. No culture can survive without Him.

  -Steven Lawson

- To the world, it is never enough, but when it comes to the kingdom of God, Christ is always found to be enough.

  -RJK

- Religious people always get upset when God uses the people they thought were unqualified.

  -FB

- It's funny how the ungodly, perverse, and demonic only encourage people in one direction. You've never heard a false prophet encourage anyone to draw closer to Jesus, and you've never heard a false teacher encourage anyone to pursue righteousness, sanctification, and holiness.

  -Micheal Boldea Jr.
  (EJ, pg. 12)

- People who put their hope in the present age value the temporary riches of the world. They strive for mansions that speak of illusive successes and happiness. They seek to make a legacy that will be passed down to following generations as a memorial to their so-called "greatness." They perceive that if their name is on some institution, street, or building that those who follow will take note that they once existed. The truth is, these people may leave some small token of history behind, but eventually the winds of time and the storms of life will wipe out all knowledge of them.

  -RJK

- Human society is built on the errors of fools. This sounds brutal, but in the context of Scriptures it is very kind. I say this because a fool acts without regard to future consequences—as though there were not another world besides this one and he was not intending to die.

  -A. W. Tozer
  (WOG, pg. 90)

- Sin is not just a part of being human in a broken world. It is what broke the world.

  -FB

Whose Destiny Do You Hold?

When we are content to live this life on an earthly plane, we never consider the power we hold when it comes to influencing others for good or bad. We figure we have our own problems taking care of our personal affairs without getting caught up with other people's lives. However, when you understand God's heart, and you feel His hand on you or know you have some type of destiny, there is also a sense that other people's destiny could very well be in your hands. You know you can't save them, but as an instrument in God's hand you will in some way impact them to the point that will even change their destiny.

To some, they may influence the destiny of individuals or a group, but there are those who influence the destiny of a nation such as the prophet Daniel did in Babylon and Medo Persian Empires. Another such man was **Joseph Hardy Neesima**. He was born Shimeta Neesima in Tokyo, Japan in 1843, during a time when the samurai warrior was still revered, class structure determined a person's value and future, and Christians were executed or exiled.

Commodore Matthew Perry would arrive in Japan ten years after Neesima's birth bringing the winds of change through treaties of friendship to a secret land. As a young boy Neesima showed passion for liberty and had a thirst for knowledge, which included knowing the true God of heaven. At age 15 he refused to worship the family idols. He was a samurai who eventually traded his sword for a Chinese Bible. With the intervention of God, he made a daring escape to America from Japan, which was a crime punishable by death. His goal was to know God who had both ordained his calling and mission before the foundation of the world

On July 20, 1865, Neesima arrived in America destitute. He had a full heart but an empty hand. Even though the Civil War was over, work was hard to find and his "pidgin" English caused its own type of barrier for him to reach his desire to learn English in order to be educated in the ways of God, he would not allow himself to be deterred. He was eventually taken in by a kind, godly couple who saw great potential in him and he became their adopted son and took on the name Joseph Hardy Neesima. They financed his education and he graduated from Amherst College and entered Andover Theological Seminary.

In 1872, he was offered the means to serve a Japanese delegation to the United States. He was provided with a passport and invitation to return to his own land. It was through this political door he made some important connections that would serve him well when it came to fulfilling his calling in Japan. He was given a vision from God for the formation of an educational program and college in Japan where those who had the calling of being preachers and teachers of Christian doctrine could be trained to fulfill their Christian destiny.

He returned to Japan ten years after his initial journey to America as a missionary to fulfill his calling. This would require him to face daunting and dangerous challenges as he would be shaking up ingrained beliefs such as Buddhism and Shintoism, which were the national religions of Japan, and facing some giant financial mountains that God clearly leveled before him as a testimony to the fact what He calls one to do, He prepares the way and enables the vessel.

He did start his college in Japan. It was named "Doshisha," or "Company of One Endeavor," and it was established in Kyoto which was the sacred city of the interior that housed over six thousand temples, and it was where Buddhism and Shintoism had flourished unchallenged for thousands of years. In spite of the religious environment, within the fifteen years Neesima had been engaged in this work, the students grew to 900 and the founder was ready to take it from Doshisha College to Doshisha University. He had even secured the funding for it. However, due to his great labors Neesima wore himself out and died at age 47 in 1890 before seeing the transition.

His widow honored his humble wishes which was, "Raise no monument after my death. It is enough, that on a wooden cross there stands the word, 'The grave of Joseph Neesima.'"

Neesima's life shows us the real monument are those who are living, and he left such a memorial to his beloved country, Japan, that would greatly impact it. More than 5,000 students passed through Doshisha in 1903. Out of that class, eighty were preachers of the Gospel, 161 became teachers, 27 government officials and 16 newspaper editors. (AMH, pgs. 39-53)

- Have we reached the ultimate stage of absurdity where some people are held responsible for things that happened before they were born, while other people are not responsible for what they themselves are doing today?

  -Thomas Sowell

- The WORLD is changed by your example, not your opinion.

  -FB

- Western civilization without Christianity is like a beef broth without beef.

  -Robert W. Keyserlingk
  (GG, pg. 33)

- Sadly, it is easy to come under the influence of darkness of this present age. In our need to please others, we can submit to their form of darkness. In our need to fit in with the world, we can justify coming into agreement with darkness. In our desire to have life on our terms, we can allow darkness to become light. In each case, the darkness will entangle our hearts, minds, and ways into a destructive web of bondage and despair.

  -RJK

- (In regard to the Middle East conflict.) At its core, this conflict is part of an epic spiritual war that's raged since the fall of Adam and Eve in the Garden. It's a war between good and evil – between God and Satan. The ultimate destiny of humanity, and planet Earth itself, hangs in the balance. The city of Jerusalem is ground zero in this epic war, and the Temple Mount is the coveted prize.

  -David Rosenthal

- Human reason is anchored in the flesh. It draws conclusions based on the flesh's experiences, desires, and interests, and if it is not regenerated and has not been renewed, it will always war against the will and plan of God.

  -Michael Boldea Jr.
  (EJ, pg. 15)

- Society has been so dumbed down and brainwashed that people automatically assume you're a conspiracy theorist for thinking outside of the box. We really do live in a clown world.

  -FB

- Exceptionalism can't be found in detours, short-cuts and just getting by to get along with the world. It is found when people look up to the One who is perfect and majestic, and choose the high road of integrity of heart, excellency in their preferences, and righteousness in their ways.

  -RJK

- Only one life, 'twill soon past; only what's done for Christ will last."
  -C.T. Studd

- When sin becomes a habit then Jesus becomes a distant memory.

  -FB

Distinction

The Bible tells us we are children of light, not darkness. Since the world is dark, as the light we must bring the contrast and distinction that we do not belong to darkness and have no part in it.

We must keep in mind that light has its attraction to those who taste the bitterness of darkness. Such individuals may not even recognize they are in darkness until they have a contrast between the indifference and hatefulness that is hidden by the darkness and the love of God which will greatly shine in the darkness.

Rev. Charles G. Grubb was a well-known clergyman of the Irish Church. He shared an incident that brought the distinction of Christ's light from the world's darkness. He was holding a mission meeting in the cathedral of an Australian city.

When settling in for the night at his hotel room, he discovered that he was within a few doors of a Spiritualist lecturer who had come to the same city to deliver a course of lectures on Spiritualism. It is the custom in England and in her colonies for the guests in the hotel to put their shoes outside the door on retiring. They are returned during the night, cleaned and polished.

When Grubb looked for his shoes in the morning, they were not there. While standing in the doorway, he heard what appeared to be a violent altercation taking place between the Spiritualist lecturer and the proprietor of the hotel.

Walking towards him in his slippers, the proprietor started offering his apologies to Grubb. He informed him in the early hours of the morning someone had stolen all the shoes in the corridor. Grubb's response was, "Hallelujah," I have another pair of shoes."

The proprietor turned to the spiritualist and said, "I intended to come and hear your lectures on Spiritualism, but I am going to hear this clergyman preach. Did you hear what he said? You have been abusing me and denouncing the management of the hotel; all this clergyman says is 'Hallelujah! I have another pair.'"

The results of Grubb shining the light of Christ is that the proprietor of the hotel was converted, along with his wife, children, and the staff at the hotel. The chef who refused to come to the meeting still heard the Gospel through the keyhole of his little room as the other staff members proclaimed it. (COS, pgs. 157-158)

It is amazing what a little bit of light shining in the darkness can illuminate when the opportunity presents itself. As believers, we must remember that darkness gives us the greatest means to allow our light to shine.

- I must constantly remind myself that I am just passing through this world and that my citizenship is not here, my future is not based on the present age, my hope is not founded in the temporary, and my expectation is not dependent on the unpredictable seasons of this present age.

-RJK

- In a world that is drowning in government lies, Hollywood lies, mainstream media lies, and educational lies, I choose to stand on God's Word which will never lie.

-FB

- Although da Vinci's *The Last Supper* is an iconic piece resonating with generations of Christians, the artist himself was not devoted "to Church or Christ." Rather, he upheld causality and unity in naturalism, with science and experience as the guiding principle. "Science is the Captain," he penned in his philosophical maxims, "and practice the soldiers."

Carl Teichrib
(GG, pg. 37)

- They make it about themselves, their ego, and their aspirations and are willing to sacrifice everything, including the truth on the altar of self.

-Michael Boldea Jr.
(EJ, pg. 17)

- I believe one of the weaknesses of much evangelicalism in America is that many Christians have not developed a consistent, Christian-theistic world view. Whether or not we admit it, we are battling ideologies and systems of erroneous thinking. We are to be pulling down "strong holds... and bring into captivity every thought to the obedience of Christ."

  -Larry Spargimino
  Jan. 2024 Prophetic Observer

- We want all the promises of heaven while holding on to the scraps of the world. We want to come up to the best God has to offer, without giving up what we think the world is promising us. In essence, we want the best of both worlds. We offer our decency to the world, our best crumbs to God, our religious self to the religious crowd, while straddling the fence of compromise to avoid being rejected by God and totally consecrating our life to the Lord Jesus Christ.

  -RJK

Creation

Taking Up the Challenge

In the past when we have challenged some people about God, they declare they believe in science—that which can be studied and proven and not something that requires what appears to be "blind" faith in something called God. This is just one of many excuses why people choose the ways of unbelief, but it will prove to be a flimsy excuse when they encounter God for themselves.

Two Scandinavians found themselves on the opposite side of the coin over this issue. One a great violinist, **Ole Bull** believed that his music could awaken any dead soul to the reality of God for it was inspired from heaven. The other one was a great inventor, **John Ericson**, who had no use for what would be considered "unscientific nonsense" that was for the sentimental and small minded.

These two men had been friends but had drifted apart but found their paths crossing when Ole Bull was on a musical tour in America. They had a delightful visit and when the violinist invited the inventor to his concert, Ericson declined by saying he had no time to waste on music.

Ole Bull knowing the supernatural affect his music had on people became curious as to whether it would awaken Ericson. Since

Ericson would not come to him, Bull decided to go to the inventor. He actually broke his precious violin down to the base so he could ask the inventor about the acoustic properties depending on the grain of wood. From there Ole went on to discuss something unseen, the sound waves that can't be reputed. To illustrate it, Bull put his violin back together, tuned it and begin bringing the bow softly down upon the tense strings drawing out a few sweet but rich tones.

In a moment the workmen in the shop dropped their tools and listened with wide-eyed wonder as Bull begin to play on until the workshop almost became a place of worship. When Ole finally paused, Ericson lifted his bowed head and revealing a face wet with tears, he said softly, with a bit of reverent awe in his voice, "Play on! I never knew before what it was that was lacking in my life." (COS, pgs. 54-55)

Man is missing something, but he is not always aware of it. He settles for what he is used to and veers away from something his mind has already rationalized as being foolish. For such a person it takes an awakening of the spirit to cause the soul to rise up in inspiration and expectation towards the unseen.

It often takes the unseen power of the Gospel to awaken a man to his need to be filled with the reality of God. Other times it takes the unseen compassion to reach the hurting with comfort that will lift them up from despair to look into the open arms of a Savior. In some cases, it takes the music of heaven to wake up the skeptic to experience the unseen inspiration and intervention of heaven.

God knows how to awaken, but are we prepared enough, caring enough or even curious enough to be used by our Creator in such a way that the unaware discovers what they have need of and realize they have a glorious inheritance awaiting them.

- We know that God spoke creation into being. A. W. Tozer made reference to this creative voice, "It was the commanding voice of God that brought things into being...Everything in creation is built upon the foundation of this creating voice." (WOG, pg. 16)

- Everything in creation speaks of life. The trees speak of the beauty of life, the river the constant flow of life, the flowers the grace that sustains life, and the wildlife the order that maintains life. Each aspect of creation has its own heartbeat that pulsates through its very fiber, always pointing to its Designer.

-RJK

Hidden

Under the Dead Sea are salt and chemical deposits hundreds and possibly thousands of feet deep. It is believed that the great destruction of Sodom and Gomorrah is what created the Dead Sea and that in Josephus' time it was called the Asphaltic Sea because it was covered with thick oil which was used to pitch ships. They do not know what happened to stop this seepage of oil but an earthquake is suspect.

It has been claimed, and most likely exaggerated by many, that the mineral and chemical wealth of the Dead Sea is more than the rest of all the world. In Deuteronomy 33:24-25, the prophecy surrounding Asher is of upmost importance. It states, "and let him dip his foot in oil."

The boundaries of the tribe of Asher extended from what is now Haifa region northward to Lebanon along the Mediterranean Sea and was in the shape of a foot attached to the part of the leg just below the knee. The area of the foot in Haifa is where oil and natural gas are being pumped. Is it coincidence or prophetic?

In God's economy there are no coincidences. Consider what Jacob prophesied about Asher in Genesis 49, (Most of this information was taken from Noah Hutchings' article in the Prophetic Observer, September 2022.)

———— • ◄═══ • ————

- Human personality is the greatest work of artistry in all of God's Creation! If God calls it into existence as we know He does, for we all know beautiful personalities that continue to flower with the passing of years, we may rest assured He would not allow His masterpiece to molder in the grave.

-Howard E. Kershner
(DPS, pg. 131)

- We are adept at inventing phrases to dismiss God and get rid of Him, and so what the writers of the Old Testament called God, we call the laws of nature.

-A. W. Tozer
(WOG, pgs. 77-78)

So Much For Theories

Scientists are once again confounded by God's creation. It seems that science can explain everything, that is unless something steps outside of popular theories such as evolution.

Apparently, they have discovered a new breed of octopus. This unique creature has something resembling a shell around it. There is nothing in evolution that shows that this octopus somehow evolved to this state. Of course, it you are a believer of God's Word, it is easy and understandable.

God made that octopus with a shell encasement and the scientist has once again discovered that even with all of their theories, the only sound conclusion is that God created the world along with all that is in it.

+——————•—————•——————+

- Creation is God's poem, witnessing to His eternal power and glory.

                                                -H. A. Ironside
                                                (GE, (E) pg. 116)

Prayer: Lord, all of Your creation speaks or sings of You. Oh, to be as Your creation. It is my heart to praise You and my inspiration to sing to You, to be part of the chorus about me that brings glory to You, for You alone are worthy. Amen.

- We think we are so big, but consider the universe. We think we are strong, but face the power of rushing water or a strong wind, and see how strong we can be against such elements. We think we are so smart, but our mind cannot imagine eternity. It is because of such foolish conclusions about personal strength that many walk in unbelief towards God.

                                                -RJK

The Road-Cutting Man

Cultures are interesting to consider because when one takes the Gospel into a different culture for the first time, they must find that one point of redemption that has been integrated into their culture or language in order to make alive and real the message of Christ's redemption.

The Maliyali people in Papua New Guinea had a struggle when it came to turning from their old beliefs to Jesus. God's Word told them that Jesus is the only way, but they could not relate to Jesus being the only way until they learned that Jesus actually "cut a road" for them but He went one step further. He not only cut a way for salvation but He also dismantled all the other roads that had been devised by Satan and man, making them inept, impassable, and useless.

After they realized that God had sent the road-cutting man, they admitted that they now "get Him," for Jesus is the only true road. How everyone needs to get Jesus! Whether He is the Way, has cut the way, prepared the way, and etc. the truth is He is the only Way to eternal life, to the Father, and to heaven.

- Creation holds some wise examples. For example, a flower does not think of competing to the flower next to it. It just blooms.

-FB

Creation's Examples

God uses different parts of creation to describe His people's place in His kingdom. He uses the branches to describe believers that must abide in the vine to produce fruit, as well as sheep who must have the disposition of a lamb to hear His voice and be led into their life in Christ.

When it came to Israel, He used the fig tree whose initial fruit comes out in the spring, the olive tree whose olives must be crushed in order for its worth and potential to be brought forth and a vineyard in which He is the husbandman who has made all of the necessary investment for the nation to produce fruit for His glory. Prophetically, the Lord used the burning bush in the wilderness to reveal that even though the nation of Israel will go through fiery tests, they will never be consumed.

———————————

- But we are on the greatest space ship of all time. The earth upon which we ride is rotating upon its axis at the rate of about 1,000 miles per hour. It is revolving around the sun at a speed of more than one and one half million miles a day. . . We are having the grandest ride of all. Surely, we want to be on good terms with the Captain.

-Howard E. Kershner
(DPS, pg. 152)

Day of Completion

The Lord occasionally reminds me that after the sixth day, His work was perfect and complete. I also realize it was after the creation of man that the Lord ceased from work and rested. In fact, His Son went to the cross as man where the most trying and complete work was finished: the work of redemption. He then was put in a grave where all work becomes silent.

In light of this knowledge, my request to Him is simple, please help me to obey in small and great ways in order to ensure a completion of a matter. After all, His ways have taught me that if a matter is completed it not only signifies order is present, but one can now come into rest. At the place of rest, there can be sweet fellowship where He not only can enjoy me, but I can enjoy Him. Therefore, the request is for Him to help me to be obedient, and it is for the purpose of being prepared to enter the Garden of sweet communion with Him. Amen.

———•———•—◆—•———•———

Prayer: Lord, Your creation reveals so much about You. Give me the eyesight to see You in it, the ears to hear it praise You, the smells that speak of Your heavenly fragrance, the touch to feel Your presence, and the means to taste Your goodness. Amen.

- Even though we may perceive ourselves to be strong, in light of the forces and power of nature, we are the weakest of all creatures. The reality is we have no strength outside of God. The strength we have will ultimately prove to be our weakness in the end. It will reveal our limitations and downfalls and that we are incompetent to see a matter through to completion.

-RJK

Stands On Its Own

Creation clearly declares the greatness and power of our Creator. He is the artist that created this masterpiece, the Potter that shaped it, the Scientist that understood how all the elements were to work together, and the Inventor that brought it to fruition. Clearly, creation reveals His wisdom and intelligence. Man may understand the working and principles behind creation, but he cannot bring such factors together. He can observe them and figure out their equations, but he cannot reproduce them.

The Bible tells us creation will not only reveal the greatness of God, but it will expose the foolishness of man. Man is forever trying to be god of his small world. In his arrogance, he believes that he can control the elements around him. He not only foolishly tries to compete with God for supreme position on his particular pile of dirt, but he foolishly rejects His existence.

Blowing the Mind

"When pregnant, the cells of the baby migrate into the mothers 'bloodstream and then circle back into the baby, it's called "fetal-maternal microchimerism".

For 41 weeks, the cells circulate and merge backwards and forwards, and after the baby is born, many of these cells stay in the mother's body, leaving a permanent imprint in the mother's tissues, bones, brain, and skin, and often stay there for decades. Every single child a mother has afterwards will leave a similar imprint on her body, too.

Even if a pregnancy doesn't go to full term or if you have an abortion, these cells still migrate into your bloodstream.

Research has shown that if a mother's heart is injured, fetal cells will rush to the site of the injury and change into different types of cells that specialize in mending the heart.

The baby helps repair the mother, while the mother builds the baby.

How cool is that? This is often why certain illnesses vanish while pregnant.

It's incredible how mothers' bodies protect the baby at all costs, and the baby protects and rebuilds the mother back — so that the baby can develop safely and survive.

Think about crazy cravings for a moment. What was the mother deficient in that the baby made them crave?

Studies have also shown cells from a fetus in a mother's brain 18 years after she gave birth. How amazing is that?"

If you're a mom you know how you can intuitively feel your child even when they are not there.... Well, now there is scientific proof that moms carry them for years and years even after they have given birth to them.

I find this to be so very beautiful.

———————————

- In Matthew 6:28, Jesus was calling man back to the center of truth by reminding him of creation in its simple beauty. The beauty of creation points to the artistry of God. It mirrors the uniqueness of His glory. God's glory is not artificial—it is pure. Temporary robes, such as those that cover the nakedness of man, do not constitute real glory, but the beauty of God's creation serves as natural robes that express His unfolding majesty.

-RJK

Adversity And Suffering

No Cost Too Great

How high is our calling? To answer that question, we must consider the tools the Lord uses. As a great artist, He will only use the best paint brushes, as a Sculptor the sharpest chisels, as the potter the right type of clay along with the proper preparation, and as the musician the best designed instruments. The process can be tedious and long, but in the end a masterpiece is brought forth that brings glory to the Lord.

The tools our great Master uses are often adversity and suffering. Adversity is a type of fire and suffering is a type of identification. Fire prepares and identification establishes authority. Those who feel the fire of adversity and taste the bitterness of sorrow must count the cost as to whether they are willing to give all up, including their life. In light of Christ's sacrifice there is no cost too great to pay, no sacrifice that is too much to offer, and no bounds too limited to reach the great heights of God.

There are many who have picked up the torch of the Gospel to carry it in dark places that would feel the fires of adversity and become identified with Jesus in His sufferings. Some of their names are known but many have simply receded into the great cloud of witnesses. It is not that they are unknown, but their purpose to make known Jesus to those lost in the darkness defined their mission. Therefore, it mattered little to them whether anyone knew their names or not.

These individuals wanted the name of Jesus implanted on the hearts of those they preached to. They wanted His name to be lifted up in praise by those who believed, the source behind the power of the witness of those who followed in Jesus' footsteps, and the last name that would be reverently spoken as they departed this earth.

One such person who had such a focus was **John Coleridge (Coley) Patteson.** He had the opportunity of experiencing the best the world had to offer, but he chose to run the race of his lifetime towards the ultimate destination of heaven.

Patteson came from a family of well-standing, was educated by the finest institutions, had traveled Europe, and was assured of eventually having like standing in the Church. He took a parish position in England, but in 1854 he received the call to leave his native country and travel as a missionary to assist his friend and mentor, Bishop Selwyn.

Selwyn was with the Church of England but had labored for years in the Melanesian Islands which are today comprised of New Guinea, Fiji, the Solomon Islands, the Maluku Islands and New Caledonia. Over time Patteson would visit Aneityum, Erronmanga, Mota, Guadalcanal, the Solomon Islands, and the New Hebrides

The challenges were great which included different dialects among those whom they ministered to. He faced hostile receptions and barely escaped with his life on more than one occasion. His travels brought him face to face with anger and fear brought on by Roman Catholic Priests who saw the missionaries as an intrusion into their kingdoms and a point of competition.

At age thirty-three Patteson became Bishop of Melanesia for the Church of England. His main way of going from island to island was to cruise to and around the islands in his schooner, *Southern Cross* to make contact with the natives. But as in many cases, natives were suspicious.

In one situation the natives were ready to take revenge on him because one of their people had been killed by a white trader. Before they killed him, he asked their permission to pray. He kneeled down, and in that prayer he committed his spirit and soul to God. As the natives witnessed his prayer, they decided he was not a murderer and after he was done with his prayer, they escorted him back to the vessel and bid him farewell.

He also suffered much with illnesses and weaknesses brought on by constant strain, but he would always rejoice in whatever state he was in. Patteson was unaware that a great shadow was falling across his name. He had worked hard among the natives of the island and had gained a trustworthy reputation. Sadly, traders of the Pacific were kidnapping natives to sell to plantations of Queensland and was using his name to gain access to their latest commodity.

In September 1871, he visited the island of Naukapu. His schooner had been stopped by a reef and low tide, and two natives volunteered to take him to the island in their light canoe. He readily agreed to go with them.

It was night time before the schooner could make it towards the island but they were met by natives in a canoe. The canoe had a bundle and when it was unwrapped, it was the 44-year-old body of Patteson. He had a smile of peace on his face and on his breast lay a leaf of the cocoanut palm with five knots tied in the long sprays.

The schooner crew later learned that the five knots represented five inflicted wounds with club, spear, and arrow that were on his body. These five wounds represented the five natives that had been taken by traders. The natives perceived them dead and according to their culture it was a tribal right for them to exact blood for blood. Like his Savior before him who had endured misunderstanding and false accusations and received five wounds to His body and died on behalf of others offenses, Patteson indeed became identified with the Lord Jesus Christ.

Today the work begun by Selwyn, Patteson, and others has taken root and the Gospel has flourished in many islands and regions, leaving Christianity the predominant religion in most of Melanesia.

As for the people of Naukapu, they have long repented of their crime. On the spot where Patteson fell now stands a memorial the people erected. It is a simple, impressive cross with this inscription upon it: "In Memory of John Coleridge Patteson, D.D., Missionary Bishop, Whose life was here taken by men for whom he would gladly have given it." (AMH, pgs. 283-298)

***

As we can see, missionaries face different challenges, but for many that treaded into the spiritually dark places of the world, they faced the constant enemy of death. Whether it was because of disease, hostile natives, rugged terrain, or endless hardships, death nipped at their heels.

However, as living martyrs, these individuals realized that regardless of the harvest field they were called to, they were always walking towards their demise. However, they could walk in confidence because God held their lives, their days were numbered, and their steps already prepared by heaven itself.

Many did enter the next world of glory while on the mission field. **James Chalmers** was such an individual. He was called to New Guinea. A man of adventure, vision, and commitment, he walked through many dangers from ravaging waters, dense forest, wild beasts and savage cannibals. It was clear that God was in the many harrowing circumstances that ended with miraculous interventions.

He outlived two wives, and made incredible inroads into the field he was in, but he was not content to stay there. He wanted to make inroads into places the light of the Gospel had not yet reached. At age 60 in 1901 after 24 years of service, he set out on an expedition to visit a tribe of fierce cannibals. He never returned.

It was later discovered that he along with the two other missionaries with him were killed, their heads disbursed as trophies and their bodies used as food. (AMH, pgs. 299-316)

***

Rev. **James Calvert** and his wife **Mary** served in the Fiji Islands which had a barbarous and bloodstained history. It was clear to missionary organizations that evil reigned supreme so much so that many abandoned any hope of the light of the Gospel ever penetrating the darkness. However, darkness will not stop the light from one day shining through it when His servants adhere to the calling that is placed on their hearts.

When the Calvert's were on their way to Fiji, the ship's captain tried to persuade them to turn back by saying to them, "You will lose your life and the lives of those with you if you go among such savages."

Calvert responded, "Sir, we died before we came here." This is the attitude of all who first count the cost when it comes to facing the throes of hell. Through this couple's lives and ministry, the love of God did break through, changing the Fiji Islands. In fact, they would spend 17 years working among the people.

Like the missionaries who labored in the South Pacific islands, the Calver's witnessed gross, decadent practices among the natives. They could not show disgust or condemn them for they were enslaved by the darkness.

Their lives were spared many times, revealing that nothing is too great for God when it comes to preserving those who shine the light of hope in the darkness. Mary passed away in 1882 at age 68 and her husband passed away ten years later at age 79.

Calvert was spared to see the islands provided with 1,300 Christian churches that were crowded Sunday after Sunday by devout congregations. (AMH, pgs. 317-329)

***

John G. Paton would face off with many warring tribes and vicious cannibals in the mission field of New Hebrides. The missionaries who had come before him beginning in 1839 were either killed or driven off by the natives. It was in 1858 that Paton's work among the people of New Hebrides would begin in earnest.

It seemed death followed Paton. Shortly after his arrival, several missionaries were murdered and within a year of his arrival, his wife Mary and his newborn son died of fever. He was eventually driven off of the island after four years of living under constant threat of death, but not for long. In 1864, he married, Margaret and together they returned to a smaller island called Aniwa. Within 15 years most of the island had turned to Christ.

This couple saw the fruit of their labors from chapels being build to Christian schools organized. John and Margaret served together in missionary efforts for forty-one years. She died in 1905 and John followed two years later at age 82. By 1907, 12,000 former cannibals of the New Hebrides had been converted and 133 native teachers had been trained and sent out as preachers and teachers of the Gospel to their own people.

Today, the majority of the population consider themselves Christians. (AMH, pgs. 331-347)

***

When I read the stories of missionaries, I realize their lives would make an incredible movie. Many had unbelievable adventures that people can read about by getting the books that they have written themselves or other authors have written about them.

These missionaries' lives have intrigue, danger, harrowing adventures, great loss, and miraculous interventions. Every missionary had to face their own fears, step over their own ineptness, and confront such thick spiritual darkness that often caused them to cling to the Rock and trust the light of the World to guide them, knowing if it penetrated the darkness, it would also save souls and change lives.

I wrote about some of these missionaries' adventures in greater detail, but in most cases they all have many similarities, but different mission fields created their own personal challenges to each one.

The reason I write about these individuals is because the church in America has no idea as to the cost that was paid through the generations so people in great darkness, such as each of us once were, could be translated into the light of Jesus Christ.

I constantly remind myself of the Apostle Paul's words in Romans 10:14-15 to keep my perspective right, "How then shall they call on him in whom they have not believed? and how shall they believe in him of whom they have not heard? and how shall they hear without a preacher? And how shall they preach, except they be sent? as it is written, How beautiful are the feet of them that preach the gospel of peace, and bring glad tidings of good things!"

- If your adversary is more committed to their cause than you are to yours, you will fold.

-Michael Boldea Jr.
(EJ. pg. 48)

- When a man became a Christian, he gave up father and mother, house and lands, nay, his own life also...But then was the age of heroes, that was the time of giants. Never did the Church so much prosper and so truly thrive as when she was baptized in blood.

-Charles Spurgeon
(WFF, pg. 196)

- Sometimes what looks like an obstacle in your path is actually a gift meant to move you in a different direction.

-Jane Lee Logan

- The purer the silver, the hotter the fire. Some of the greatest saints have been the most sorely tried. We may shrink from the furnace of trial, but our heavenly refiner knows how to temper the fire...we shall not be thoroughly free from the dross of iniquity until we awake in His likeness.

-Herbert Lockyer
(APB, pg. 121)

- People are not persecuted for living a holy life, it is the confession of Jesus that brings the persecution.

-Oswald Chambers
(CWC, pg. 17)

- Trials are intended to make us think, to wean us from the world, to send us to the Bible, to drive us to our knees.

-FB

Thorns

Thorns in Scripture make an interesting study. The first mention of thorns was in Genesis when a curse was pronounced on Adam that pointed to the bitterness that would come forth from the land due to sin. They also represented what the idolatrous and pagan nations would prove to be to Israel if they did not rid the Promised Land of them. Thorns are found among beauty such as the rose bush, and were used in parables to bring a contrast between good and bad fruits. It is what also was used to show how the world chokes out the Word of God.

Thorns are found in much of creation but they cast a glorious shadow in Genesis 22:13 where the ram was caught in a bush that Abraham used as a substitute burnt offering in place of his promised son. Many bushes in that area are thorny. The ram most likely was caught in one of those thorny bushes that would quickly entangle it.

Horns represent authority in Scripture. We know that the ram pointed to Jesus as our Burnt Offering whose life was used up for our sake and became a sin offering who would die on our behalf. However, the Lamb of God who held all power and authority as Kings of kings, and Lord of lords would be crown by a crown of thorns. He would allow Himself to become the curse, so man would no longer have to live under the curse of death. In the midst of His great suffering, like the rose bush, beauty was found because His sacrificial action came out of a love so sweet, so wonderful, and so breath-taking that to this day it still remains indescribable.

- Separation from the world only causes suffering if we think we're missing something worthwhile.

-Ruth Hunt
(VPH, pg. 163)

- There is no wine if grapes are not pressed, no perfume if flowers are not crushed. If you feel any pressure in life, it means God is bringing the best out of you.

-FB

- The enemy of our souls does not care from which angle we approach our service to him, as long as we do not serve the true God of heaven. If we do, he will oppose us.

  -RJK

- What we take for granted is never ours until we have bought it by pain. A thing is worth just what it costs. When we go through the suffering of experience, we seem to lose everything, but bit by bit we get it back.

  -Oswald Chambers
  (CWC, pg. 25)

- Endurance is a cultivated virtue. It is not something you are born with; it is something you build up over time. That we lack the endurance to push back the darkness and grow weary before the other side even warms up should be an indictment against contemporary Christianity.

  -Michael Boldea Jr.
  (EJ, pg. 49)

- A Sudan Christian worker began to sing a song that was written by a man whose home was bombed during one of the Sudan's previous civil wars. Here is what it says, "Even in war, we can sing. Even if death is our destiny, the difficulties will be easy for us, because Jesus remains our hope. This is our peace, true peace."

  -The Voice of the Martyrs
  (Special Report)

Rubies In My Eyes

The love of God is an impartial love. Although controversial and considered a mystic, this impartial love was displayed by Madame Guyon when she was imprisoned for the sake of Christ in the French prisons, including the celebrated Bastille from 1695 to 1705.

Madame Guyon was a cultured, refined, educated woman, and, until smitten with smallpox had been an exceedingly beautiful woman. She admitted that no beauty should outshine the beauty of Christ that must come from within the believer, and that her smallpox scars were a point of blessings from her Savior and identification with Him.

In 1698 she wrote about her time as a prisoner in Vincennes. She shared how she passed the time in peace as she sang songs of joy which the maid who served her also learned by heart. During that time, she came upon a sentence which she always read in amazement, "The stones of my prison walls shone like rubies in my eyes."

She went on to state, "I esteemed them more than all the gaudy brilliances of this vain world. My heart was full of that joy which thou givest to them that love Thee in the midst of their greatest crosses." (COS, pgs. 156-157)

Guyon wrote one of her loveliest hymns during her ordeal:
"A little bird I am,
Shut from the fields of air;
Yet in my cage I sit and sing,
To Him who placed me there.
Well pleased a prisoner to be,
Because, my God, it pleases Thee.

"Nought have I else to do;
I sing the whole day long;

And He whom most I love to please,
Doth listen to my song;
He caught and bound my wandering wing
But still He bends to hear me sing.

"My cage confines me round;
Abroad I cannot fly;
But though my wing is closely bound,
My heart's at liberty.
My prison walls cannot control
The flight, the freedom of the soul.

"Oh! It is good to soar
These bolts and bars above,
To Him whose purpose I adore,
Whose Providence I love;
And in Thy mighty will to find
The joy, the freedom of the mind."

- Grief changes us, the pain scripts us into someone who understands more deeply, hurts more often, appreciates more quickly, cries more easily, hopes more desperately, loves more openly.

  -Unknown

- God can turn your most painful heartache into a beautiful testimony.

  -FB

- It is only when I realistically face how weak I am that I have been able to discover just how strong God is. It is in weakness that I will fling myself on His mercy, cry out for help, and wait on Him to show me grace so He can intercede on my behalf out of pity because I am so weak and helpless.

-RJK

Prayer: Lord, we are a blessed people. Whether in the ovens of adversity, the fires of persecution, or the abyss of hopelessness, You are our immovable foundation of hope, sanity, and promise. Thank You for being who You are. We can rejoice in You. Amen.

- What matters most is how well you walk through the fire.

-Charles Bulowski

- Tribulation will teach us how to express things, our circumstances will teach us, temptations of the devil will teach us, difficult things will teach us.

-Oswald Chambers
(CWC, pg. 211)

- After a week in jail, losing his home and the destruction of all he owned, this evangelist made this statement, "Persecution is not an accident. It is the expectation." (WFF, pg. 72)

Wrestling Verses Clinging

One of the patriarchs I like to study is Jacob. He often gets a raw deal because he is an incredible mirror to the fleshly, carnal man. Jacob was a dichotomy. He was a "plain" man which in the Strong's Concordance defines as meaning "perfect." In this case it means that Jacob was perfect in his motives towards the things of God.

241

You could tell he was struggling with lying to his father. He knew if his father caught him in the lies to obtain the blessing, Isaac would curse him instead of bless him, but his mother told him to let the curse fall upon her if he was caught.

It is important to note that Isaac was losing his eyesight and that he heard and recognized Jacob's voice, but went with the touch of the arm of Jacob that was disguised as well as the smells of a hunter. At this point Isaac chose to believe the presentation even though his hearing had been correct.

Unlike his fleshly brother Esau, Jacob did value the eternal matters of heaven beginning with the birthright. He sought God concerning his herds, did right by his cheating uncle and was willing to serve his brother to make amends for the past.

He had one more aspect of his character to confront and that was his strength. Strength often expresses itself in self-sufficiency. As believers we know our sufficiency is of God, but we fail to recognize that we rely on our personal strength until self-sufficiency is kicked from underneath us.

Jacob had to face this when he had to face the heavenly entity the night before he was to meet Esau. He first wrestled with this entity until his thigh was knocked out of joint. Keep in mind the strongest sinew in Jacob's body that maintains the body's ability to wrestle had shriveled up by one little touch from the heavenly being. So much for strength that maintains self-sufficiency.

The next and only thing Jacob, in his now "insufficient" state could do, was simply cling to the being until He blessed him. In the first blessing Jacob had to become part of a lie and in this one he started out wrestling for it and ended up clinging to it until it was so.

This is when the heavenly entity asked his name. Name has to do with character. Strength of character comes with endurance in challenges, is refined in testing, and is brought forth in adversity. It was then his name, Jacob, was changed from that which revealed the workings of the carnal to that which expressed his real potential, Israel, "the prince that prevails with God."

It is natural to wrestle with God in our own strength, but we will lose in the end. However, in defeat we will wisely learn what it means to cling to God as we wrestle before Him in prayer. In such times our strength will be left in the dust as we cling to Him until He has had His way or has left us with a blessing.

J. Gregory Mantle best summarized this in his book, *The Counterfeit Christ,* "He (Jacob) had to be crippled before he could be crowned. Many are never crowned because they have never been willing to be crippled." (pg. 94)

- Suffering is a big part of the Christian walk. If a person is truly walking according to heaven, suffering will come from every direction in the form of adversities. These adversities come from life, the world, and Satan.

  -RJK

- Much of your persecution will come from lukewarm Christians.

  -FB

- Suffering is the touchstone of saintliness, just as temptation is, and suffering wrongfully will always reveal the ruling disposition because it takes us unawares.

  -Oswald Chambers
  (CWC, pg. 232)

- God delights to increase the faith of His children. Our faith, which is feeble at first, is developed and strengthened more and more by use. We ought, instead of wanting no trials before victory, no exercise for patience, to be willing to take them from God's hand as means. I say—and say it deliberately—trials, obstacles, difficulties, and sometimes defeats, are the very food of faith.

-George Muller

- Persecution is like fire. I use a word similar to *purify*. If we want pure gold, we have to let it go through the fire.

-Mr. Xi
(WFF, pg. 142)

Fight the Good Fight

A soldier must be convinced that he is fighting for something that is worth dying for. In fact, it must be greater than his life in importance or he will not see any need to offer himself up on the battlefield in order to risk all that he values in this present life. This is why patriotism must be stirred up before men will choose to go into a war where there is the possibility of dying on a foreign field.

The Apostle Paul tells us in 1 Timothy 6:11-12, "But thou, O man of God, flee these things; and follow after righteousness, godliness, faith, love, patience, meekness. Fight the good fight of faith, lay hold on eternal life, whereunto thou art also called and hast professed a good profession before many witnesses." In this Scripture, we are told what it will take to fight the good fight of faith.

We first must follow after that which is honorable and worthy. For believers, it is godly character that will sustain them through the battles that will ultimately test, establish, and refine their faith. As believers, we have righteousness. This is just. We have godliness. This is worthy. We have faith. This is valuable. We have love. This is honorable. We have patience. This is virtuous. And, finally we have meekness. This attitude points to strength under control.

By pursuing these qualities, we will be able to profess a good profession before those who witness our lives in the harvest field or on the battlefield.

244

* Jesus embraced the cross because of love. He preferred man in his lost state above Himself. We cannot imagine how far the incredible loving arms of God would have to reach. We know they reached from heaven and embraced a cross for our sake. They reached from the glories of heaven into the very depths of sin-laden souls to establish the way of forgiveness. They reached as far as the grave to embrace mankind in its grave darkness of delusion, disobedience, and death to ensure life.

  -RJK

* Our desire therefore is not that we may be without trials of faith, but that the Lord graciously would be pleased to support us in that trial, that we may not dishonor Him by distrust.

  -George Muller

* The suffering of the saints at heart is not what is ensnaringly known as "Deeper Death to Self"; it springs from an active submission and determination to accept the intensely individual responsibility of doing God's will.

  -Oswald Chambers
  (CWC, pg. 328)

* Our hope, our acceptance of the invitation to the banquet, is not based on the idea that we are going to be free of pain and suffering. Rather it is based on the conviction that we will triumph over suffering.

  -Brennan Manning
  (WFF, pg. 147)

* Sometimes you must hurt in order to know,
  fall in order to grow,

lose in order to gain.
Because most of life's greatest lessons
Are learned through pain.

-FB

Are You Carrying Your Cross?

To be separated from the old life and the old way, we must take up our personal cross. Every Christian must carry their personal cross, knowing each cross will vary.

Some carry a light cross, but for them it is great because they still must die daily upon it. Others may carry unusual crosses, but nevertheless, they will not glory in them because they will cease to be as they were as their particular cross begins to impart death to all that is associated with the old way. There are those who carry heavy crosses. They may look noble in carrying such a burden, but they will not seek such recognition because there is no honor in the death of the old life.

These people have also realized that the cross is meant to discipline their focus, ways, and walk. It is all about becoming identified with Jesus. There is no glory in carrying such a cross. The glory is found when the cross has its way of death in the person's life and the glory of the Son of God begins to shine forth in their lives.

◆————•—◀——•————◆

- In weakness and sympathy we would save our loved ones from struggle and suffering if we could, but in so doing we would be depriving them of the opportunity to grow strong, to achieve character and to become sons of God.

-Howard E. Kershner
(DPS, pg. 37)

- It's during the worst storms of your life that you will get to see the true colors of the people who say they care about you.

  -FB

- The whole purpose for denying our self-life and crucifying the lusts of the flesh is so God can have His way to bring forth life that produces fruit for His glory.

  -RJK

- When you come to Jesus, you have to be ready. There is a cross on your shoulder; there is a cost you had to take. Sometimes it's your life, sometimes it's your country, sometimes it's your family.

  -Zamir
  The Voice of the Martyrs
  August 2023

- The ship of the Church never sails so gloriously along as when the bloody spray of the martyrs falls upon her deck. We *must* suffer, and we *must* die, if we are ever to conquer this world for Christ.

  -Charles Spurgeon
  (WFF, pg. 196)

- My story is filled with bad choices, broken pieces and a lot of hurt. It is also filled with a major comeback, freedom in my life, peace in my soul and a Savior that restored everything.

  -FB

- Grief never ends...but it changes. It's a passage, not a place to stay. Grief is not a sign of weakness, nor a lack of faith—It is the price of love.

  -John Gray Writer
  (FB)

Prayer: Lord, we know that You allow the night to come upon our souls. It is a time for You to go deeper so that eventually we can come higher in You. I know these things, but knowledge does not take away the impact of such darkness upon my soul, even though I choose to trust You. However, in the end I will not be ashamed or disappointed that I put my complete faith in You. Amen.

THE TABLECLOTH

When we consider the beauty of something, we must acknowledge that we are also admiring the abilities or the handiwork of the artist. The following story was written by Pastor Howard C. Schade of the first Reformed Church in Nyack, NY for *Reader's Digest* in 1954. It may simply be a good story or taken from actual events, but no matter how your look at it there are many unwritten stories that involve the miraculous, where God used the inspirational abilities of others to connect the dots of history and the people who lived during tumultuous times to bring forth reconciliation of broken hearts and restoration of downtrodden souls.

***

The brand-new pastor and his wife, newly assigned to their first ministry, to reopen a church in suburban Brooklyn, arrived in early October excited about their opportunities. When they saw their church, it was very run down and needed much work. They set a goal to have everything done in time to have their first service on Christmas Eve.

They worked hard, repairing pews, plastering walls, painting, etc., and on December 18 they were ahead of schedule and just about finished. On December 19 a terrible tempest — a driving rainstorm — hit the area and lasted for two days. On the 21st, the pastor went over to the church. His heart sank when he saw that the roof had leaked, causing a large area of plaster about 20 feet by 8 feet to fall off the front wall of the sanctuary just behind the pulpit, beginning about head high.

The pastor cleaned up the mess on the floor, and not knowing what else to do but postpone the Christmas Eve service, headed home. On the way he noticed that a local business was having a flea market type sale for charity, so he stopped in.

One of the items was a beautiful, handmade, ivory colored, crocheted tablecloth with exquisite work, fine colors and a Cross embroidered right in the center. It was just the right size to cover the hole in the front wall. He bought it and headed back to the church.

By this time, it had started to snow. An older woman running from the opposite direction was trying to catch the bus. She missed it. The pastor invited her to wait in the warm church for the next bus 45 minutes later.

She sat in a pew and paid no attention to the pastor while he got a ladder, hangers, etc., to put up the tablecloth as a wall tapestry. The pastor could hardly believe how beautiful it looked and it covered up the entire problem area. Then he noticed the woman walking down the center aisle. Her face was white as a sheet. "Pastor," she asked, "where did you get that tablecloth?"

The pastor explained. The woman asked him to check the lower right corner to see if the initials 'EBG' were crocheted into it there. They were. These were the initials of the woman, that had made this tablecloth 35 years before, in Austria.

The woman could hardly believe it as the pastor told how he had just gotten "The Tablecloth". The woman explained that before the war she and her husband were well-to-do people in Austria.

When the Nazis came, she was forced to leave. Her husband was going to follow her the next week. He was captured, sent to prison and she never saw her husband or her home again.

The pastor wanted to give her the tablecloth; but she made the pastor keep it for the church. The pastor insisted on driving her home. That was the least he could do. She lived on the other side of Staten Island and was only in Brooklyn for the day for a house cleaning job.

What a wonderful service they had on Christmas Eve. The church was almost full. The music and the spirit were great. At the end of the service, the pastor and his wife greeted everyone at the door and many said that they would return.

One older man, whom the pastor recognized from the neighborhood, continued to sit in one of the pews and stare, and the pastor wondered why he wasn't leaving.

The man asked him where he got the tablecloth on the front wall because it was identical to one that his wife had made years ago when they lived in Austria before the war, and how could there be two tablecloths so much alike?

He told the pastor how the Nazis came, how he forced his wife to flee for her safety and he was supposed to follow her, but he was arrested and put in a prison. He never saw his wife or his home again in all the 35 years.

The pastor asked him if he would allow him to take him for a little ride. They drove to Staten Island and to the same house where the pastor had taken the woman three days earlier. He helped the man climb the three flights of stairs to the woman's apartment, knocked on the door and he saw the greatest Christmas reunion he could ever imagine.

Holidays

Is It a Memorial?

Throughout the world, different cultures and people take holidays from their regular routines. In America we have managed to adjust some of our holidays around weekends so we can extend our time off from work.

As I consider the diverse way people use the idea of holidays, I began to wonder how much of our culture understands the difference between holidays, days off, and celebrations. As I began to consider the excuses for partying, watching sports, and getting away from daily activities, I began to see how the world fudges the reason for our days off, our holidays, and days of celebration.

God established the first day off, but it was a day of rest. In a sense it was to celebrate a finished work, that of creation. It was His way of delighting in what He had created, and since it was complete, He now could cease from all activity and enjoy it.

There is nothing wrong with having fun, but when it is a person's sole pursuit and reason for having time off, then it can become idolatrous. Remember, in the last days people will be lovers of pleasure more than lovers of God. The problem with pursuing fun, fun, fun is that it creates a party spirit that is void of any sane, safe and realistic boundaries and in some cases, it becomes like a drug that people can't live without and must constantly chase after.

Now we come to the concept of holidays. These are days set aside, but for what? The problem is that people look for any excuse to have a holiday in America and the reason or purpose of it is often lost in the idea of the activities they can now plan around the particular day. Our society has created all kinds of holidays and how many of them hold any real significance? Perhaps we just need to admit that such holidays can become traditions where certain activities take center stage, or in many cases, they remain a day off without any real significance except we have a time out from our daily demands and responsibilities.

Then we come to the concept of celebration. Celebration is actually commemorating or memorializing something of great importance. When you consider the Jewish feasts, they celebrated life and blessings as they remember God's deliverance or great intervention on their behalf.

America has set certain memorials apart. Two of them are Memorial Day and Thanksgiving. We may see them as a day off, but we are to soberly remember the sacrifice of our soldiers and the blessings that God has bestowed on this nation. When I see the general attitude of people at such times, I am reminded of what Jesus said to His disciples on the night He was betrayed, "What, could ye not watch with me one hour?" (Matthew 26:40b).

Can we not take at least one hour out of our self-serving activities to remember what the celebration is about, soberly consider it, and examine our attitudes about what we are celebrating. Or, is it a tradition that, as opportunists, we are capitalizing on. If so, Jesus' next statement would apply, "Sleep on now, and take your rest." In other words, remain asleep about the spiritual significance of the real purpose behind the celebration.

Other celebrations that point to some type of memorial in which Christians celebrate, are Resurrection Sunday, and as being part of this nation, the 4th of July. Both celebrations contain some type of memorial to cause us to look back in order to examine our present attitude in light of the sacrifice that was made to ensure proper respect. This respect is necessary to maintain the significance of the memorial so we will never forget the present blessings because of past sacrifices.

Days are days for the most part as they become lost in succeeding days, but whether we truly remember certain days comes down to whether they represent a true memorial. Memorials remind us of the past. For Christians, our greatest memorial is known as "Communion," and in that celebration we have very important lessons as to what it means to commemorate the death, burial and resurrection of Christ.

His memorial causes us to examine ourselves in light of our attitude about His sacrifice that was made to obtain the blessings we now enjoy. It reminds us that if Jesus' sacrifice had never taken place, we would have no present in which to commemorate our deliverance and no hope for the future.

This section is called, "Holidays" because in American culture even our memorials are considered holidays. There are a couple of reasons a memorial becomes a mere holiday. 1) There is no foundation that has been established or maintained as to its importance. 2) Man is using it for his own agenda which will render it into a mere tradition. 3) The emphasis has changed as to why we celebrate it, and what is being highlighted has no memorial established in it.

As Christians, we must consider our "holidays" and make sure it is just another day off. However, if there is a memorial established in it, we must take the time, even if it is an hour, and humble ourselves as we sit in sober meditation about what it means. We must remember the sacrifices made, to ensure that gratitude arises out of the dung of the world's mockery and ingratitude to embrace the blessings in order to enjoy the type of life we have been given by God Almighty through the sacrifices of others.

———————

Memorial Day

Memorials all about, standing as remembrances,
Remembering sacrifices far and near too great to describe,
Marked by flags erected on hollow ground,
Grounds sanctified by tears of what was,
Clothed in sorrow deep for what will never be,
Distinguished with simple memorials and names,
Surrounded by invisible tombs of questions left unanswered,
Encased in broken dreams: "What if," "Was is worth it," "If only,"
Highlighted by flowers that point to life once lived,
Like the painful memories of old will fade with time,
Among the masses only a few remembered,
Lives offered up to enter into fires of trials and testing,
All accepted, some broken, some wounded, some lost,
Thoughts of those who enter the sacred grounds,
Taken captive by the vastness of the graves that lay silent,
Silence only interrupted by muffled cries,
Silence that lingers through the day,
Till the night falls, till the lonely sound of taps,
Reaching through generation afore to the present,
For the night has indeed come,
Laying to rest the fallen, the brave,
  and the unsung heroes of the past and present.

-RJK

———————

- Gratitude can transform common days into Thanksgivings, turn routine jobs into joy, and change ordinary opportunity into blessings.

-William Arthur Ward

Thanksgiving

Thanksgiving, a time to ponder the life I have been given,
To consider my blessings that are indescribable,
To remember the sacrifice of others,
To recall the opportunities that came my way.
Thanksgiving a time to take note of the abundance,
The promises of old that prepared the way,
The possibilities of the present that stand before me,
The hope of tomorrow that reaches beyond this world.
Thanksgiving a day to relearn gratitude,
An event to put to bed past regrets,
Restore struggling relationships,
To partake of labors, not in sorrow, but in appreciation.
Thanksgiving, a time to offer up the sacrifice of praise
    with a thankful heart,
To come to the place of worship in a humble spirit,
Not in service, but in celebration to exalt that which is worthy
    of all consideration.
To rejoice that I know the One from whom all blessings flow.

-RJK

WHERE WAS JESUS BORN?

Migdal Eder, better known as the "Tower of the Flock" or "Shepherd's Field" in Bethlehem was where the royal flocks were raised and cared for by Shepherds who served the sacrificial system of the Temple. These were special lambs destined to be used for the twice daily temple sacrifices and the annual Passover lambs in Jerusalem.

The Shepherds who watched over them were not ordinary Shepherds; they were priestly shepherds, men who were specifically trained for this royal, priestly task. The surrounding fields is where the Shepherds grazed their flocks. In ancient times, these Shepherds would care for the ewes out in the fields and bring them into the sheltered tower when they were about to give birth to their lambs. The top level of the tower was the watch tower where the Shepherds could observe the flock in the fields, and the lower portion of the tower was where the newborn lambs were birthed.

One of the priest's duties in conformity with the Law was to verify that the lambs born were without spot or blemish, with no bones broken during the birthing process, and without defect as an acceptable sacrifice for the Temple. It was also their responsibility to swaddle the newborn lambs in the white linen swaddling clothes and lay them in the ceremonially clean manger to protect them from injury. [The mangers were not used as feeding troughs.] The swaddling clothes were from the priestly robes of linen that were no longer in good repair; they were torn into strips and placed in mangers.

When Mary and Joseph could not find room in the inn, they went to the ceremonially clean and sheltered building known as the Migdal Eder, the Tower of the Flock. There would have been no other animals present, only lambs. Staying in the royal compound of Migdal Eder would not have been a hospitality offered to everyone in Israel. It would have been off limits for the average Jew. But

Joseph and Mary were from the lineage of David and it would have been their right to stay there. [Luke 2:4] It was in this special stable at the Tower of the flock that I believe Jesus was born. The Tower of the Flock was the birthplace of thousands of lambs, which had been sacrificed to prefigure Christ. As the ultimate Passover lamb, what more appropriate place could "the Lamb of God, who takes away the sin of the world" be born?

When Mary placed Jesus in swaddling clothes he was being wrapped in priestly garments from the moment of His birth — a symbolic connection and foreshadowing of Christ's office as our Great High Priest.

When the angel found these Shepherds in the field, he told them "Today in the town of David a Savior has been born to you; he is the Messiah, the Lord. This will be a sign to you: You will find a baby wrapped in cloths and lying in a manger." [Luke 2 11-12] If you notice, the angel did not give them any further directions to the place of birth. This is because these men were Shepherd Priests, and they knew exactly which manger the angel was speaking about – it could only mean THEIR manger at the Tower of the Flock! Luke 2:15 says "When the angels went away from them into heaven, the Shepherds said to each other, "Let us now go to Bethlehem and see what has happened, which the Lord has made known to us." Verse 16 says without hesitation they hurried off to Bethlehem and found Him wrapped and lying in the manger like their precious lambs after its birth.

For further confirmation read Genesis 35:21 where the Migdal Eder is mentioned as being near the place where Rachel died and was buried after giving birth to Benjamin. The tower of the flock is mentioned in both the Mishnah and the Talmud as being where the announcement of the Messiah would be declared. There is a prophecy in Micah 4:8-10 that speaks of the tower of the flock in conjunction with a woman giving birth. It speaks of a flight to Babylon [Egypt is where Joseph and Mary with the Christ child fled shortly after His birth to escape Herod]. The Shepherds undoubtedly knew about this prophecy speaking of the restoration of the kingdom of David and that the birth of their anticipated Messiah would be at Migdal Eder [the tower of the flock].

-Lynette Hughes

THE HOTEL IS FULL

A Jewish lady named Mrs. Rosenberg many years ago was stranded late one night at a fashionable resort — one that did not admit Jews.

The desk clerk looked down at his book and said, "Sorry, no room. The hotel is full."

The Jewish lady said, "But your sign says that you have vacancies."

The desk clerk stammered and then said curtly, "You know that we do not admit Jews. Now if you will try the other side of town..."

Mrs. Rosenberg stiffened noticeably and said, "I'll have you know I converted to your religion."

The desk clerk said, "Oh, yeah, let me give you a little test. How was Jesus born?"

Mrs. Rosenberg replied, "He was born to a virgin named Mary in a little town called Bethlehem."

"Very good," replied the hotel clerk. "Tell me more."

Mrs. Rosenberg replied, "He was born in a manger."

"That's right," said the hotel clerk. "And why was he born in a manger?"

Mrs. Rosenberg said loudly, "Because a jerk like you in the hotel wouldn't give a Jewish lady a room for the night!"

-FB

Rayola Kelley

The Wonder and Promise
of Christ's Birth

Wonder filled the night air,
Glorious light parted the darkness,
Rejoicing heard all around,
A declaration stirring up the humble in heart,
Can this be, the consolation of Israel?
Has the Promised Messiah come into the world?
Is the Glory of Israel now clothed in humanity;
Destined to become a light to the Gentiles.
Hope causing the insignificant to rise,
Trust taking hold of the prophetic,
Ready to seek the promises of old,
A star highlighting the way to a lowly place.
What will one behold in a stable?
Mere sheep standing guard,
Shepherds kneeling before a simple structure,
A couple standing in awe,
What were the claims?
In the city of David, a son was born,
Is this baby held by a crude wooden structure amidst the hay,
The promised Christ the Lord?
A child pointing to redemption,
Unveiling glimpses into heavenly glory,
Foreshadowing another wooden structure,
Lifting Him up as the Lamb of God for the world to see,
Fulfilling the claims of old, the promises from above,
A King who was born among great rejoicing.
Becoming Savior who would die in the midst of great
    darkness.

Born when man was taxed by autocracy,
Lived when man was oppressed by tyranny,
Died to redeem in the midst of despotism,
Rose in the middle of hopelessness,
Ever living as King of an eternal kingdom,
Lord of a great household and High Priest of an everlasting
  priesthood.
Coming back in the midst of great tribulation as Judge.
Rightfully taking His place on the throne as King of kings
Ruling over receptive hearts as Lord of lords,
Bringing peace as the Prince of peace,
Fulfilling the claim on that night so long ago,
"Glory to God in the highest,
  and on earth, peace, good will toward men."

-RJK

- In the Church calendar: Advent, is the beginning of the Christian's new year. Advent is all about asking these questions: Why are we here? What do we do? Why do we do what we do?

- K. P. Yohannan
K.P.'s Corner
GFA World's Ministry Newsletter
December 2023

New Year Proclamation

There was an important proclamation made on New Year's Day in 1863. The president at the time knew it would not be popular with the political pundits who either thought it political suicide to do it or felt passionately opposed to it for personal and financial purposes. However, the president knew it was the right thing to do for the people. It did cause jubilation in many cities where canons even were fired to commemorate it. Who was this president and what was the proclamation? The president was Abraham Lincoln and the proclamation was His Emancipation which became the Thirteenth Amendment, abolishing slavery. (Imprimis—December 2022)

Church Matters

The Seeds of the Church

One of the most neglected teachings in the church is about the Church. The Church of Jesus Christ is not some building, denomination, or doctrine, it is a living organism of people who have been called out of this world into an eternal kingdom.

In her foreword in her fifth book about those who knew their God, author Lillian Harvey wrote this about these people's devotion, "Such devotion as we read about shames our shallowness and our failure to make a vacuum for God in the busy materialistic scramble for higher living standards."

Harvey points out our expensive homes and cars, along with vast riches and resources, and then goes on to bring her concern for Christians today to the forefront. "Our ideas are so low, and our zeal so lukewarm, and our stocks of grace so pitifully small that we need to remember great saints who all remind us, we too can make our lives sublime, and departing leave behind us, footprints in the sands of time." (TK, pgs. 4)

This Church is made up of lively (living) stones that have been and are being positioned in a spiritual building by the Holy Spirit. This living building has been placed on a sure foundation of the revelation of Jesus Christ, and is lined up to the cornerstone of His teachings and examples.

This church is considered precious to God because it has been purchased by His Son. Marriages in many cultures require some type of dowry and God provided the dowry of His Son on behalf of the Church, and Jesus redeemed it or purchased it with His sacrifice on the cross.

The question is, was Jesus' redemption enough to purchase a bride for Himself? The answer is yes, He paid the necessary and complete price for the Church but Jesus made an important statement in John 12:24, "Verily, verily, I say unto you, Except a corn of wheat fall into the ground and die, it abideth alone: but if it die, it bringeth forth much fruit."

It has been said on more than one occasion that "the blood of the martyrs is the seed of the Church." As pointed out by the author, John C. Lambert, in *Adventures of Missionary Heroism,* "From an earthly perspective the death of a Christian witness seems a tragic event. Yet from a heavenly perspective it is but the continuation of that seamless plan, conceived before time began, by a just and loving God to accomplish his ultimate redemption of man" (pgs. 111-112).

The English missionary, **James Hannington** gave his life for the cause of Christ and ended up becoming one of those precious seeds that would be planted in the ground of Africa. Oftentimes it is the blood of martyrs that has inspired others to become witnesses. Keep in mind witnesses are also known as "martyrs."

Hannington felt called to the shores of the Victoria Nyanza after reading about two missionaries who had been murdered for their faith. He saw the need to pick up the torch of the Gospel and continue to carry it in that same region regardless of the possible price.

Jesus tells His followers to count the cost and for those who know what the ultimate cost might be are also realistic about their calling and their destination. I have often wondered if such brave Christian souls are going forth as a matter of honor or out of a sense that if others are willing to give their lives for the Gospel, surely it is worth it for them to lay all *before* the Lord for His work, lay all *up* to Him for His use, and lay all *down* for His glory.

Hannington left his parish and his wife as well as their three young children in England in 1882 to take up the work with the Church Missionary Society in Africa. He was appointed leader of a new party that consisted of six men, and his main instructions were to reach Uganda from Zanzibar, where his parish would be East Central Africa. He was the first to volunteer to make the dangerous journey, and he and his party were to reinforce the work of MacKay who was holding the ground with a single companion in the face of infinite difficulties.

His journey was rugged and difficult, but he entered his new experiences with the zest of his boyish days. He would write home of his many adventures embellishing them with descriptive words and drawings. His encounters with murderous robbers, staring down lions, surviving dangers from leopards, rhinos, buffaloes, and hippopotamus highlighted his many adventures.

He reached the Victoria Nyanza around Christmas in 1882, but during the time he tried to find means to cross the river, he had a violent attack of malarial fever. He was reduced to such a state he had to be returned to England until he regained his strength. His recovery was described, "as one alive from the dead."

It was his desire to return to Africa after regaining his strength and the directors of the Church Missionary Society appointed him as the Bishop of East Equatorial Africa, the diocese which embraced not only Uganda but the immense region that lies between the Victoria Nyanza and the coast.

His first failure to reach his destination caused Hannington to be more determined to succeed on his second attempt. He wanted to bring comfort and relief to the persecuted Christians who were under the cruel oppression of a wicked king.

After setting in order the missionary stations near the coast, Hannington paid a visit to Mount Kilimanjaro for the purpose of planting the banner of the cross upon it very slopes and it was there that he began to make plans for his second and last journey towards Uganda.

Although he and his group encountered much mistreatment by indigenous tribes on their journey, he wrote in his diary, "I strove in prayer; and each time trouble seemed to be averted."

He along with 50 men traveled towards Uganda. Even though Mackay was trying to assure the wicked king overseeing this region that this determined man with his company was not any threat to him, he still arranged with a puppet king under him to arrest them. For a week the men were kept in close confinement until a band of the king's soldiers arrived with secret orders to put them all to death.

Hannington's men were stripped and bound, and his clothes were roughly torn off when he reached the place of execution. Although he was weak from fever and greatly reduced by his trying imprisonment, his courage did not fail him and he gave his murderers the message he had brought for the king, and then kneeling down he committed his soul to God. All of the men's blood but three, were spilled on the ground as they were all killed with spears.

No doubt God kept the three alive to bring back Hannington's diary and tell what had happened. Because of his courage to face lions, murderers, and death, Hannington is referred to as the Lion-hearted Bishop. At his death in 1885, he was only 38, but there is a saying that fits his life, "We live in deeds, not years." (AMH, pgs. 111-128)

***

Hans Knevel was a man of strong Christian convictions but in 1572 he learned that even a man's convictions could mean being dragged to court over theological differences. He was a citizen of Antwerp, but was arrested as an Anabaptist.

After being tortured for many days, he was told that his crime was not his convictions but that he did not "obey the authorities." Hans knew the reason he was in jail, tortured and on trial. He cut through the façade by making this statement, "We will gladly obey the authorities in all taxes, customs and excises..." But he went on to make it clear that to change his Christian conviction in order to align with the magistrate, that he would not do.

Hans we executed by being burned alive. (GG, pg. 41, footnote 28)

- May it never be true that persecutors value their lies more than we value God's truth. We must serve our young Christian brothers and sisters at *any* cost.

  -Cole Richard
  President of The Voice of the Martyrs
  January 2024 (Magazine)

- As a preacher, based on nothing less than revelation, and the authenticity of the revelation depends on the character of the one who brings it. Our Lord Jesus Christ put His impress on every revelation from Genesis to Revelation.

  -Oswald Chambers
  (CWC, pg. 14)

- The one fruit that always identifies the spoiled, selfish, worldly, immature Christian is ingratitude. They are so used to the empty fluff of the world that they can't be grateful or excited about the milk of doctrine because it lacks worldly additives. As for the Bread from heaven, it is too mundane; therefore, they easily become bored with it because the world offers variety; and as for the meat of the Word, they have developed no teeth to chew it and as a result, they choke on it in utter disgust.

-RJK

- We need preachers who preach that hell is still hot, that heaven is still real, that sin is still wrong, that the Bible is God's Word, and that Jesus is the only way of salvation.

-FB

- The wolves, false teachers, and false prophets see themselves as kings searching for a kingdom, a lord searching for a fiefdom. Their intent is not to serve but to be served, and whenever their authority is challenged, they react instinctively to protect their piece of the pie.

-Michael Boldea Jr.
(EJ, pg. 74)

- Many folks want to serve God, but only as advisers.

-Author Unknown

- There are no self-made Christians or Christian workers in Christ's service, they are all *Christ made*.

-Herbert Lockyer
(APB, pg. 146)

- A preacher should have the mind of a scholar, the heart of a child, and the hide of a rhinoceros.

-Vance Havner

- This lukewarm Church is only producing happy sinners instead of holy saints.

  -FB

- Give people liberty where the Bible doesn't, and you'll always have an audience.

  -Michael Boldea Jr.
  (EJ, pg. 9)

The Dichotomy

As believers, we struggle with the influence of three worlds, the world, the flesh and the devil. We find ourselves in a quandary because the flesh is natural in what it often needs, the world provides us with what we need, and Satan has the ability to magnify our needs in such a fashion our desire for them become obsessive, abusive, and oppressive.

We strive to overcome the world as a means to subdue its attractions upon the flesh, humble ourselves before God in order to push Satan back until he is under Jesus' feet, and discern what is of the Holy Spirit so that we can be in line with the ways of righteousness. Our flesh wars with the spirit, while our soul becomes confused by the attacks of Satan and the temptations that bombard us. Even in the dark world of the demonic, evil can be made to look alluring and good.

However, the enemy that seems to almost bring us down to the utter abyss of despair are those who we use to call friends. We trusted them enough to turn our back on them, thinking that they will watch it and not see it as a target when we are vulnerable and already fighting off frontal attacks.

Sadly, some of these friends are like Judas Iscariot. Although Jesus was not blindsided by his attack, we usually are because we trusted such individuals to be our friend, not our adversary. Here is one we loved that now shows animosity towards us for no cause. We called them friend, now they are an enemy. We trusted them with deep things of the heart and now they are using it to bring accusation against us. We fought with them and for them when they were under it, now they are at the forefront of bringing us to utter destruction.

It is a challenging dichotomy that King David often wrote about in his psalms. He bemoaned all of his enemies, but the ones who caused the greatest bitterness to his soul were the ones that shot forth the arrows of betrayal that truly will destroy the peace of one's inner being the most.

The bitterness of betrayal is not something you can swallow without choking on it. It seems so unfair and unjust causing you to wrestle with a type of insanity that does not make sense, ending up with you being thrown down on the mat of hopelessness by raw emotions such as hurt, anger, and bitterness that are running amuck.

The questions bombard you. You are to love your enemies but how can you trust such a one again? That is when you find out how much trust strengthens a committed, sacrificial love, and without it how can such love stand? We must pray for those who betray us and, in the past, you had prayed with such fervency for them, but now that your heart is broken, how can you in all sincerity pray for them to ensure your words are not hollow and empty before the throne of God? It is not only a dichotomy but a terrible dilemma.

In *Psalm 102:6-12* David talks about how such darts of betrayal made him feel. He related it to the different fowls. He remembered a bird could be brought down in flight by unexpected darts and arrows. He talked about being like a pelican of the wilderness or the owl of the desert. How many pelicans will you see in the wilderness and how many owls can survive the desert for long if they don't have water and the right prey available?

Like the birds he mentioned, David was a man out of his element. He did not know what to do about these enemies. He was like a lone sparrow on the roof top watching and waiting for possible destruction to come. It was clear that such enemies were bent on destroying him and David wrestled with whether God was using these individuals to bring something to his attention about his own spiritual status. He knew his days were like shadows and his strength would wither like the grass.

However, even a lone sparrow can take courage because God's eye is on the sparrow and nothing happens to it without God knowing it. Spurgeon said it best when He said, "God attends the funeral of every sparrow."

Each time David came to the end of his emotional despair and his wrestling match in the soul, he looked up with confidence, accepting that even though he didn't have the answers, God was still who He is and never lets anything happen unless it is for the good of His servants, and in light of bringing glory to Himself (*Psalm 102:12-11*). He is the believer's hope, strength, and source of love. At the end of self, the believer has nothing to offer, but in the Lord, he has everything he needs in order to do right, even by his enemy.

Prayer: Lord, I choose to trust You, but the battle rages for my mind and heart. Keep my heart still before You and my mind sound in You. I need to trust You as I discern the environment around me. Amen.

- As Christians, we are to hate sin in our own lives, be indifferent to its temptations, reject its cruel ways, show utter contempt towards its destructive ways, shun its prejudices, flee its arrogant attitude, resist its anger, and despise its murderous fruit. In essence, we must never have any part or agreement with the ways of wickedness. As the Bible instructs, we must come out and be separate.

-RJK

- I am quite sure that the root of nine-tenths of all heresies that have ever afflicted the Christian Church, and are the cause of the weakness of so much popular Christianity, is none other than the failure adequately to recognize the universality, and the gravity of transgression.

-Dr. Alexander Maclaren
(COS, pg. 36)

- We need a generation of preachers who love the secret place more than the public place and who love the Presence more than the platform.

-Holy Spirit & Fire
(FB)

- If you sit under a true shepherd who has led you to green pastures, then learn what the green pastures look like so that you might avoid the dried-out and sickly ones.

-Michael Boldea Jr.
(EJ, pg. 10)

- Persecution leaves the church full of believers serious about their faith—serious enough that threats of arrest or physical pain can't keep them from meeting. Those who are there only because it's "cool" quickly fall away.

-Todd Nettleton
(WFF, pgs. 142-143)

- We are not here to heap upon ourselves blessings, we are here to be a blessing.

-RJK

- The only reality in life is moral reality, not intellectual or aesthetic. Religion based in intellectualism becomes purely credal, Jesus Christ is not needed in it.

    -Oswald Chambers
    (CWC, pg. 80)

- He that is ashamed to speak the truth has need to be ashamed of himself.

    -Charles Spurgeon

- The best speakers for God are frequently they who are least gifted with human eloquence: for if that be richly present – the mighty power of moving men – there is an imminent peril of relying on it, and attributing the results to- its magnetic spell.

    -Herbert Lockyer
    (APB, pg. 52)

- We laugh off the pulpit pimps of today, thinking them benign and in offensive, but they are not, and when their poisoned fruit is fully ripened, there will be scores of souls so turned off by the idea of God that they will actively seek to persecute those who still cling to the hem of His garment.

    -Michael Boldea Jr.
    (EJ, pg. 75)

- Our churches don't need more coffee bars, laser lights, cool worship songs, celebrity pastors, and topical sermons having your best life now. We need men who will teach the whole word of God, who will magnify Jesus above all else, who won't minimize sin, but call people to repent, and who will make it clear that Jesus is the only way to be saved and without faith in Him, you won't go to heaven.

    -Jordan Riley

- The greatest heresy in the church today is we think we are in the entertainment business. It is scarcely possible in most places to get a person to attend a meeting where the only attraction is GOD.

  -A.W. Tozer

- If you are a follower of Christ, in the world's eyes, you are, by virtue of your association with Him, a second-class citizen.

  -Michael Boldea Jr.
  (EJ, pg. 56)

- The church cannot be the salt of the earth if we keep sugar-coating the Gospel.

  -FB

- What is God requiring from you? He does not want your strength, but your heart. He does not want your deeds, but your obedience to what is right. He does not want your offerings, but He wants you to learn His ways so that you can walk in confidence of who He is. It is time that, as believers, we give Him what He desires for He is worthy of the best, rather than what we are willing to throw His way out of convenience and selfishness.

  -RJK

Time Is Short

There is no time in eternity, but being of this world means we are creatures of time. We are subject to time and in light of eternity, our life is nothing more than a vapor, our trouble temporary, and our footprints quickly taken away by the winds of the world.

When you consider time in light of eternity, the Bible speaks of dispensations, ages, and the fullness of time. Dispensations have to do with how something is administered. For instance, we live in a dispensation of grace which means everything is measured, considered, and executed according to grace.

Ages have to do with certain time frames in which something will function. Each age has its philosophies, idols and pinnacles, which point to the age as having a beginning and an end. In between is the story of progression of civilizations based on the strength of armies, only to end up on the great slide of digression that is marked by the moral weakness of man as he is taken down into the cesspool of sin and failure, ending with one civilization after another being buried by the sands of time.

The fullness of time has to do with God fulfilling His plan or purpose. When Jesus' came it was because everything was in place, and when He comes again it will be when the fullness of the Gentiles have been brought to fruition for judgment.

I know there are many days I have foolishly wasted because of vain activities and squandered because of foolish thoughts. The problem with time is you can't ever get it back.

We have a tendency to think time is eternal when we are children looking forward with some great expectation toward some event that seems like it will never happen. It eventually does because time comes and goes. In our youth at the peak of our strength, we take for granted there is still much time left when in reality our days are numbered.

In our 30s and 40s we feel that time is still on our side but have we acquired wisdom to properly run the race so our lives will count in light of eternity? We get a bit reflective about time in our 50s, but have we realized that time is a gift that can't be wasted. We feel a bit of urgency in our 60s because the strength of our youth is now waning, and frustration in our 70s because we can't do as much due to time that is marking our lives, reminding us life as we know it is becoming like graveclothes. For those who make it to their 80s they admit they're surprised they are still here, and in their 90s they know they are on borrowed time. And what about when one hits the 100 mark—do they still believe they have much time left?

The Bible tells us how to look at time, our lives in regard to time, and what we must do in light of time. We can't redo time. We can't recapture what we lost due to time, and we can't rewind time. This is why Paul tells us to redeem the time for the days are evil, and as we can see, winding down to a destructive climax.

- We Christians try to put God's stamp of approval on our sometimes worldly or fleshly activities. We try to take the lemons this life presents us and make it into lemonade, but we must be honest that in spite of breaking a matter down with our logic and adding what we call justification to it that in most cases it will be considered sour to God and He will spit it out.

  -RJK

- A creed is necessary, but it is not essential. If I am a devotee of a creed, I cannot see God unless He comes along that line.

  -Oswald Chambers
  (CWC, pg. 27)

- Christian expectation in the average church follows the program, not the promises. Prevailing spiritual conditions, however low, are accepted as inevitable. What will be is what has been. The weary slaves of the dull routine find it impossible to hope for anything better. We need today a fresh spirit of anticipation that springs out of the promises of God. We must declare war on the mood of non-expectation, and come together with childlike faith.

Only then can we know again the beauty and wonder of the Lord's presence among us."

-A. W. Tozer

- Too many Christians think their feelings prove their heart, but it is actions that prove the heart.

-FB

- The modern story of Western Christianity abounds with examples, pulling from both secular and mystical visions.... Many churches and ministers subsequently drank from the fountain of collectivism. Corresponding is the popular social justice movement, its roots in the dual history of Catholic common-good teachings and Marxist-based class warfare.

-Carl Teichrib
(GG, pg. 546)

- False teachers and false prophets pose the greatest danger to the church, and every New Testament writer saw the truth of it and warned against them...We were warned to be watchful because they are effective and oftentimes sprinkle enough truth into their deception to cause division, confusion, and strife.

-Michael Boldea Jr.
(EJ, pg. 14)

- The 1900s saw the technology of radio and motion pictures become a highly favored instrument for Christian communication. In spreading the gospel, those devices seemingly held the potential for good. However, the reality is that they have spread a leaven that continues to corrupt the body of Christ by undermining *sound doctrine* and leading Christians astray *unto fables.* It is called the leaven of *entertainment.*

-T.A. McMahon
The Berean Call
January 2024

- If a word comes to you, calls itself God's message, and does not start with man's sin, nor put in the forefront of its utterances the way by which the dominion of that sin can be broken in your own heart, and the penalties of that sin in your present and future life can be swept away, it is condemned—(in the very fact itself), as not a gospel from God or fit for men.

-Dr. Alexander MaClaren
(COS, pg. 36)

- Some people aren't in Christ, they're just in Church.

-FB

Passing on the Legacy

How important is it to pass on the spiritual legacy to our children and grandchildren? Remember, children are God's legacy that has been entrusted to every parent for a season. When on that great day we meet our Lord, how many parents will be able to hand the legacy back to the Lord without shame and dread?

In most cases, Americans are more concerned with leaving some worldly inheritance behind than leaving a spiritual one that will carry their families into eternity. It is clear that those who are only concerned with the earthly, have no real vision of the heavenly.

A widow woman by the name of Prisca, who was among the Yembi Yembi group of Papua New Guinea, had such a concern. She knew her time on earth was coming to an end. At such a stage, one has nothing to lose in light of reputation or of a worldly nature. She challenged the parents of her village with these words, "I am not worried to die. I will see Jesus at death. God has straightened the road before me. I am hanging on the death of Jesus to pay the penalty of my sin. I just have this one worry about my grandkids. Will I see all of them in Heaven? I don't know. You parents better not slack off with your number one work in life! Teach them Messiah's road. Teach them!" She kept this urgent challenge up until her ultimate graduation from this life into God's glory. They said of her graduation that with a smile and a tear coming down her face, she took her last breath.

Was her urgent request the end of the story? It was not. Her words did make inroads into the parents and they wasted no time in sitting their children down and having the most important conversation they could have with them about their soul. They shared their grandmother's concern for them and how important it was to her that they understood the gospel message. Many of her grandchildren admitted they were not sure of their destination, exposing the great need for their parents to continue to teach what the Word of God states about all matters pertaining to life and godliness.

Children are a lot like the talents mentioned in Matthew 25. Children are God's most precious gifts and we must not bury them under the vain, endless rhetoric of the world; rather, we must invest in them the things of heaven

- We have forgotten heaven and become enamored of this world, living our lives as though the only plans God has for us pertain to earth.

-Dave Hunt
The Berean Call, July 2023

- To clothe the outer man with religious discipline, but allow him to still remain unregenerate in disposition, is to make a religious bigot out of him.

  -RJK

- The church is to feed the Sheep, NOT to entertain Goats!

  -A.W. Tozer

- Beware of preaching the gospel of temperament instead of the Gospel of God. Numbers of people today preach the gospel of temperament, the gospel of "cheer up."

  -Oswald Chambers
  (CWC, pg. 172)

- Instead of designing a church service to attract people, have a service that attracts God. He will draw the people.

  -FB

- Love for the sheep is exhibited in protecting them from the wolves, not ushering them into their open jaws.

  -Michael Boldea Jr.
  (EJ, pg. 37)

- Next Sunday you are to talk about heaven. I am interested in that land because I have had a clear title to a bit of property there for more than 55 years. I did not buy it. It was given to me at a tremendous sacrifice. I am not holding it for speculation, since the title is not transferable. It is not a vacant lot.

  -Dr. Harry Rimmer
  Scientist & Bible Scholar

- Jesus invested in a few men for over three years. He walked with them, supped with them, slept with them, and traveled with them. He served as their patient, anointed teacher and their constant companion, example, and leader. He was a leader in authority, attitude, and conduct. He was as big as the outdoors, yet He was meek and humble. He was powerful, yet obedient and disciplined. He was great, but as a servant to all He became the least among men. He was God, but became man. His purpose was to save people out of this world for Himself and build a Church that could not be moved by hell, but only by the Spirit of the Living God.

-RJK

- The weakness of so many modern Christians is that they feel too much at home in the world.

-A. W. Tozer

- I think the greatest weakness in the church today is that almost no one believes that God invests His power in the Bible. Everyone is looking for power in a program, in a technique, in anything and everything except where God has placed it: His Word.

-R.C. Sproul

- Unity without the Gospel is a worthless unity, it is the very unity of hell.

-J.C. Ryle

- Turning a blind eye to false teaching, false prophets, and false teachers is not a sign of love; it is a sign of cowardice and a self-serving narcissism that cares nothing for the welfare of those who see you as a spiritual leader, mentor, or teacher.

-Michael Boldea Jr.
(EJ, pgs. 37-38)

- If only Christians would allow the love of God to compel them to give the best, and give it all for the work of God. Unresponsiveness towards that which is righteous and benevolent causes hearts to become hardened. How many hearts are becoming hard? How many visions are being lost because Christians are heaping so much of the world upon themselves that they have lost sight of heaven? How many ears have become dull to the cries of the lost, due to a lack of love and compassion? How many eyes have become blind to the plight of others in order to avoid responsibility? The Apostle Paul tried to stir up the Church with these words, "Wherefore he saith, Awake thou that sleepest, and arise from the dead, and Christ shall give thee light" (Ephesians 5:14).

  -RJK

- Nothing is more important than persistence in this habit of cultivating Christ's indwelling presence. Every habit grows out of a succession of little acts. No habit comes full-grown into the life.

  -J. Gregory Mantle
  (COS, pg. 176)

- Our pulpits need Biblical preachers not motivational speakers.

  -FB

- The foundation of the Church has been the cross of Christ and His shed blood, the growth and expansion of the Church has been through martyrdom, the depth of the Church has been developed through suffering, the victory of the Church has been through obedience and faithfulness, and the life of the Church has been Christ's life and the ministry and power of the Holy Spirit.

  -Larry M. Brown
  CEO of Ethnos 360

- Outward reformation may change practices, but it is inward revival that transforms the hearts and minds of the people.

  -RJK

- We aren't called to be like other Christians; we are called to be like Christ.

  -FB

- A shepherd who is willing to put himself between the wolves and the sheep is a true shepherd.

  -Michael Boldea Jr.
  (EJ, pg. 36)

- God had made man an extension of Himself—in His own "image." Man *belonged* to God in a very unique way. That same sense of belonging exists today, thousands of years after the Fall. Augustine declared, "Thou hast made us for Thyself, O God, and we are restless until we find our rest in Thee."

  -Ruth Hunt
  (VPH, pg. 19)

- It is hard for some people to believe that they are sowing every day into their spiritual lives and in the lives of others. We tend to think our words, examples, and conduct mean nothing. However, our words serve as the plow, our examples water, and our conduct cultivates. Each aspect of our character will cut into, make impressions, and leave its mark on people's lives, memories, and decisions.

  -RJK

- Jesus didn't eat with the sinners and tax collectors because He wanted to appear inclusive, tolerant, and accepting. He ate with them to call them to a changed, fruitful life, to die to self and live in Him. His call is transformation of life not affirmation.

-Anglican Christian Prayer

- One of the most troubling problems with the church today is the unwavering loyalty to a "Christian" personality rather than to Christ and His Word. The unwillingness to test every man's teaching with God's Word coupled with a stubborn lack of discernment, produces fertile ground for deception to flourish.

-FB

- Through His Son, the Father did a great work (redemption), and through His Spirit He is doing a greater work (sanctification). Through His children He is doing a glorious work according to His plan by ensuring the Church is brought forth for His glory, His purpose, and His work.

-RJK

- See to it that you do not rest in a worldly religion; to give God your knee, while the world carries away your heart.

-Joseph Alleine
(TK, pg. 38)

Are You Trifling
With Heavenly Glory?

What does the word "glory" mean? I have done much to research this word. Everything has some type of glory attached to it. For example, man's glory is vainglory for in the end it will prove useless, the world's glory is a glitter that will fade, man-made religion carries a false glory that has no substance to it, and then there is God's glory.

As believers who are part of the body of Christ, Colossians 1:27 tells us our glory is Christ in us, which is the hope of glory. Notice the hope of glory is because Christ is in us, not because we have any measurable glory in and of ourselves.

Hope points to a future realization. We may by faith know we have the essence of glory in us because of redemption, but we will never know the fullness of this glory until the next world.

As J. Gregory Mantle points out, this word "glory" is a word that has lost its crown and needs to be reevaluated. He compared it to a coin that long ago lost its mint and that it has become cheapened and debased. This is when Mantle brought out that a man's real glory consists not in what he has but in what he is.

This brings us back to the essence of glory. It has to do with the quality of one's character. Man's base character is in a fallen state, the world's character is profane, and God's character is holy. This is why Mantle described true glory as the glory of character, and holy character is nothing less than the Divine image more and more fully incarnated in man.

Although imperfect in man, the image of Christ is being brought to fruition by the Holy Spirit through the work of sanctification. Mantle describes this glory in this manner, "Christ in us coming to fruitage— His growing beauty, His increasing mastery, His complete dominance of thoughts and affections and will, that in all things He might have the pre-eminence. What a Gospel to proclaim! To put the hope of such glory within the reach of every man! Limitless possibilities of exaltation are here to those who have fallen the lowest." (COS, pg. 177)

As believers, there is no greater glory to reflect in this world than Christ. It is part of our high calling because all that is done in us, through us, and with us is His glorious work and intervention. It is for this reason He deserves to be glorified with our lips, in our service, and with our life. We must not touch His glory or trifle with it by taking personal credit for His righteous ways, His incredible wisdom and

His perfect works. It is for this reason we are not to glory in anything except our Lord.

———————

- If a man can keep humility as his constant companion and give glory to God for all He does through him, there is no limit to what God can do.

  -Michael Boldea Jr.
  (EJ, pg. 135)

- Religion defines us. It can serve as our conscience, but much of religion is just an outward cloak that allows many to hide their filthy rags behind a religious façade. For example, it hides insensitivity, compromise, wickedness, and sin. Today, much of religion has become professional entertainment instead of a high calling. It is all outward conformity, rather than inward transformation. It is about worldly kingdoms, rather than an unseen kingdom made up of believers of Jesus Christ.

  -RJK

- Wrong is still wrong even if everybody is doing it; right is still right even if nobody is doing it! Therefore, stand for what is right even if you have to stand alone.

  -FB

- What we need as the Church isn't marketing techniques and strategies, but a transcendent Word that confronts challenges, and rescues fallen sinners.

  -Michael Horton
  Whitehorse Inn.org

- Early in my Christian life, the difference between Christianity and religion was defined. I have never forgotten the diverse difference between these two arenas. However, this has not kept me from falling into religious traps. I equated a church building with serving God, rather than being available to serve people. I have defended leaders, rather than standing for truth and holding the line of righteousness. I took up causes, instead of maintaining the only cause set forth in Scripture: Jesus Christ and Him crucified.

  -RJK

- With the nation being in crisis economically and spiritually, it is not the primary responsibility of Washington DC to fix it. In truth, it is the burden and duty of the Church of the Living God.

  -David Lane
  American Renewal Project

- Ministry is about looking for a place to SERVE not a place to shine.

  -FB

- Do you know who you are in Christ? Are you looking elsewhere for your identity or life? If you are, you will find yourself lost in the ridiculousness of it all. You may not realize the state of your spiritual condition at this point, but down the line, emptiness will mock you, disillusionment will rob you, vanity will consume you, and hopelessness will overtake you.

  -RJK

- A watered-down gospel may get a lot of people into pews, but it won't get anyone to the cross.

  -David Alan Campbell

- We do have problems in the churches, and it is because we do not seek God's hand. We do not know what God is trying to do, and we do not see as God sees.

-A. W. Tozer
(WOG, pg. 94)

- For the Church, the danger is not in being left behind, but in being caught off guard.

-Marvin Rosenthal
Zion's Fire
May/June 2023

- A church that will not confront sin, will eventually end up conforming to sin.

-FB

- The problem with the organized church in America is that it is not desperate enough for the things of God. The church may be suffering from malnutrition, but it has failed to recognize it because many continue to gorge themselves on vain religious diets of man and the world.

-RJK

- When the Church tolerates the very things that God hates, it finds itself in bed with the devil.

-Brad Law

- It is hard for God's people to realize that when it is time for them to follow Jesus, they are the most vulnerable. If they linger behind or stop to graze on bits of worldly "grass," they will find themselves falling prey to wolves. Jesus is clear that all disciples must first deny themselves of the luxury to linger a bit longer, crucify the tendency to graze on that which has no substance or

287

purpose, and become serious in following Him up the path of righteousness, in spite of the loss of this present world.

-RJK

- The world may see fit to normalize depravity, but the Word of God does not, and the children of God should not.

Michael Boldea Jr.
(EJ, pg. 152)

- Unless we purposely live in view of the next world, we cannot make much out of our present existence.

-Charles Spurgeon

- The preacher may seem to be too much like the winter night, very bright, but very cold.

-Joseph Alliene
(TK, pg. 37)

- My observation is that we have maintained the church of Jesus Christ as an ascetic ward in the hospital and never managed to get anybody out of it.

-A. W. Tozer
(WOG, pg. 55)

- Inaction is unbelief. Wrong action is rebellion. Half-hearted action is disobedience because we must do all things with our whole heart when it comes to our service to the Lord.

-RJK

- The mark of an effective church is not how many people come, but how many live differently as a result of having been there.

-FB

- That very church which the world likes best is sure to be that which God abhors.

  -Charles Spurgeon

- If the children of God were in no danger of being deceived, led astray, or otherwise sidelined by the enemy, why are there so many warnings in the Bible about being vigilant, on guard, and aware of the devil's machinations?

  -Michael Boldea Jr.
  (EJ, pg. 90)

- As believers, we often perceive we can't be touched by deception, but deception is wrapped up in good things, clothed in religious garbs, adjusted to feed religious pride, and designed to seduced the most ardent religious zealot. After all, Satan can come as an angel of light and his cohorts can come across as ministers of righteousness. When a Christian is operating from the religious pinnacle of self-sufficiency and not from the base ways of need and humility, that is when they are the most vulnerable to deception.

  -RJK

Man's Challenges

Small But Fierce

What determines the size of a man? His height, his talents, his abilities, his strength, his means to survive, or his character? The world looks on the outside of man to determine his worth. This can be based on prejudices, biases, agendas, and priorities. If he passes the first test, the next one is what can he contribute to society in light of work ethic, productivity, and accomplishments? In most cases the test stops with the second one, but there are those few who consider a man in light of his character.

The depth of character determines much about a man--whether he is trustworthy, his word means anything, or if he possesses inner disciplines that make him reliable and trustworthy.

The real issue for man is how God considers him. He weighs man's spirit, tests his heart, tries the character of his faith, and seeks out true worshippers and those who are righteous before Him.

The next question is what does the soul and spirit weigh? Upon death, it has been noted the loss of two ounces, which they figure is what air weighs in the body. However, spirit is breath and it is believed that the soul, which is made up of our will, emotions, and mind also houses the spirit. This brings us down to a simple truth, man's soul weighs the same but his spirit is weighed by God, which is based on his motivation. Therefore, the motive of man determines the real weight of a man's soul.

Man determines what he will allow to motivate him based on what he chooses to believe. What he chooses to believe will also govern what master he comes under that will greatly influence him. Man's soul may be heavy due to sin, weighed down because of spiritual darkness, ugly because of wickedness, and depraved because of evil reigning, or it can be the Spirit of light because it has been redeemed by the blood of the Lamb, and the spirit set free to soar in the Spirit of God.

True missionaries do not regard the size and status of those they are called to minister among. To them such people are lost souls who need to hear the liberating message of the Gospel. They are aware that pagan culture oppresses the people, the darkness of ignorance and superstition will manifest itself in their murky attitudes, their fear will cause them to be unpredictable, and their true master will cause them to gravely test or silence the witness of heaven. However, if the burden is there, missionaries can't ignore it regardless of the darkness that lies before them, for they know they have been entrusted to carry the only torch of hope to bring the light in the midst of darkness. **Rev. A.B. Lloyd** had such a burden for a unique, intriguing human race that was buried deep in the Ituri Rainforest of Central Africa. This tribal group was set apart from all other tribes. They are known as the Pygmies, a group of humans who were small in stature but their reputation was that of being fierce, causing fear.

In spite of the rumors that circulated about these individuals, most Europeans doubted their existence, but at the turn of the 20th century, explorer Henry Morton Stanley came upon them. Shortly afterwards in 1897, Lloyd set out on a remarkable journey in order to bring the light to this tribe that was disbursed throughout a region six times the area of England.

Lloyd was not only a missionary, but his services in Africa included being a war correspondent with the British army, an interpreter and a makeshift surgeon. His journeys from Uganda deep into the forests of the Congo brought him into contract with the Pygmies.

In his journals he poured out his heart for these people located in the heart of Africa. The following entry shows his burden and passion for these individuals, "The time has come when we in this civilized land of ours should stretch out our hands to these poor ignorant cannibals, and seek to lift them out of their darkness and gross superstition into the light of the Gospel of Christ. Their blood will surely be upon us…if we knowing their state, seek not to break their age-bound chains of heathenism and proclaim liberty to the captives and the opening of the prison to them that are bound."

Like those before him, he encountered various obstacles. Lloyd had been involved with eleven skirmishes along with British soldiers that took place on African soil to suppress rebellion against the Queen. He had narrow escapes and later succumb to malarial fever.

The soldiers were ordered home to do more recruiting. Ninety-nine left for England, while Lloyd, who was the 100th man, decided to strike westward right across the continent, by way of the Pygmy Forest. He secured a guide who knew the land, furnished himself with provision for three months; gathered a few porters; and with a bicycle, camera, donkey and a faithful little dog named Sally, set out to explore and bring the light to the unknown. In the end the camera proved useless, the donkey was sold and sadly Sally who survived many adventures as well as hairbreadth escapes became food for a crocodile, but the bike proved valuable when small snake trails presented themselves to him.

Prepared by his experience in Africa, he was used to the creatures, insects, and terrain he would encounter. His shooting skills came in handy to provide food and protection. He described both the beauty of the landscape as well as its unmanageable ways that buffeted them.

After seven days of fighting their way through the unforgiving terrain of the forest, Lloyd caught a glimpse of what he thought was a gorilla in his gun scope, to be immediately informed that it was a man. His first encounter with the dwarfs proved to be a standoff as both with mutual fascination they silently gazed at one another.

Lloyd expected to be plummeted with poison arrows, but as the missionary peacefully sat in his chair, he called out a salutation to them and one shyly responded. He then asked him if he would sit and talk with him.

The full-grown man of four feet, but displaying a well-knit figure and powerful limbs turned out to be the chief. He informed Lloyd that they had been observing his caravan for six days but due to the smallness of the company and what was obviously peaceful intentions of the caravan, it disarmed their suspicions. It became clear that when not feeling threatened that these individuals proved to be good natured and were ready to give the right hand of fellowship to those who displayed peace and friendliness.

The Pygmies took him to their camp where he discovered that the women were comely little creatures, averaging 3 feet 10 inches. He found out they were a traveling people and learned about their ways of hunting and surviving in the midst of giants. He also found the people to be intelligent and possessed religious ideas which would offer a foundation for a higher faith and worship than their own.

Lloyd's last part of his journey was for the most part by canoe which proved to be one of ease after traveling through a jungle, but even that was not without its challenges. He almost drowned and he had to travel through the region where cannibalism was openly practiced. He had some harrowing experiences and witnessed great depravity that is always attached to cannibalism, which is based much on the darkness of superstition.

However, he came out with a passion for the Pygmies and cannibals who were in darkness. He knew if the light penetrated the darkness, that heirs of salvation would be discovered. The truth is that this is true for all humanity. (AMH, pgs. 159-175)

We live in the barren wilderness of the world, are hedged in by the dark forest of paganism, oppressed by depraved superstition, and blinded by the false lights of witchcraft, idolatry, and cultural practices. Man's soul is often heavy, shrouded in confusion, overwhelmed by disillusionment, and lost in darkness. What is light to him, is darkness to God. What is acceptable to the world is profane to our Creator, and what is good to man's way of thinking is filthy rags to our Lord.

How the light needs to shine in the great darkness of man's heavy souls, and the one who carries that light are those who have received it in their souls. They are the container, Jesus the light, the Holy Spirit the oil, and the Word of God the flint. We must pray that the light is lifted up, the flame of passion burns bright in our hearts, and the burden for souls becomes great as the Word lights the path to the deliverance, the salvation of those who are lost, but seeking an eternal refuge.

- Most people don't really want the truth. They just want constant reassurance that what they believe is truth.

  -FB

- Knowledge of good broadens a man's mind, makes him intolerant of all sin, and shows itself in intense activity.

  -Oswald Chambers
  (CWC, pg. 154)

- A.W. Tozer points out in discourse about wisdom how man has a deep restlessness because he was created in the image of God to be used for His purpose and pleasure. The way he was created would enable him to experience God in His fullness. However, the thing that has stopped man from experiencing God is that he relies upon his own wisdom that is comprised of scholarship, business, inventions, psychology, and theology. He goes on to say, "No matter how successful a man is in these endeavors, there still remains a void within that can never be filled." Clearly, the only way that void is filled is when we begin to experience God. (WOG, pg. 72)

- That sin is here, conscience and universal experience attest. The evidences of its presence are not slight or intermittent. Turn in what direction one will, sin confronts one as a face of human life, an experience of the heart, a development of history, a crimson thread in literature, a problem for science, and enigma for philosophy.

  -Dr. James Orr
  (COS, pg. 36)

- Humanity has three Great desires: To be as God, to be Masters of Meaning and Destiny, to build Heaven on Earth.

  -Carl Teichrib
  (GG, pg. 4)

- We'd rather blame God for the thing we do than take personal responsibility for our actions and admit it's our own shortcomings, failures and duplicity that kept us from following through.

  -Michael Boldea Jr.
  (EJ, pg. 19)

- Classy is when you have a lot to say but you choose to remain silent in front of fools.

  -FB

- The reality of human nature is that we are lazy unless a matter serves our purpose. But, if we are prepared to work, we will learn there is tremendous satisfaction in it when we actually finish or accomplish a job or reach a goal.

  -RJK

- If a rhetorician teaches a politician to do what is unjust, he does that man and his city more harm than good.

  -Socrates

- That which lies in the well of your thought will come up in the bucket of your speech.

  -Charles Spurgeon
  (APB, pg. 212)

- Pride is the central citadel of independence of God.

  -Oswald Chambers
  (CWC, pg. 171)

- There is no one more deceived than the one who professes to be a Christian, then habitually walks into the devil's den.

  -FB

- Our tongue often proves to be a loose cannon. It is not only used to shoot others full of holes, but we will inevitably turn around and shoot ourselves in the foot with it.

  -RJK

The Reality of Independence

Man wants to be independent from all rule. He strives to be his own master and God. He wants to rule His home, control the events that flow in his life, and somehow make his own Eden on earth that serves his deepest desires and pleasures. This independence from his Creator is rebellion.

Rebellion comes in different forms. Man uses personal strength to create the idea he is self-sufficient and has no need for God. He uses his talents to believe he can create his own reality and can do it in spite of the unseen powers that greatly influence his existence. He strives for that which is supposed to give him purpose, reason, and power, but like Esau he ends up selling his birthright for a bowl of food. He rebels against the norm to break free of the conventional and ends up becoming a slave to everything. He decries about his right to live life as he will, but ends up succumbing to silly trends, peer pressures, worldly presentations, and deadly activities.

In her book, *A Very Present Help,* Ruth Hunt talked about how individualism has characterized the philosophy of the culture of the youth for the past five decades. They call it "freedom" but in reality, it is conformity where everyone looks exactly alike and behaves as others while doing the same thing. If you dare step out of that conformity you are not labeled as an individual but someone who is not loving or tolerant to the change of cultural attitudes. (VPH, pg. 73)

The truth is we have been conditioned even in rebellion to conform to a few, while being seduced and deceived to believe we are being our true selves. Unless we have found our identity in a relationship with our Creator, we become lost in the deception that raging against authority is a way to establish independence, mocking the conventional is the way of being different from the norm, and becoming part of the latest acceptable crowd puts one on the right side of a matter. It is all a lie and we are simply being indoctrinated into a sick reality that is far from individualism, sanity, and a meaningful life.

Man's digression always leads him into a surreal world where there are no absolute truths, no real consequences, and that somehow everything will work out for his benefit. However, a line has been drawn in the sand by an old rugged cross. The choices are clear, the results irreversible, and the ways clearly marked. Man will not be able to ignore, fudge, or move the line; rather, he must choose, and in doing so, he will choose his destiny: that or tormenting hell, forever separated from any life or a blissful life in the presence of his Creator.

- There is a three-fold foot that carnal self stands upon: our own wisdom, our own righteousness, our own strength. These three feet must be cut off, and we must learn to have no subsistence in ourselves, but only in Christ, and to stand only on His bottom.

  -Joseph Alleine
  (TK, pg. 36)

- The funny thing about intolerant people is that they are only tolerant when you agree with them.

  -FB

- We chose half measures rather than the full amount. We tried to resist the devil without submitting to God, and that's like trying to row across the ocean with just one oar.

  -Michael Boldea Jr.
  (EJ, pg. 19)

- The greatest enemy to human souls is the self-righteous spirit which makes men look to themselves for salvation.

  -Charles Spurgeon

- You are free to believe whatever you want to believe. I'm just here to tell you the Scripture says, life is short, death is real, hell is hot, eternity is long. Jesus saves!

  -C.L. White
  Christian Rider Ministry

- Darkness is my own point of view; when once I allow the prejudice of my head to shut down the witness of my heart, I make my heart dark.

  -Oswald Chambers
  (CWC, pg. 178)

- Man's life is but for a moment in light of eternity, a season in light of maturity, and entails a lifetime of challenges. As a result, there is change in some ways, but drudgery in other ways. However, people avoid change and most resent being at the place of drudgery. The truth that remains consistent is God's faithfulness and man's mortality.

  -RJK

- We live in a generation of emotionally weak people. Everything has to be watered down because its offensive, including the truth.
  -FB

- We all long for Eden and are constantly glimpsing it. Our whole nature is soaked with the sense of exile.

  J. R. R. Tolkien

- Today's society appropriates the blessings while despising the very ethos that created them.

-Carl Teichrib
(GG, pg. 42)

- I find no enemy so dangerous as self.

-Joseph Alleine
(TK, pg. 38)

- We may seek God by our intellect, but we can find him with our heart.

-FB

Wisdom Recognizes
the Inevitable

In light of man's limited wisdom that sets him up to be wrong most of the time. Rev. James Snyder made this statement in his introduction to A.W. Tozer's book on wisdom, "What many people do not understand is that the unknown unknowns *can* and *do* sabotage lives. It is the arrogance of a fool who believes he knows everything and therefore qualifies him for making all the decisions in his life and that of others around him." He goes on to say this is especially true when it comes to others' spiritual life. (WOG, pg. 7)

True wisdom teaches us to hear both sides before judging and yet even after knowing both sides, wisdom will take you one step further and reveal the inevitable about man in his limited state. Even after hearing both sides, a wise person recognizes they still know nothing unless it is revealed from heaven and confirmed as being so.

- You can be so full of religion yet have no relationship with Jesus Christ.

  -FB

- Today we find ourselves in a contradicting world of limitless possibilities, even as we scramble to erase distinctions. Of course, the animal kingdom operates in a male-female binary. We, however, are at war with all forms of otherness. *Never mind what is natural or factual.*

  -Carl Teichrib
  (GG, pg. 88)

- Many people are banking on being the exception to the rule and not treating the prospect of eternity and where they will spend it with the requisite seriousness. True, you only live once and can only die once, but after this, the judgment. It's that last part nobody wants to consider because it puts a damper on the whole life in the fast lane mindset.

  -Michael Boldea Jr.
  (EJ, pg. 25)

- Sin never promised liberty. It only promises that you can experience all the world can offer without any restraints, but it is incapable of sparing you of consequences. The world promises temporary happiness, but not satisfaction. The flesh promises temporary satisfaction, but never lasting contentment. Self promises temporary exaltation, but never any real peace.

  -RJK

- The *hand* of ambitious rudeness should be *cut* off; The *eye* of ambitious coveting should be *plucked* out. The *foot* of ambitious will fulness should be *cut* off.

  -Robert Glover
  (APB, pg. 217)

- It is not human nature that needs altering, it is man's spirit that needs to be brought back into right relationship with God, and before that can be done the disposition of sin has to be dealt with.

  -Oswald Chambers
  (CWC, pg. 243)

- God does not guide those who want to run their own life.

  -FB

ANYONE FOR CHANGE

I once wrote, people desire change, but fear and resent it when it comes because it often tears up their present comforts, brings them to abysses of hopelessness because they can't control it, pits of failures because they can't adjust it to their way of thinking, and caves of despair because change will be what it is. Yet there must be change that involves reconciliation with God, transformation of the soul, and revival of the spirit. Here are some thoughts I wrote down.

> Your family will not change until you change.
> You community will not change until your family changes.
> Your nation will not change until your community changes.
> The power of change is found in one place, one message:
> **The Gospel**.

In regards to substitutions:

We have become religious instead of children of God in order to fit in with what is normal.

We have become fleshly and politically correct to exist in a doomed world, rather than become spiritual in order to live.

We have become judgmental, rather than compassionate to avoid any real cost.

We have become gods of our worlds, rather than servants of the Most High God.

Necessary change for environments must begin with local churches.

The face of the visible Church will not change
until each believer makes Jesus Lord of their lives,
and the Church makes Jesus its only head.

Real change always begins with the person who looks back at you in the mirror,

A person who is humble enough to be wrong, repents in tears of brokenness,

A person who cries out for mercy, knows that only God can change their hopeless state of death and destruction.

Prayer: Lord, change begins with me, but it can only take place in the secret places of communion with You. Lord, bring me into that place of change through humility and repentance. Amen.

- Oh, how fickle we human beings are! How self-centered and self-serving we can prove to be. It is true; at the door of every unbroken and unrepentant man lays incredible treachery against God.

-RJK

- A true believer is at war with his sin, a false believer is at peace with it.

-FB

- There are two ways to be fooled. One is to believe what isn't true. The other is to refuse to accept what is true.

-Soren Kierkegood

- We are spoiled, coddled, self-obsessed, petulant children who balk at the idea of personal accountability, taking responsibility, pursuing the way of righteousness and truth, or considering the laying down of our burdens (sins) at the foot of the cross.

-Michael Boldea Jr.
(EJ, pg. 33)

- When you come amongst those whose morality and uprightness crown them the lord of their own lives, there is no affinity with you, and they leave you alone.

-Oswald Chambers
(CWC, pg. 421)

- People need to quit living in light of the past as they live from one memory to another. Such people miss the moments and opportunities to embrace the small gifts that life will allot to each of us. I have watched so many people rage against what is, try to manipulate what is not, and totally miss what could be, that I have come to realize why so many end up regretting the missed opportunities that will not pass their way again.

-RJK

- Sin is always a choice. Obeying God is always a choice. No one will force you to do either one.

  -FB

- It is better to suffer wrongdoing than to do wrong oneself.

  -Socrates

- The power of willing ignorance is unbelievable.

  -Unknown

- Men should be more afraid of wealth, less afraid of poverty. Wealth tends to pride, indulgence and selfish power.

  -Herber Lockyer
  (APB, pg. 220)

- David defeated Goliath but lost to Bathsheba. Our real giants are the desires we haven't killed.

  -FB

- In my lifetime, I have sought for that which I thought would make me happy. I have pursued after that which I perceived would give me purpose. I have desired those things that I thought would bring me inward satisfaction. However, all of it proved to be vanity. Whether my search brought me to disillusionment, my pursuits ended in despair, and my desires proved to be unrealistic, it all proved useless. The reality is, all that I need and desire are found in Christ. To look for anything outside of Christ is to know and taste the bitterness of vanity.

  -RJK

Prayer: Lord, save me from the foolish, worldly, wishful thinking of the "old man." Amen.

- An apology without changed behavior is just manipulation.

  -Pieces of Soul
  (FB)

- I know in my own case when I allow Satan, self, or the world to rock my boat, my heart becomes subject to fear instead of to the Prince of Peace. When I take matters into my own hands to try to figure out a situation, I hit confusion and doubt. As I try to look into the future with my physical eyesight instead of looking into the face of my Lord, I fall into despair and hopelessness.

  -RJK

- "And be not drunk with wine, wherein is excess; but be filled with the Spirit." It is easy for many men to obey the first part of this injunction while they disobey the latter. We must be thrilled, and if human nature does not get its thrills from the right place, it will take them from the wrong.

  -Oswald Chambers
  (CWC, pg. 438)

- Anxiety does not empty tomorrow of its sorrows, but only empties today of its strength.

  -Charles Spurgeon

- If one does not discipline himself to do what he knows should be done, but follows his momentary inclinations, he will become a wishy-washy, spinless creature without determination and drive toward any worthwhile goal.

  -Howard E. Kershner
  (DPS, pg. 142)

- First, we overlook evil. Then we permit evil. Then we legalize evil. Then we promote evil. Then we celebrate evil. Then we persecute those who still call it evil.

  -FB

- Carl Teichrib summarizes the same temptation and lie put forth in the Garden of Eden as being passed down to each generation, "The temple of man beckons; come, *let us build our Bable – let us play our game of gods.*" (GG, pg. 552)

- Sin is a contagious disease of the soul. It invades our perception, making us spiritually dull. It deceives us about our personal condition, making us indifferent towards its work of death in our lives. It operates within the confines of vain imaginations, creating ignorance and superstition towards God. It makes our hearts hard toward truth, our necks stiff with arrogance, and our knees diseased with independence. As a result, man is forever walking in the ways that seem right to him, but they lead to destruction.

  -RJK

- People will forgive you for being wrong, but they will never forgive you for being right, especially when events prove you right while proving them wrong.

  -Thomas Sowell

- Evil preaches tolerance until it is dominant then it tries to silence good.

  -FB

- By delay of repentance, sin strengthens, and the heart hardens. The longer ice freezes, the harder it is to be broken.

  -Thomas Watson

- We are not seeing terrible things in our culture because we vote the wrong way. We are seeing terrible things in our culture because men love darkness rather than light.

  -Voddie Baucham

- "MAN WANTS TO BE GOD." This Last Generation has tried to make man more like God and has tried to make God more like Man. There is no fear of God in most people. They speak and want God to serve them. They want to call down fire from Heaven. They want to play God and decide Who God uses and saves and who He does not. They want God to fit into their little boxes. They want to build an External Kingdom while God is trying to Build an Inward Kingdom in the hearts of all Believers. JESUS Does not dwell in Temples built by Human Hands. He dwells in You and me. He is purifying that Kingdom now because He is Coming Soon for His Church

  -Alan Brayshaw

- Sin is not what society says it is. Sin is not what the media says it is, sin is what God says it is, and His laws do not change.

  -FB

- Our problem *today* is that we are engrossed with *things*. We are pursuing things instead of pursuing God. We are running after things instead of running after God.

  -A. W. Tozer
  (WOG, pg. 86)

- Loneliness always turns one inward. To be free, one must turn outward, away from self to others…Give yourself to others. You're not the only lonely one…It's not so much the number of friends but rather the quality that makes for fulfillment.

  -Ruth Hunt
  (VPH, pg. 27)

- Vision, or any emotions at all are the greatest snare imaginable to spiritual life, because we are apt to build these things round our reasoning and go no further.

  -Oswald Chambers
  (CWC, pg. 452

- Eventually everything established by man will collapse in complete ruin. It will be judged by the Law of God, buried by the dust of vanity, lost in a maze of ineptness, marked by the ash of decay and death, and forgotten as the sands of time erase away all memory of its existence.

  -RJK

- Because a body of men holding themselves accountable to nobody ought not to be trusted by anybody.

  -Thomas Paine

- Hell can't be made attractive so the Devil makes attractive the road that leads there.

  -FB

- Morality may keep you out of prison, but only the blood of Christ can keep you out of hell.

  -Michael Boldea Jr.
  (EJ, pg. 99)

- Today's new concept of freedom misses it so completely here. The need is not to belong to oneself but to someone other than oneself. Not to be loved but to love.

  -Ruth Hunt
  (VPH, pg. 28)

- ...the story of mankind or the history of any community or family is littered with the wrecks of those who lacked firmness and were more like putty than flint.

  -Howard E. Kershner
  (DPS, pg. 143)

- The basis of things is tragic, and intellect makes a man shut his eyes to this fact and become a superior person. One of the great crimes of intellectual philosophy is that it destroys a man as a human being and turns him into a supercilious spectator; he cuts himself off from relationship with human stuff as it is and becomes a statue.

  -Oswald Chambers
  (CWC, pg. 80)

- It is clear that activities that originate, operate according to, and are maintained by the arm of the flesh stand cursed. There will be no life found in any of it. Controlled chaos may reign, but strife will prove to be the ripples beneath the façade of peace.

  -RJK

- If you start worrying what other people think, you build up a sort of self-importance of yourself which is very toxic. Let go of how others perceive you.

  -Tartaria & History Channel
  Telegram

- When a man gets to despair, he knows that all his thinking will never get him out, consequently he is in the right attitude to receive from God that which he cannot gain for himself.

  -Oswald Chambers
  (CWC, pg. 48)

- It was obvious that the weaponry contained within this earthly life had the means to knock me off my high horse, cause me to fall off my pinnacle of self-importance, and pull me down from my position as king of my particular molehill. Ultimately, these weapons are constantly being used to bring me down into the dust of failure, the cesspool of need, and the endless pit of ineptness.

  -RJK

Bits And Pieces

Smile

Time for a story to make you smile that I found on Facebook...Psalm 126:2, "Then our mouths were filled with laughter and our tongues with joyful songs."

A pastor and two of his deacons are out on the river fishing in their rowboat. Twelve o'clock rolls around, and one of the deacons notices a nice spot on the bank to have lunch. He turns to the others and says, "That looks like a nice spot for lunch. What do you say we lunch over there?"

The other deacon agrees, and so does the pastor. The deacon stands up in the boat, steps out onto the river and walks over to the bank. The pastor looks on with amazement, and thinks to himself, if his deacon is holy enough to walk on water, surely he can.

The other deacon stands up, picks up the picnic basket, steps out of the boat, and walks over to the bank and sits with the first deacon. Again, to his amazement, the pastor thinks again, if his second deacon is holy enough to walk on water, surely he can.

The pastor stands up, steps out of the boat, and sinks into the water. The first deacon turns to the second deacon and says, "Think we should have told him where the rocks were?"

- Life brings tears, smiles, and memories. The tears dry, the smiles fade, but the memories last forever.

  -FB

- George Washington gave a sober warning 232 years ago that should be taken seriously by this nation, "The propitious smiles of heaven cannot be expected on a nation that disregards the eternal rules of order and right that heaven itself has ordained."

  -David Webber
  Prophetic Observer
  June 2022

- Today it is practically impossible to find a country that does not incorporate socialist elements...With state socialism the difficult and honorable road of free enterprise is softened through group solutions, and the slower-to-come social benefits of capitalism.

  -Carl Teichrib
  (GG, pg. 48)

- The main reason we can be sure that totalitarian control cannot be successful in the end is that it would violate a fact that undergirds the entire universe. Mankind will never have it within his power to make an algorithm that emulates the knowledge of God. It won't work.

  -Larry P. Arnn
  President of Hillsdale College
  Imprimis, November 2023

- A bad attitude is like a flat tire, you can't get very far until you change it.

  -FB

Prayer: Lord, I so need balance to my life. You are the center that brings balance, the reality that ensures balance, and the hope that tips the weights of life to embrace balance. Lord, become my all in all. Amen.

- Nations do not die from invasion; they die from internal rottenness.

  -Abraham Lincoln

- For Marxists, class conflict motivates human action; for feminists, it is patriarchal domination; and for critical race theorists, it is whiteness.

  -Jon Harris
  (CSJ, pg. 100)

- Within the halls of government, business, academia, healthcare, entertainment, and organized religion, corruption and greed have taken hold. Humanism and its accompanying Earth-centered ethics (disguised by green-agenda proponents as "sustainability)" are replacing Judeo-Christian standards of morality that are now looked upon with scorn. It's no longer a matter of Christianity getting squeezed out of these arenas – it's now getting shoved out the doors.

  -David Rosenthal

- The good news is that human beings, by nature, don't like tyranny. That is why, as Aristotle explains in Book Five of his *Politics,* tyrants must infantilize their people to maintain their hold. We are seeing uprisings of parents in our country these days. They are angry that schools are dividing their children into groups labeled "oppressed" and "oppressors" according to their skin color. They are angry that the schools are encouraging their children to believe they are a different sex than their biology dictates. Parents are pushing back because parents love their children. That is nature. Nature can be tortured and otherwise set upon, but it cannot be overcome in the end.

-Larry P. Arnn
President of Hillsdale College
Imprimis, November 2023

- Ungodly governments attack the sacred role of parenthood because they know it is their only path to victory.

-Cole Richard
President of Voice of the Martyrs
January 2024 (Magazine)

- You're not grown until you know how to communicate, apologize, be truthful, and accept accountability without blaming someone else.

-FB

Beware of Looking Over While Looking Around

It is natural to see what sticks out in our world that proves inconvenient, irritating and frustrating. We look around for some solution and often end up looking over what is significant.

The world is always looking over what does not fit in its narrative, while looking around for means to fit it in, control it or silence it. It has no patience to contend with something that leaves it without options, or the time to observe something long enough to maybe figure out what is really going on. After all, if a matter can't be dealt with within the acceptable confines of the accepted methods or means of the world, there is no hope for it.

A seven-year-old girl by the name of Gillian presented such a challenge to her parents and teachers. She could not sit still in class, and in spite of the many disciplinary measures taken at school and at home, none ever managed to corral her into the acceptable mode that would win her the recognition of being a well-behaved child at school.

Gillian's mother was called to the school to discuss her daughter's problem. As her mother along with a couple of educators speculated about what to do about the situation, an older teacher who knew about Gillian arrived. He asked everyone in attendance to follow him into another room.

He left Gillian in the room and told her that they would be back. He then turned on the radio. Without any awareness of being observed from the window and being left alone in the room with music, Gillian immediately got up and began to move up and down, chasing the music in the air with her feet and heart.

The wise teacher smiled as he looked at the mother and his colleagues as they looked shocked and surprised at her gracefulness and ability to express her inner being. He stated that Gillian was a dancer and that her mother needed to take her to dance lessons.

In 1981 after a successful career as a dancer, opening her own dance academy, and receiving international recognition for her art, Gillian Lynne became the chorographer of the acclaimed musical, "Cats."

This is a secular story with an important principle. How much do the powers that be in churches or even in the congregations overlook who they consider insignificant? In essence, they fail to discern and recognize the talents and abilities of those who could further the Kingdom of God because they fail to fit into the mode of what is considered normal and acceptable.

- It is curious that physical courage should be so common in the world and moral courage so rare.

  -Mark Twain

- Life has no remote, get up and change it yourself.

  -FB

- In life you will fall out with people you never thought you would. Get betrayed by people you trusted with all of your heart. And get used by people you would do anything for. But life also has a beautiful side to it. You will get loved by someone you never knew you would have. Form new friendships with people that will establish more meaningful and stronger relationships. And overcome things you never thought you would ever get over. We all have chapters that end with people at some point in our life. But take both comfort and courage in knowing that the very best part of your book is still being written.

  -Author Unknown

- The best weight you'll ever lose is the weight of people's opinions.

  -FB

- For a long time, history was "philosophy teaching by example," that is, the account of men's actions as good or evil in relation to the health of their societies. In the new form of history, actions are not good or evil in themselves, but only to be praised or condemned to the degree they forward or retard progress as defined by ideology. One effect is this...historians do not care about the of evidence, but only about cherry-picking facts to suit the predetermined theory. The duty of historians, they think, is to make a better world, not to tell the truth.

-Clyde Wilson
Historian
(CSJ. Pg. 102)

- It is not what a man does that is of final importance, but what he is in what he does. The atmosphere produced by man, much more than his activities, has the lasting influence.

-Oswald Chambers
(CWC, pg. 51)

A great woman
Still Shines in Memories

For years, I have watched insanity tie up history, hoodwink the innocent, ride on the shirttails of ignorance and prejudice, and try to pervert what s pure. Due to woke and political correctness, exceptionalism is not allowed, uniqueness is ignored, goodness is mocked, and purity is stomped on.

One such historical figure was a woman. I grew up looking at this woman whose face was on a particular brand of syrup. The product she backed was exceptional, but it was that smiling face that made me feel good about the morning and about life in general.

This exceptional woman, Nancy Green, was born into slavery in 1834 in Kentucky. However, her past never became an excuse; rather, she seemed to use it as stepping stones of betterment. She became famous because of her ability to tell stories while selling her products. The branding of the syrup alone was a tribute to this woman's gifts and talents.

She made her debut in 1893 at a fair and exposition in Chicago. Her ability to tell a good story along with her warm and appealing personality highlighted her exceptional showmanship. Needless to say, her booth became so popular they had to assign special security personnel to keep the crowds moving. She demonstrated such skill with the products before her as she served it to the crowd that she was later signed to a lifetime contract that kept her trustworthy face before the public.

Nancy Green traveled on promotional tours. She secured financial freedom and became a national spokesperson as well as a leading advocate against poverty in favor of equal rights for all Americans. She maintained her job until her death in 1923, at age 89.

Sadly, due to our insane cultural emphasis, she has been ERASED by politics. Due to the wickedness and stupidity of despots in power, future generations will not even know this beautiful woman existed. What a shame. The world knew her as "Aunt Jemima", and she was a true American success story.

- If you didn't hear it with your own ears or see it with your own eyes, don't invent it with your small mind and share it with your big mouth.

  -FB

- Whether a government be Democratic, Republican, or Autocratic it must have some central authority. Without that central authority society cannot exist, and its overthrow inevitably leads to anarchy and chaos among the people.

  -J. Gregory Mantle
  (COS, pgs. 117-118)

- The chief modern rival of Christianity is "liberalism." An examination of the teaching of liberalism in comparison with those of Christianity will show that at every point the two movements are in direct opposition.

-J. Gresham Machan
(COS, pg. 141)

▪ The best things in life aren't things.

-Joshua Becker

Common Sense

If you fail, never give up because F. A. I. L. means
First Attempt In Learning.
END is not the END. In fact, E. N. D.
Effort Never Dies.
If you get <u>NO</u> as an answer, remember N. O. means
NEXT OPPORTUNITY
CHANGE YOUR MINDSET about how you look at something.

-Unknown

Beauty With Engineering Skills

I have to admit I grew up teething on Hollywood's presentation of life. The people I watched on screen became the people they portrayed. I would later learn that the characters some portrayed would never match the real character or impact that some of the actors/actresses left behind the scenes. Granted, many actors/actresses had terrible reputations when it came to morality, but they occasionally would rise up to meet some formidable events and use their means and gifts in other ways. For example, Edward G. Robinson, who was a Jew, helped finance the French Resistance during WWII. They even had a code name for him that kept his identity a secret until after the war, "Manny."

Another person who had an impact on the warfront was a Jewish actress with Austrian roots who had immigrated, ended up in America, and ultimately avoided the horrors of Nazi occupation. By 26 she was a recognized actress, but her direction changed in 1940 after a Nazi U-boat sunk a cruise ship resulting in 90 British children drowning.

She fought back by applying her engineering skills to develop a sonar sub-locator that was used in the Atlantic, greatly benefitting the allies. The principles behind her technology kept on giving by way of wi-fi and Bluetooth. Perhaps you know her. Her name was Hedy Lamar.

+————————•————•————+

- Heaven requires a reservation. Hell only has general admission.
  -Church Sign

- To those who think slavery started in America, get a reality check! Quit the delusion and Grow Up! Slavery as always been around. Those who are realistic are sick of the foolishness that abounds, the wickedness that is justified and the evil that is preferred by those in darkness—always insisting everyone must come under the same darkness that enslaves them into their insane realities.
  -RJK

- In order to keep up with the times, evangelical industries reinvent themselves almost every 10 years. Yet nowhere is this thinking represented in Scripture…The overall effect of associating egalitarianism and activism with the gospel, attaching "quality-of-life" issues to the "pro-life" movement, assuming conservative views conflict with public witness, and attributing worldly motives to conservative causes has been to move evangelicals toward the left politically.

-Jon Harris
(CSJ, pgs. 130, 131)

- When a nation gets away from a vibrant faith in Christ, life loses its means and Satan has an open door to promote death, his ultimate objective.

-Battle Cry periodical
Published by Chick Publications
(Jan/Feb 2024 pg. 7)

- There are some things that money just can't buy. Like **manners, morals,** and **integrity.**

-FB

Who Is He?

There is a lot of speculation about the anti-Christ. There are those who believe that since lawlessness is associated with the anti-Christ then it must not be a man but lawlessness itself. Is this a correct perception or just another vain theory of man?

There was an interesting question made by Dr. Larry Spargimino in the November 2023 Prophetic Observer, "Could the Antichrist be some kind of a super robot, or a cyborg powered by the latest AI technology? A few years ago, the possibility of this actually occurring was very low. Today it is very high."

It is true there are clones that will last up to three years, as well as robots and cyborg powered by AI technology. However, we must go to Scripture and see what it says about this figure, "And the beast was taken, and with him the false prophet that wrought miracles before him, with which he deceived them that had received the mark of the beast, and them that worshipped his image. These both were cast alive into a lake of fire burning with brimstone" (Revelation 19:20).

It is very hard to keep things straight in Revelation. There is Babylon which is a system that is related to as a beast but will be destroyed, and we are told that another breast will come up out of the earth in Revelation 13:11 who exercises all the power of the first beast.

We see in Revelation 19:20 that this beast has an image he will give power to. No doubt this image could entail AI technology that can be controlled by man, but this beast has the same criteria as the Son of Perdition does in 2 Thessalonians 2:2-9. Refer to Revelation 13:13-15. The beast will be cast into the lake of fire which means he has a soul. God is not going to cast into the lake of fire some robot or some technical human like cyborg. In this case Revelation is not talking about an environment of lawlessness either.

We have various opinions about this matter, but in the end, we know whatever happens will be Scriptural. We know that the only ones who will be deceived by this beast are those who have taken the mark. As a believer, I know what I am looking for so if I see it, I will not be deceived, but how many know what to look for? How many are keeping their eyes open, and being prepared to stand even in the midst of possible persecution for the true faith first delivered to the saints? How many know the Word of God and how many instead know acceptable man-made doctrines?

I may try to understand and interpret prophecy according to my understanding, which in the past has been based on man's teaching and doctrines, but the Bible tells me we know in part. We are always trying to fit prophecy into our own understanding and what we end up with are good-sounding theories but when put to the test they will often fail.

It is up to us to know what God says about such matters, believe it instead of interpret it, thereby, giving the Holy Spirit the freedom to highlight matters in order to be properly interpreted and understood. After all, it is not only about discerning the times and knowing the signs, but being prepared to stand in them with faith, withstand with truth, and continue to stand because of the unfailing promises of God.

———————————————

- Little hugs, can dry big tears. Little candles, can light the darkness. Little memories, can last for years. It's the little things in life that bring the greatest happiness.

-FB

Sand Pounders

Have you ever heard of the "sand pounders?" They were a big part of guarding our beaches and shores during WWII. These sand pounders worked in teams and were part of the Coast Guard. They covered more than 3700 miles of coast and it took 24,000 men to work them properly.

They worked 100 feet apart, covering a two-mile stretch. They were able to cover difficult terrain quickly and efficiently. And who were these sand pounders? They were horses.

Contributors

I gave my friend Stephen Truss, *More Nuggets From Heaven.* He liked it enough to request the first Nuggets book. He had one suggestion, he wanted to know the time period that the different people that I quoted from lived. I could relate to him because before I read a person's book, I read about them to get an idea of the times they lived in. Instead of asking questions about some of them as I have in previous books to show unique things about their life or character, I decided to take his suggestion and give a summary of those who shared what I consider heavenly wisdom in all six of my nugget books.

For saints it proves a couple of things. 1) Truth will stand in the end no matter what. 2) God's wisdom is like drops of water that falls on dry, thirsty ground that is capable of bringing forth beauty, inspiration, and life; and 3) their works will follow them.

Here are most of the names and some information of those who God has used to touch, challenge, and cause me to think outside of the different "boxes." Some of these individuals may surprise you, but remember nuggets can be found in deep, dark places because those who have shared the nuggets may not be heirs of salvation. The summaries of individuals were obtained from internet searches and the valuable resource book, *Encyclopedia of Christian Biographies,* by Ed Reese.

As I considered these individuals, it was easy to see that God has always provided His wisdom through the generations, as well as established a sure witness through His committed servants.

Adams, Abigail: (1797-1801) Wife and closest advisor to her husband, John the second President of the United States and mother of the 6th President of the United States, John Quincy Adams.

Adams, John: (1735-1826) American statesman, attorney, diplomat, writer and Founding Father who served as the 2nd President of the United States.

Agnon, Samuel (Shmuel) Yosef: (1887-1970) Austrian-Hungarian born Israeli novelist, poet, and short story writer.

Alden-Tirrill, Anna: Author of the Annie series for teenagers as well as devotions for women. She is a co-author of *Cyber Love's Illusions.*

Alleine, Richard: (1610-1681) English Puritan clergyman, an ordained priest and later appointed as Chaplin to Sir Ralph Hopton.

Alighieri, Dante: (1265-1321) Italian poet, writer and philosopher.

Allender, Dan: American Christian therapist, author and professor.

Alexander of Jerusalem: (175-251) A Bishop of Asia Minor. He was imprisoned and martyred.

Alward, Gladys: (1902-1970) A British-born evangelical Christian missionary to China whose story has been told in both a book and a movie.

Ambrose of Milan: (339-397) A theologian and statesman who served as Bishop of Milan.

Anderson, Sir Robert: (1841-1918) Second assistant Commissioner of the Metropolitan Police (Scotland Yard). He was also an intelligence officer, theologian, and writer.

Arnobuis: (d: 327) Latin philosopher, teacher of rhetoric and apologist.

Arthur, K. (Kay): (b 1933) Missionary to Mexico with her husband, but emerged as a bible teacher who hosted a daily radio, television, and online Bible study teaching called *Precepts for Life.*

Athanasius: (328-373) Christian Theologian and the 20th patriarch of Alexandria, Church Father and chief defender of Trinitarianism.

Augustine of Hippo: (354-430) Christian theologian and philosopher and was the bishop of Hippo Regius.

Aurelius, Marcus: (d. 180 at age 58) Roman Emperor from 161-180 and a Stoic Philosopher.

Baker, H. A.: (1881`-1971) American author and Pentecostal missionary to Tibet, China, and finally to Taiwan until his death.

Barclay, William (1907-1978) Theologian, Scottish minister and professor as well as author, radio and TV presenter. His popular set of Bible commentaries on the New Testament sold 1.5 million copies.

Barker, Matthew: (d. 1698) English Puritan and author.

Barnhouse, Donald: (1895-1960) Presbyterian pastor, radio pioneer, preacher, journalist and author.

Basil: (329/330-379): Ascetic theologian and bishop of Caesarea.

Baucham, Voddie: (b. 1969) Pastor, author, and academic who teaches and writes on biblical apologetics and Christian theology.

Baxter, Richard (1615-1691) 17th century English Puritan, church leader and theologian. He was described as "the chief of English Protestant Schoolmen."

Baxter, Sidlow: (1903-1999) A pastor, theologian and later served as an evangelist. He authored as many as 30 books.

Beck, Fred: Pastor, missionary and leadership training as well as in administrating missionary work.

Begg, Alistair: (b. 1952) Scottish pastor, author, and Christian radio ministry of preaching and teaching.

Benham, Jason: (b. 1975) Along with his identical twin brother, David, they are authors, speakers, entrepreneurs, former minor league Baseball players, and filmmakers who are known for their Christian and conservative views.

Benjamin, Jerry: Author of *The Little Nuggets Series* booklets as well as an itinerant Bible teacher who traveled the world to proclaim the pre-eminence of Christ in all things.

Bernard: (1090-1153) Canonized as a saint, an abbot, mystic and co-founder of the Knights Templar.

Briscoe, Stuart: (1930-2022) British evangelist, author, international speaker and senior pastor of Elmbrook Church in Brookfield Wisconsin.

Blacklock, Thomas: (1721-1791) A blind Scottish poet and author who studied for the Church because the church people would not accept him as their minister due to his inability to see.

Bliss, P. (Phillip) P. (Paul): (1838-1876) An American composer, conductor, writer of hymns and a bass-baritone singer. His hymns include "Almost Persuaded," "Wonderful Words of Life," and the melody for "It Is Well With My Soul."

Boldea, Michael Jr.: The grandson of a potato farmer, and the son of a glass blower. He came to America at the age of nine, and began ministry at the age of twelve as his grandfather's (Dudeman) interpreter. He is a preacher and author of challenging books that will not leave the reader sitting at ease in their pews.

Bonar, Horatius: (1808-1889) Scottish churchman and poet.

Bonhoeffer, Dietrich: (1906-1945) German theologian, author and dissident anti-Nazi. A founding member of the Confessing Church. He was arrested and executed.

Boniface: (675-754) English Benedictine monk who was made bishop of Mainz and was martyred.

Bonner, Mickey: (1932-1997) Evangelist and author who died of a heart attack while preaching.

Boom, Corrie ten: (1892-1983): Dutch watchmaker who after her ordeal in a WWII Nazi German Concentration camp for hiding Jews, became an author and international Christian speaker. The book about her ordeal, *The Hiding Place* has not only been read by many following generations, but it has been made into a movie.

Booth, William: (1829-1912) English Methodist preacher who along with his wife, Catherine, founded the Salvation Army.

Boston, Thomas: (1676-1732) Scottish Presbyterian church leader, theologian, and philosopher.

Bounds, E. M.: (1835-1913) He was an American author and member of the Methodist Episcopal Church, South Clergy.

Bowen, George: (1816-1888) A new England atheist who was converted to Jesus Christ and went as a missionary to India to never return to his homeland.

Boyle, Robert: (1627-1691) Author and renowned natural philosopher and Chemist, who was considered a Christian Scientist. (Not to be confused with the "Christian Science" cult.)

Brainard, David: (1718-1747) American Presbyterian minister and missionary to the native Americans. His life and commitment served as an inspiration to others such as missionaries William Carey and James Elliot.

Brengle, Samuel Logan: (1860-1936) A commissioner in the Salvation Army and a leading teacher and preacher of the doctrine of Holiness.

Brooks, Phillip: (1835-1893) American Episcopal Clergyman, preacher, Bishop of Massachusetts and author of the song, *O' Little Town of Bethlehem.*

Browning, Robert: (1812-1889) English poet and playwright.

Buck, Pearl S. (1892-1973) American writer and novelist.

Buechner, Frederick: (1926-2022) American writer, Presbyterian minister, preacher and theologian.

Bullinger, E. W.: (1837-1913) British Anglican clergyman, biblical scholar and theologian.

Bunyan, John: (1628-1688) Pastor and author of *Pilgrim Progress.* He wrote this book along with others while he was in prison for his faith.

Campbell, Duncan: (1898-1972) A Scottish evangelist, who is best known for being a leader in the Lewis Awakening or Hebrides Revival in the mid-20th century.

Campbell, Micca: Christian author, speaker and teacher.

Carey, William: (1761-1834) English Christian missionary to India, Baptist minister, translator, social reformer, and cultural anthropologist who founded the Serampore college and university in India.

Carlson, Tucker: (b. 1969) Former Fox News host. An American conservative, political commentator and writer who now hosts, *Tucker on X.*

Carlyle, Thomas (1795-1881) Scottish essayist, historian, and philosopher who exerted a profound influence on 19th century art, literature, and philosophy.

Carradine, Beverly: (1848-1931) American Methodist Minister, author, and evangelist for the holiness movement.

Carmichael, Amy: (1867-1951) Famous Irish Christian missionary to India. She founded a mission and opened an orphanage.

Catt, Michael C.: (1952-2023) An American film producer (Fireproof), author and senior pastor of Sherwood Baptist Church until he retired in 2021.

Chadwich, Samuel: (1860-1932) One of the greatest preachers of English Methodism. He served as president of the Wesleyan Methodist Conference.

Chafer, Lewis Sperry: (1871-1952) American theologian. He co-founded Dallas Theological Seminary with older brother Robin Thomas Chafer.

Chisholm, Thomas: (1866-1960) American hymnwriter, poet, and Methodist Minister.

Chambers, Oswald: (1874-1917) An early 20th century Scottish, Baptist evangelist and teacher. He never wrote a book but his wife, who was a court transcriber, transcribed his many priceless teachings that were later published in devotions and books.

Chapman, Mary Beth: A speaker, author, and co-founder of *Show Hope* an adoption advocacy orphan care. She is the wife of Christian music singer and song writer, Steven Curtis Chapman.

Chapman, Robert (1803-1902) Known as the Apostle of love. He was a pastor, teacher and evangelist in England and Europe.

Charnock, Stephen (1628-1680) 17th century Puritan theologian and paster who wrote classic works.

Chesterton, G. (Gilbert) K. (1874-1936) English author and Christian apologist, as well as a literary and art critic.

Chrysostom, John: (347-407) Outstanding preacher and patriarch of Constantinople.

Church, J. (Jerry) R. (Rolan): (1938-2011) American Clergyman and author who founded the television ministry, *Prophecy in the News.*

Churchill, Winston: (1874-1965) British statesman, Prime Minister of England and writer.

Cleary, Steve: Started his work in missions in 1989 as a volunteer for *The Voice of the Martyrs* and joined the staff in 1990. He founded Revelation Media where he provides sound quality media for mission efforts.

Clement of Alexandria: (150-215) Converted from paganism he became the first known Christian Scholar.

Clement of Rome: (30-100) Converted by the Apostle Paul. Known also as Pope Clement. He was considered one of the first Apostolic Fathers of the Church and the bishop of Rome.

Clendennen, B. H.: (1922-2009) Ordained minister with Assemblies of God. Founded Victory Tabernacle in Beaumont, TX and served as its pastor until 1992 when he became a missionary to Russia at age 70.

Clow, William: (1853-1930) He was a highly educated man that studied Scripture on his own. From his personal study, he reflected in his sermons the incredible wealth he had accumulated. He was true to Scripture and the message of the cross.

Comfort, Ray: (b. 1949) New Zealand born minister; evangelist and author who lives in the United States and started Living Waters Publications.

Comenius, Jan (John) Amos: (1592-1670) A Moravian philosopher, teacher, and theologian.

Cowper, William: (1731-1800) English poet and hymnodist.

Crabb, Larry: (1944-2021) American Christian counselor, author, Bible teacher, and seminar speaker.

Crossman, Eileen Fraser: The author who wrote the biography about her missionary father, James O. Fraser's life and adventures in China.

Cyprian: (210-258) Bishop of Carthage and Christian writer.

Cyril of Jerusalem: (310/315-386) Bishop of Jerusalem.

de Vauvenargues, Marquis: (1715-1747) French writer and moralist.

DeHann, M. R. (1891-1965) American Bible teacher and founder of Radio Bible Class and the devotional guide, *Our Daily Bread."*

DeMoss, Nancy Leigh: A popular author and speaker in Christian living and biblical womanhood.

Denney, James: (1856-1917) A Scottish theologian and preacher. He is best known for his theological articulations of the meaning of atonement within Christian theology.

Des Gerlaise, Nanci: Author of *Muddy Waters.*

Dickey, Samuel Gordon: (1859-1936) A prolific author and evangelical lay minister active in the latter part of the 19th century.

Dixon, A. (Amzi) C. (Clarence): (1854-1925) A Baptist pastor, author, Bible expositor, and evangelist who was popular during the late 19th and early 20th centuries.

Doddridge, Philip: (1702-1751) English Congregationalist leader, educator, and hymnwriter.

Douglass, Frederick: (1818-1895) African American social reformer, abolitionism, orator, writer, and statesman.

Drucker, Peter: (1909-2005) American business consultant, educator and author. His writings were mainly due to underlying Christian value system.

Duewel, Wesley: (1916-2016) He was invested in the cause of missions for 70 years. He served as President of One Mission Society (CMS). His devotional classic, *Ablaze for God*, is his most popular book.

Duncan, Campbell: (1898-1972) A Scottish evangelist, wo is best known for being a leader of the Lewis Awakening or Hebrides Revival in the mid-20th century.

Dyer, William: (1632-1696) Fervent pastor in London expelled from his church in the Great Ejection of 1662.

Edwards, Jonathan: (1703-1758) American revivalist, preacher, philosopher, and congregational theologian.

Edwards, Tyron: (1809-1894) American theologian and minister.

Elliot, Elisabeth: (1926-2015) Christian author and speaker. Her first husband, missionary James Elliot was killed with four other missionaries in 1956 in Ecuador after contacting the Auca people who saw them as a threat.

Elliot, James: (1927-1956) An American Christian missionary that was killed in an attempt to reach the Huaorani people of Ecuador. His writings from his diaries have been published.

Einstein, Albert: (1879-1955) German-born theoretical physicist who is widely held to be one of the greatest and most influential scientists of our times.

Epictetus: (50-135) Greek Stoic and philosopher.

Erdman, Charles R. (1866-1960) Author and an American Presbyterian minister and professor of theology at Princeton Theological Seminary.

Faber, George Stanley: (1773-1854) Anglican theologian and prolific writer including hymns such as *Faith of our Fathers.*

Felix, Marcus Minucius: (d. 250) Earliest Christian apologist to write Latin. He was also a Roman lawyer.

Fenelon, Francois: (1661-1715) French Catholic archbishop, theologian, and author.

Finney, Charles: (1792-1875) An American lawyer, author, evangelist, and minister leader in the Second Great Awakening in the United States. He was the central figure in the religious revival movement in the early 19th century.

Fisher, C. H.: Pastor of a house church in Asheville, North Carolina.

Flavel, John: (1627-1691) English Puritan Presbyterian minister and writer.

Flint, Annie Johnson: (1866-1932) Prolific writer of poems and hymns.

Franklin, Benjamin: (1706-1790) American Founding Father, polymath, leading writer of his time, scientist, inventor, statesman, diplomate, printer, publisher, and political philosopher.

Fraser, James 0.: (1886-1938) British Protestant Christian missionary to China with the China Inland Missions.

Froude, James Anthony: (1818-1894) English historian, novelist and biographer.

Fuller, Thomas: (1608-1661) British scholar, preacher, and one of the most witty and prolific authors of the 17th century.

Fulgentius of Ruspe: (462-527) A North African Christian prelate who served as Bishop of Ruspe.

Gandhi: (1869-1948): Indian independent activist.

Gentle Shepherd Ministries (GSM): Founded in 1989 by Jeannette Haley and Rayola Kelley. Main goal is to disciple people to be followers of Christ by presenting the Word of God through any vehicle available from teaching, preaching, evangelizing, and written materials (books, articles, FB devotions).

Gerth, Holley: A bestselling author, speaker, and introvert advocate.

Glover, Richard (1712-1785) English poet and politician. Author of *The Letters of Junius.*

Godbey, W. (William) B. (Baxter) (1833-1920) A significant evangelist in the early stages of the Wesleyan-holiness movement.

Godet, Frederic: (1812-1900) A Swiss Protestant theologian. He authored New Testament Commentaries and was considered an expert on the life of Paul and the Pauline Epistles.

Goforth: Jonathan: (1859-1936) First Canadian Presbyterian missionary to North China who evangelized, trained Christian workers nearly 40 years. Thousands were converted and he founded many churches.

Gordon, A. (Adoniram) J. (Judson): (1836-1895) American Baptist preacher, writer, composer, and founder of Gordon College and Gordon-Cornwell Theological Seminary.

Gowdy, Harold (Trey) Watson: American television news presenter, former politician and former prosecutor who served as an U.S. Representative for South Carolina.

Grant, Alisha: A name that Rayola Kelley uses with some of her writings.

Greenly, Ray: Pastor of National Prayer Chapel and host of Living Water Radio.

Gregory of Nazianzus: (325-389) Eastern church father and patriarch of Constantinople.

Grimes, E. (Emily) May: (1864-1927) Hymn writer and missionary to Africa.

Groves, Anthony Norris: (1795-1853) English Protestant missionary who has been called the "Father of faith missions."

Gurnall, William: (1616-1679) English author and Anglican Clergyman.

Guthrie, Thomas: (1803-1873) Popular Scottish preacher of his day in Scottland and was associated with many forms of philanthropy.

Guyon, Madame Jeanne-Marie: (1648-1717) French Christian accused of advocating Quietism which was considered heretical by the Catholic Church.

Haley, J. (Jeannette): (b. 1943): Co-founder of Gentle Shepherd Ministries, Christian teacher, author of articles and books as well as a professional artist. She painted the fourteen murals (5 ½' by 10') in the Chapel of the Resurrection in Bothel, Washington.

Hammarskjöld, Dag: (1905-1961) Swedish economist and statesman who served as the second secretary-general of the United Nations from 1953 until his questionable death in 1661.

Haney, M. L.: Evangelist and author of *Inheritance Restored.* His book *Pentecostal Possibilities* about his life was published in 1906.

Harris, Jon: An author who has been involved in college/career and music ministry for much of His Christian life.

Harvey, Lillian G.: (1911-2008) She and her husband, Edwin were missionaries to England. Founded M.O.V.E (Message of Victory Evangelism) and were led to building up a large resource of selected material to put into paperback books that span centuries, denominations, gender, and class to inspire the reader to a fuller and deeper faith in Jesus Christ.

Harvey, Paul: (1918-2009) American radio broadcaster for ABC News Radio. He is best known for *The Rest of the Story*. His program reached as many as 24 million people.

Hatch, Sidney A.: He served in WWII and after the war he proceeded to work in ministry in various locations and states.

Havergal, Frances Ridley: (1836-1879) British poet and hymnwriter. She wrote hymns, melodies, religious tracts and works for children.

Havner, Vance: (1901-1986): Pastor of a country church but became known as a powerful preacher and author who is greatly quoted today for his sometimes funny one-liners that carry a punch.

Hay, Alex R.: Author of the New Testament order for church and missionary work.

Heasley, Jacquelyn K.: Writer, Christian singer author and theologian.

Henry, Matthew (1662-1714) A British Non-conformist minister and author. He is best known for the six-volume biblical commentary exposition of the Old and New Testaments.

Henry, Patrick: (1736-1799) American Founding Father, orator, and politician.

Heschel, Abraham: (1907-1972): Polish American Rabbi and one of the leading Jewish theologians and philosophers of the 20th century. He was professor of Jewish mysticism and authored many books.

Hession, Roy: (1908-1992) British evangelist and author.

Hibbs, Jack: Founder and president of Real Life and pastor of Calvary Chapel in Chino Hills. CA.

Hilary of Poitiers: (300/315-368) Bishop of Poitiers. Devoted his tongue and pen to fighting the Arian heresy.

Hilton, Conrad: (1887-1979) American businessman who founded the Hilton Hotel chain.

Hodge, Bodie: A speaker, writer and researcher for Answers in Genesis, a Christian organization that promotes Biblical creation.

Holtz, Lou: (b. 1937) American former successful college football coach and television analyst.

Holtzmann, H. (Heinrich) J. (Julius): (1832-1919) German theologian.

Howse, Brannon: A radio and television host who covers news, politics and culture from a Christian perspective.

Hugel, Baron Von: (1852-1925) Influential Austrian Catholic layman, religious writer and Christian apologist.

Hughes, Lynette: A published journalist. She and her husband were founders of the Freedom in Truth Ministry and have ministered together as a team for 38 years. She is a former associate pastor in the Four Square Gospel Church and pastored two home churches.

Hughes, Selwyn: (1928-2006) Welch Christian minister and author of over 50 Christian books. Founded the Christian Ministry Crusade for World Revival (CWR).

Hulme, Kathryn: (1900-1981) American novelist.

Human, Maureen: A Christian herbalist who owns and runs an herbal business with her husband, Larry and daughter Laura. She experienced a Job situation and was able to express her journey through her poems and continues to write poetry.

Hunt, David and Ruth: David (1925-2013) was an American Christian apologist speaker, radio commentator, and author. He founded the Berean Call and was in full time ministry until his death. His wife Ruth (d-2013) was an author as well. One of her books is *East Wind.*

Huss, John: (1369-1415) Bohemian Reformer who believed the common people should be allowed to read the Bible. He was arrested, imprisoned, and burned at the stake.

Hutchings, Noah: (1922-2015) Author and former President of Southwest Church Ministries, a Christian broadcasting company in Oklahoma City. He spent six decades hosting the radio show, *Your Watchman on the Wall.*

Hyde, John: (1865-1912) Known as *Praying Hyde* and the Apostle of prayer. He was also an American missionary to India.

Jefferson, Charles E.: (1860-1937) American Congregational Clergyman.

Jefferson, Thomas (1743-1826) American statesman, diplomat, lawyer, architect, philosopher, Founding Father, and the third President of the United States.

Jerome: (342-347-420) Known as Jerome of Stridon. An early Christian priest, confessor, theologian, translator, and historian.

Jones, Bob Sr. (1883-1968) American evangelist and broadcaster. The founder and 1st President of Bob Jones University.

Jones, E. Stanley: (1884-1973) American Methodist, Christian missionary, theologian, and author.

Jones, Martyn Lloyd: (1899-1981) Welch pastor, author and physician.

Jowett, John Henry: (1864-1923) Influential British Protestant preacher who wrote books on topics related to Christian living.

Justin (Martyr): (100-165) Platonic philosopher and apologist as well as a teacher and author who defended his faith against scornful critics. He was scourged and beheaded for his faith. After his death, "Martyr" was added to his name.

Ignatius: (d. 110) An early Christian writer and patriarch of Antioch. He met his martyrdom on his way to Rome.

Isidore of Seville: (560-636) A Hispano—Roman scholar, theologian, and archbishop of Seville.

Irenaeus: (125/130-202) Spiritual son of Polycarp. He was a Greek Father of apologist, and apostle of Gaul and the second bishop of Lyon.

Ironside, H. A.: (1876-1951) Canadian American Bible teacher, preacher, theologian, and author.

Kalley, Robert Reid: (1809-1888) Scottish physician and Presbyterian, later Congregationalist missionary to such places as Madeira and Bazil.

Kelley, Rayola: (b. 1955) Co-founder of Gentle Shepherd Ministries in 1989, teacher, speaker, preacher, spiritual counselor and prolific writer of books, Bible Studies, devotions, and articles for a monthly newsletter, as well as a publisher.

Kelly, Stewart E.: A professor of philosophy and is an author of *Understanding Post Modernism, A Christian's Perspective.*

Kennedy, John F. (1917-1963) Decorated war hero, author, and the 35th President of the United States.

Kempis, Thomas: (1380-1471): Ecclesiastes mystic and writer. Wrote, *The Imitation of Christ.*

Kershner, Howard E.: (1891-1990) Founder and president of Christian Freedom Foundation.

Kettering, Charles (1876-1958) American inventor, engineer, businessman and the founder of Delco and head of research at General Motors.

King, Guy H.: (d. 1956) author and clergyman of the church of England. He was gifted in opening the Word up to those that heard him.

Knox, John: (1514-1572) Scottish clergyman, writer, historian and a foremost leader of the Scottish Reformation.

Kuhn, Isobel: (1901-1957) A Canadian Christan missionary to China and author.

Lactantius: (250-260-340) Latin apologist and writer. Studied with Arnobuis.

Laidlaw, Robert: (1885-1971) A New Zealand businessman who founded the Farmer's Trading Company. He was also a Christian writer and a well-known lay preacher in the Open Brethren Movement.

Larson, Steven: (b. 1951) Pastor and founder and president of OnePassion Ministries whose goal is to educate pastors in order to seek another church reformation.

Law, William: (1686-1781) A priest of the Church of England and a writer.

Lewis, C. S.: (1898-1963) British writer, lay theologian and scholar.

Lincoln, Abraham: (1809-1865) Statesman and lawyer who served as the 16th President of the United States.

Littenas, Haldor: (1885-1959) A 20th century American gospel hymn writer and publisher.

Livingstone, David: (1813-1873) British Colonialist and missionary to Africa. He was known for his epic discoveries in the heart of Africa.

Lockyer, Herbert Sr.: (1886-1984) English author of 50 Christian books. He held many Bible conferences, and preached in Scotland for 25 years and came to America in 1936.

Longfellow, Henry Wadsworth: (1807-1882) American poet and educator.

Luther, Martin (1483-1546) A German priest, theologian, author, hymnwriter, professor, and Augustinian friar.

Lyle, H. (Henry) F. (Frances): (1793-1847) A Scottish Anglican hymnodist and poet.

MacDonald, William: (1917-2007) President of Emeritus Bible College, teacher, Plymouth Brethren theologian and a prolific author of over 84 published books.

Macfarlane, Alice: (1866-1945) Missionary who worked with China Inland Mission.

MacLaren, Alexander: (1826-1910) From Scotland: First president of Baptist World Alliance, and pastor at Union Chapel in Manchester, England.

Machen, J. Gresham: (1881-1937) An American Presbyterian New Testament Scholar and educator in the early 20th century.

Mackintosh, C. (Charles) H. (Henry): (1820-1896) 19th century Christian preacher, writer of Bible commentaries, and magazine editor.

Madison, James: (1751-1836) American statesman, diplomat and Founding Father who served as our 4th President of the United States.

Mann, Horace: (1796-1859) American educational reformer and politician.

Mantle, J. (John) Gregory: (1853-1925) Author and ordained minister who was a popular speaker and had a ministry that was well known in Great Britian, America, and around the world.

Manton, Thomas: (1620-1677) Puritan preacher, theologian, and writer.

Markell, Jan: Founder of Olive Tree Ministries as well as a popular author and speaker across North America.

Marshall, Catherine: (1914-1983) American author of non-fiction, inspirational and fiction works. She was the wife of well-known minister Peter Marshall.

Marshall, Peter: (1902-1949) Scottish American author and preacher. He was the pastor of the New York Avenue Presbyterian Church in Washington D.C. He was appointed Chaplain of the United States Senate.

Matheson, George: (1842-1906): A blind Scottish minister, hymn writer and prolific author.

Maxwell, L. E.: (1895-1984) American born Canadian educator and minister.

McCartney, Clarence E.: (1879-1957) American pastor and writer.

McCheyne, Robert Murray: (1813-1843): A minister in the church of Scotland. He died at age 29.

McCracken, Robert: (1905-1973) Author and Baptist minister.

McKay, Claude: (1889-1948) Jamaican American writer and poet.

McMahon, T. A.: Author and President and Executive Director of the Berean Call Ministry.

Melito of Sardis: (d. 180) The Bishop of Sardis. Held a foremost place in terms of bishops in Asia due to the influence of his literary works.

Melville, Herman: (1819-1891) American novelist, short story author and poet of the American Renaissance period.

Meyer, F. B.: (1847-1929) A Baptist pastor and evangelist in England who was involved in ministry and inner city work on both sides of the Atlantic.

Meyer, H. (August) W. (Wilhelm): (1800-1873) A German Protestant who wrote commentaries on the New Testament and published an edition of it.

Miller, J. R.: (1840-1912) Popular Christian author, Editorial Superintendent of the Presbyterian Board of Publication as well as served as pastor in Pennsylvania and Illinois.

Moffat, Robert: (1795-1883) Scottish Congregationalist missionary to Africa. His daughter Mary became the wife of missionary and explorer David Livingstone.

Moody, Dwight L.: (1837-1899) American Evangelist and publisher and founder of Moody Bible Institute and its original ministries.

Moore, W. C. Author of classic Christian writings.

More, Hannah, (1745-1833) English religious writer, philanthropist, poet and playwright.

Morgan, G. Campbell: (1863-1945) A British evangelist, preacher, leading Bible teacher, and a prolific writer.

Morris, Henry M.: (1918-2006) American young Earth Creationist, Christian apologist and engineer. One of the founders of the Creation Research Society and the Institute for Creation Research.

Morrison, Robert: (1728-1834) An Anglo-Scottish Protestant missionary and preacher. He is most notable for his work in China.

Mott, John R.: (1865-1955) American Methodist layman and evangelist who shared the Nobel Prize for Peace in 1946 for his work in international church and missionary movements.

Murray, Andrew: (1828-1917) South African writer, teacher and Christian pastor.

Muggeridge, Malcolm (1903-1990) English journalist and satirist.

Mulinde, John: The founder and global overseer of World Trumpet Mission.

Neighbour, R. E.: (1872-1945) Pioneer missionary and evangelist who served as pastor, founded four churches, and published some 30 volumes and more than 50 booklets on religious subjects plus hymns and sheet music.

Nettleton, Todd: Host of The Voice of the Martyrs Radio, and in his service to this ministry for more than 20 years, he has traveled to numerous hostile and restricted nations to interview hundreds of believers who've faced persecution for their Christian witness.

Newton, Isaac: (1642-1726) English polymath active as a mathematician, physicist, astronomer, alchemist, theologian and author.

Newell, William R. (1868-1956) A famed Bible teacher and hymn writer who pastored in Chicago and served as the assistant Superintendent of Moody Bible Institute.

Nichols, J. (John) W. (William) H. (Hugh): (1867-1960) Preacher and teacher of God's Word and the author of a number of commentaries of the various books of the Bible.

Nicholson, W. (William) P. (Patterson): (1876-1959) An itinerant evangelist in the United Kingdon, the United States and Australia.

Niebuhr, Reinhold: (1892-1971) An American Reformed theologian, professor, ethicist, and commentator on politics and public affairs.

O'Leary, Brad: Author of 15 books on American politics, romantic travel, and religion in politics.

Origen: (185-254) Greek Christian writer and teacher.

Ortlund, Raymond C. Jr.: (b. 1949) American pastor and author.

Owens, John: (1616-1683) An English Non-conformist church leader, theologian, and academic administrator at the University of Oxford.

Oxenham, John aka William Arthur Dunkerley: (1852-1941) a prolific English Journalist and poet.

Pacian of Barcelona: (310-died before 392) Though married and a father, he became bishop of Barcelona.

Packer, J. I.: (1926-2020) English born Canadian evangelical theologian, clergy and writer.

Paige, Leroy "Satchel": (1906-1982) American baseball pitcher who played in both the Negro League and Major League Baseball. His career spanned five decades.

Parker, Joseph: (1830-1902) One of London's greatest preachers who served as a Congregational pastor. He traveled widely and one of his works was the 25 volume, *The People's Bible*.

Penn, William: (1644-1718) English writer, religious thinker and influential Quaker who founded the Province of Pennsylvania.

Pickett, L. L.: (1859-1928) Evangelist, pastor and hymn/song writer. His songs were found in hymnbooks of the Holiness movement.

Pink, A. (Arthur) W.: (1886-1952) English Bible teacher who sparked a renewed interest in the exposition of Calvinism or Reformed Theology.

Piper, John: (b. 1946) American reformed Baptist Theologian, pastor and chancellor of Bethlehem College and Seminary in Minneapolis, Minnesota.

Plato: (428/423-348 BC) Ancient Greek philosopher. A student of Socrates.

Polycarp (69-155) Believed to be a disciple of the Apostle John. He was an apostolic Father and Greek bishop of Smyrna. He was martyred for his faith.

Poplin, Mary: A professor emerita and author. Her work spans K-12 to higher education. Attended a left leaning church until she had a vivid dream that made the Jesus of Christianity undeniable to her.

Porter, Bessie: (1849/1850-1936) Hymnwriter

Postman, Neil: (1931-2003) An American author, educator, media theorist, and cultural critic.

Powell, Paul: (1933-2016): Considered a great pastor and communicator and author. Dean of Baylor University Geoge W. Truett Theological Seminary.

Prentis, Henning Webb Jr.: (1884-1954) An American industrialist known as the President of the Cork Company.

Quayle, Steve: A prophet and author who shares his insights on global chaos and end times.

Rader, Paul: (1879-1938) An American Evangelist and a college football player and coach. He was the first nationwide radio preacher in the United States and served as senior pastor of Moody Church and second president of the Christian and American Alliance.

Ravenhill, Leonard: (1907-1994) English Christian Evangelist and author.

Reagan, Ronald: (1911-2004) The 40th President of the United States, who was not only a politician above his class but an actor whose humorous lines easily won the spotlight.

Reddin, Opah: (1921-2005) Author and Bible professor at Central Bible College where she was active in educating ministers.

Rees, Seth C. (1854-1933) Leading figure in Holiness Movement, founded the Pilgrim Holiness church which was the forerunner of the Wesleyan Church.

Reidhead, Paris: (1919-1992) American Christian missionary that was devoted to communicating the Gospel message.

Riley, Jordan: Christian recording artist who shares his message of hope and God's love through his music.

Roberts, Evan: (1878-1951) Welsh evangelist that was a major figure in the Welsh Revival.

Roberts, Frances J.: (1918-2009) Best known for her classic devotional, *Come Away My Beloved.* She founded the King's Press.

Robbins, Duffy: Professor of Christian Ministries of Biblical and religious studies.

Rosenthal, Marvin: (1935-2022) The founder and President Emeritus of Zion's Hope and an author. His son David took over Zion's Hope after his death.

Rosser, Dois L. Jr.: (1921-2019) An American businessman best known for founding the POMOCO Auto Group and the International Cooperating Ministries (ICM).

Rossetti, Christina: (1830-1894) English poet who wrote devotionals and poems for children.

Rousseau, Jean-Jacques: (1712-1778) A Genevan philosopher, writer, and composer.

Ruth, C. (Christian) W. (Wismer): (1865-1944) An evangelist and one of the 10 founding fathers of the church of the Nazarene for the Holiness Movement.

Rutherford, Samuel: (1600-1661) Scottish Presbyterian pastor, author and theologian.

Ryle, J. C.: (1816-1900) English evangelical Anglican bishop and author. Known for his powerful preaching and extensive tracts.

Saint, Nate: (1923-1956) An Evangelical Christian missionary pilot who along with four other missionaries were martyred in Ecuador.

Sanchez, Stacy J.: Teacher, Christian speaker and author.

Sangster, W. E.: (1900-1960) British Methodist preacher who called for biblical roots and evangelism in the 20th century.

Saphir, Adolph: (1831-1891) A Hungarian Jew that was converted to Christianity and became a missionary and writer.

Saver, Erich: (1898-1938) Author who was raised in the Open Brethren Church.

Scarinci, Thomas Patrick: (1942-1997) Dr. Scarinci was the founder and Executive Director of Outreach Ministries.

Schweitzer, Albert: (1875-1965) French-German theologian and philosopher, organist, musicologist and writer.

Scofield, C. I.: (1843-1921) American theologian, minister, writer of a bestselling annotated Bible.

Scott, Rachel (1981-1999) The American student who was the first fatality of the Columbine High School massacre.

Scroggie, William Graham: (1877-1958) Most influential evangelical preachers and teachers of the first half of the 20th century.

Secker, William: (d. 1681) A preacher and the rector of Leigh, Essex.

Shafer, Barry: Youth leader, pastor, author, and speaker. Founded InWord Resources in 1996.

Simpson, A. B.: (1843-1919) A Canadian preacher, theologian, author and founder of Christian and Missionary Alliance.

Skoog, Pastor Phil and his wife Donna: (Phil's b. 1953) Phil is a retired successful business man who was refined as a believer through many trials that allowed him to see God's miraculous deliverances and interventions in his life. He is now a pastor, preacher, and part of a Christian quartet. With his wife Donna by his side, he founded the *Cleft of the Rock Ministries*. She is now carrying on her mother's legacy as she serves as the Coordinator of *Missions with a Heart* that her mother, Effie Ehler founded.

Slessor, Mary: (1848-1915) Scottish Presbyterian missionary to Nigeria.

Smith, Amanda (1837-1915) A Methodist preacher and former slave who founded an orphanage for African American children. She was a leader in the Wesleyan—holiness movement.

Smith, Chuck: (1927-2013) American pastor who founded the Calvary Chapel Movement.

Smith, Gypsy: (1860-1947) A British evangelist who conducted evangelistic campaigns in the United States and Great Britain for over 70 years.

Smith, Hannah Whiteall: (1832-1911) She was a lay speaker and author in the Holiness Movement in the United States and the Higher Life Movement in the United Kingdom.

Smith, Walter C.: (1824-1908) Hymnist, poet and minister. He is chiefly remembered for his hymn, *Immortal, Invisible God Only Wise.* Some of his works were written under other names such as Orwell or Hemann Kunst.

Socrates: (470-399 BC): Greek Philosopher from Athens who is credited as the founder of Western Philosophy.

Solzhenitsyn, Aleksandr (1918-2008) Nobel Prize Winner for literature, a historian Russian author who exposed the horrors of Communism and the dangers of materialism.

Spargimino, Larry: Active in Bible teaching, writing books and radio scripts on news items, a pastor, leads Bible conferences engages in overseas mission work, and is a host on the *Watchman on the Wall* broadcast.

Sparks, T. Austin: (1888-1971) A British Christian evangelist and author.

Sproul, R. C.: (1939-2017) American Reformed Theologian and ordained pastor in the Presbyterian Church in America.

Spurgeon, Charles: (1834-1892) English preacher, evangelist, and author who is highly influential today. He is known as the "Prince of Preachers."

St John, Harold: (1876-1957) Missionary to Bazil. He was called, *The Maestro* (genius) because of his Bible knowledge. In a way his legacy continued on through his daughter Patricia (1919-1993), who wrote over 25 books including biographies, poetry and Christian stories for children.

Stagner, Barry: Pastor, author, and speaker who teaches the Bible, pastor of Calvery Central OC in Tustin, CA.

Stedman, Ray: (1917-1992) Evangelical Christian pastor and author.

Stewart, James A.: (1910-1975) A Scottish born missionary, evangelist, and author who became an US Citizen and settled in Asheville, North Carolina where he died at home.

Stockmayer, Otto: (1838-1917) Part of the Keswick or holiness movement in England, and the United States.

Studd, C. T.: (1860-1931) He was a skilled Cricket Player that made his name famous throughout England. His conversion to Christ and his call led him to India where he began as a pastor. After returning to England, he received a call to go to Africa as a missionary where he established four missions.

Swinnock, George: (1627-1673) English Non-conformist clergyman and writer.

Tada, Joni Eareckson: American evangelical Christian author, radio host, artist, singer, and founder of *Joni and Friends.* She is a quadriplegic due to an accident in 1967 at age 17. She has shared her journey with others to encourage them in their challenges.

Tauler, Johannes: (1300-1361) German mystic, a Roman Catholic Priest and a theologian.

Taylor, Hudson: (1832-1905) Author and British Baptist Christian missionary to China. Founder of China Inland Mission.

Taylor, Jeremy: (1613-1667) Cleric in the Church of England who achieved fame as an author during the Protectorate of Oliver Cromwell.

Tersteegen, Gerhard: (1667-1769) German Reformed religious writer and hymnist.

Tertullian: (160-225) Lawyer and a theologian and first ecclesiastical writer.

Thatcher, Margaret: (1925-2013) British stateswoman and conservative politician who served as Prime Minister of England from 1979-1990. She was not only the first woman Prime Minister, but the longest serving one in the 20th century.

Theophilus of Antioch: (130-183-185) An apologist and sixth Bishop of Antioch from 169-183. He was converted from paganism by reading Scriptures.

Thomas of Alexandria: (d. 300) Gave his life over to serving God and spreading the teachings of Jesus Christ.

Thomas, W. (William) H. (Henry) Griffith: (1861-1924) An Anglican cleric and scholar from the English-Welch border.

Torrey, R. A.: (1856-1928) American evangelist, pastor, educator and writer.

Toussaint, Stanley: (1928-2017) Considered a spiritual giant and hero of the faith. He was a preacher and a professor emeritus of Bible exposition.

Tosefta: A compilation of the Jewish Oral Laws from the late 2ⁿᵈ century, the period of Mishnah and the Jewish Sages known as the Tannaism.

Toynbee, Arnold J.: (1889-1975) English historian, a philosopher of history, and an author of numerous books.

Tozer, A.W.: (1897-1963) American Christian pastor, author, magazine editor, and spiritual mentor.

Trail, Robert: (1793-1847) Clergyman in the established church of Ireland. He was a rector of Schull, County Cork.

Trapp, John: (1601-1669) English Anglican Bible commentator and his large five-volume commentary is still read today.

Trotter, Lilias: (1853-1928) British artist and a protestant missionary to Algeria.

Underhill, Evelyn: (1875-1941) English Anglo-Catholic writer and pacifist known for her numerous works on religion and spiritual practice, in particular Christian mysticism.

Vanderbreggar, Cornelius Jr. (1915-2015) A Bible teacher and missionary serving in missions all over the world. He also founded the *Reaper's Fellowship* and wrote numerous books.

Vaughn, Ellen: New York Times bestselling author and speaker who has written and co-written twenty books including the authorized biography of missionary Elisabeth Elliot.

Victorinus, Gaius Marius: (289-291- death after 365) He was a Roman grammarian, rhetorician and Neoplatonic philosopher. He translated two of Aristotle's book into Latin and had a religious conversion from Paganism to Christianity.

Vine, W. (William) E. (Edwy): (1873-1949) English Biblical scholar, theologian and writer who is best known for *Vine's Expository Dictionary of New Testament Words.*

Vincent of Lerins: (d. 445) A Gallic Monk and author of early writings.

Washer, Paul: (b. 1961) American missionary evangelist, author and speaker who founded the Heart Cry Missionary Society.

Washington, George: (1732-1799) Political leader, military general, statesman, Founding Father and the first President of the United States.

Watchmen Nee: (1903-1972) Chinese Church and Christian leader who was imprisoned for his faith. He also wrote several books.

Watson, G. D.: (1845-1924) Wesleyan Methodist minister and evangelist based in Los Angeles.

Watson, Thomas: (1620-1686) An English Puritan, preacher, and writer.

Watts, Isaac: (1674-1748) English hymnwriter and theologian.

Wells, Kenneth H.: Poet, author and publisher who lived in Whitefish, Montana, in the 1980's.

Webster, Daniel: (1782-1852) American lawyer and statesman.

Weichert (Kalisher), Zvi: He was ten years old when the Germans invaded Poland in 1939. He has been brought to an orphanage by his mother because he did not look Jewish and it was her way of saving him. He never saw his family again. What he did discover is he did have a true Savior in the person of Jesus Christ. His life was put into a book

Weistling, Morgan: (b. 1964) American 21st century Realist Artist. His painting of Jesus and Mary depicts the universal theme of light.

Wesley, Charles: (1707-1788) Brother of John Wesley. English leader of the Methodist movement. He was a prolific hymnwriter who wrote over 6,500 hymns during his lifetime.

Wesley, John: (1703-1791) An English cleric, theologian and evangelist as well as a leader of a revival movement known as Methodism.

Wesley, Suzanne: (1669-1742) Mother of John and Charles Wesley who by faith endured many hardships and became a strong pillar to many in her lifetime.

Whately, Richard: (1787-1863) Anglican archbishop of Dublin, author, educator, logician and social reformer.

Whitefield, George: (1714-1770) Anglican cleric and evangelist who was one of the founders of Methodism and the evangelical movement.

Wiersbe, Warren: (1929-2019) American Christian clergyman, Bible teacher, conference speaker, and a prolific writer.

Wilberforce, William: (1759-1833): Abolitionist, philanthropist, author, and had deep Christian roots due to being reared by an evangelical aunt and uncle.

Wigglesworth, Smith (1859-1947) British evangelist who was influential in the early history of Pentecostalism.

Wilson, Clifford, (1923-2012): Author of over 50 published books. He was a well-known speaker with a worldwide Christian radio outreach.

Wilson, David: Author and poet.

Wilkerson, David: (1931-2010) American Christian Evangelist, best known for his book, *The Cross and the Switchblade*. He was the founder of Teen Challenge and of Times Square Church in New York City and served as its pastor until he retired.

Winslow: Octavius: (1808-1878) Known as "The Pilgrim's Companion", he was a Baptist Minister as well as a prominent 19th century evangelical preacher in England and America.

Wise, Stephen S.: (1874-1949) 20th century reformed rabbi and Zionist leader in the progressive era.

Woods, C. Stacey: (1909-1983): A moving force in the mid-20th century in American evangelism.

Wurmbrand, Richard and Sabrina: Richard, (1909-2007) was a Romanian Luther priest of Jewish descent who was imprisoned and tortured for his unwavering faith and devotion to Jesus Christ. He is an author as well as the founder of The Voice of the Martyrs. Sabrina (1913-2000), Richard's wife was also persecuted for her faith and was an author who wrote about her experience.

Wurtz II, Robert, (b. 1969) Author of *Televangeliscalism*.

Yancey, Phillip Yancey (b. 1949) An American author who writes primarily about spiritual issues.

Xenocrates: (396/b-314/3 BC) Greek philosopher, mathematician, leader of the Platonic Academy and student of Plato.

Yohannan, K. P.: Prolific writer of 200 books and founder of Gospel for Asia.

Zacharias, Ravi: (1946-2020) Indian and born Canadian, an American Christian ordained, evangelical minister and author who founded a radio program.

Glossary

Most of the following definitions come from the book, *Game of Gods* except for definitions marked with (*) which came from the book, *Christianity and Social Justice.*

Biblical Higher Criticism: Views Scripture as being allegory.

*Egalitarian: Is a school of thought within a political philosophy that points to a free Democratic society that builds on the concept of social equality, prioritizing it for all people, which points to the idea of equal distribution regardless of personal contribution. Jon Harris summarizes goal of those promoting such a philosophy was to produce, "egalitarian equality instead of equality before the law." (CSJ, pg. 118)

*Epistemology: Imagines a two-dimensional world composed of red people, who represent the oppressed, and blue people who represent the oppressors.

Evolutionary Christianity: Pushes cosmic evolution in a way that dovetails with spiritual transhumanism.

Materialism: is the idea that the only reality is the physical matter of the universe, and that everything else, including thoughts, will, and emotions comes from physical laws acting on the matter.

Naturalism: is the view that the only way to understand our universe is through the scientific method.

Neo-Paganism: Paganism has to do with cultural expression of its beliefs, ways and practices, which are profane and idolatrous, but Neo-paganism is the religious expression of Re-enchantment

Oneness: Becoming "universal, total beings" – a unity of collective divinity.

Par Excellence Theophany: Expression that has to do with Jesus' appearance the second time.

Parousia: Is a Greek word that is used to describe the Second Coming.

Perennial Philosophy: That all religions share a common truth, expressing an inner mystical divinity, and then through psychedelic substances, ventured into the experience of chemically induced oneness.

*Presentism: It is where they interpret history according to modern priorities, fashions, and values.

Progressive Christianity: An experience of the Sacred and the Oneness and Unity of all life.

Psychological Cult of Selfism: A form of secular humanism based on the worship of self that attempts to fill the vacuum of lost value.

Re-enchantment: The assembly of meaning and purpose within a matrix of wonder and mystery, aesthetic expressions, symbolism and sentiment, all pointing to a paradigm of holism.

Rosicrucianism: Also known as the rosy Cross, is an esoteric school of thought dating back to the 17th century and the legendary figure of German mystic, Christian Rosenkreuz. Over the centuries various orders and societies have claimed Rosicrucian credentials. Some still exist and it is clear that it has influenced modern occultism and Western mysticism.

Secularization: Is always an intermediate stage between a religious society on the way out and the appearance of a new religious structuring.

Spiritism: Message of self-perfection through reincarnation of the soul: To evolve towards God.

Sufism: The annihilation of the individual ego, an "inner dimension of experience," altering the mind and bringing in new actions.

Bibliography

(WOF) The Wisdom of God, A.W. Tozer, © 2017 by James L. Snyder, Compiler and Editor, Published by Bethany House Publishers

(VPH) A Very Present Help, Ruth Hunt, © 2012, Published by The Berean Call

(DPS) Diamonds, Persimmons and Stars, Howard E. Kershner, © 1965, Published by The Bookmailer Inc.

(AMH) Adventures of Missionary Heroism, John C. Lambert, © 2017 by Generations, Master Books

(COS) The Counterfeit Christ and Other Sermons, J. Gregory Mantle, Reprint 1968, Christian Publications, Inc.

(GG) Game of Gods, © 2018 by Carl Teichrib, Whitemud House Publishing

(GE) Galatians/Ephesians (Commentaries), H. A. Ironside, Combined Edition 1981, Published by Loizeaux Brothers, Inc.

(APB) All the Parables of the Bible © 1963 by Herbert Lockyer, Zondervan

(TK) They Knew Their God (Volume 5) © 1998 by Lillian Harvey, Harvey Christians Publishers, Inc.

(VS) Voices of the Spirit, George Matheson, Reprinted from the 1904 edition, © 1979 by Baker Book House Company

(CSJ) Christianity and Social Justice, Religions In Conflict, © 2021 by Jon Harris, Reformation Zion Publishing

(EJ) The Epistle of Jude, © 2023 by Michael Boldea Jr., Boldman Publishing

(CWC) The Complete Words of Oswald Chambers, © 2000 by Oswald Chambers Publications Association, Limited, Barbour Publishing, Inc.

(WFF) When Faith is Forbidden by Todd Nettleton, © 2021 by The Voice of the Martyrs, Moody Publishers.

Encyclopedia of Christian Biographies, © 2007 by Edward Reese, Published by AMG Publishers

Other books by Rayola Kelley:

Hidden Manna (Original)
Battle for the Soul (Book & Workbook)
Stories of the Heart
Transforming Love & Beyond
The Great Debate
Post to Post: (1) Establishing the Way
Post to Post: (2) Walking in the Way
Post to Post: (3) Meditations Along the Way
Post to Post: (4) Inspirations Along the Way

Volume One: Establishing Our Life in Christ
My Words are Spirit and Life
The Anatomy of Sin
The Principles of the Abundant Life
The Place of Covenant
Unmasking the Cult Mentality

Volume Two: Putting on the Life of Christ
He Actually Thought It Not Robbery
Revelation of the Cross
In Search of Real Faith
Think on These Things
Follow the Pattern

Volume Three: Developing a Godly Environment
Godly Discipline
Prayer and Worship
Don't Touch That Dial
Face of Thankfulness
ABC's of Christianity

Volume Four: Issues of the Heart
Hidden Manna (Revised)
Bring Down the Sacred Cows
The Manual for the Single Christian Life
Parents Are People Too

Volume Five: Challenging the Christian Life
The Issues of Life
Presentation of the Gospel
For the Purpose of Edification
Whatever Happened to the Church?
Women's Place in the Kingdom of God

Volume Six: Developing Our Christian Life
The Many Faces of Christianity
Possessing Our Souls

Experiencing the Christian Life
The Power of Our Testimonies
The Victorious Journey

Volume Seven: Discovering True Ministry
From Prisons and Dots to Christianity
So You Want To Be In Ministry?

Devotions
Devotions of the Heart: Books One and Two
Daily Food for the Soul: Books One and Two

Gentle Shepherd Ministries Devotion Series:
Being a Child of God
Disciplining the Strength of our Youth
Coming to Full Age

Nugget Books:
Nuggets From Heaven
More Nuggets From Heaven
Heavenly Gems
More Heavenly Gems
Heavenly Treasures

Gentle Shepherd Ministries Series:

The Christian Life Series
What Matter Is This?
The Challenge of It
The Reality of It

The Leadership Series
Overcoming
A Matter of Authority and Power
The Dynamics of True Leadership

Books By Jeannette Haley

Books co-authored with Rayola Kelley:
Hidden Manna (original)
The Many Faces of Christianity (Volume 6)
Post to Post 3: Meditations Along the Way
Post to Post 4: Inspirations Along the Way

Other Books:
Rose of Light, Thorn of Darkness (Volume 7)
The Pig and I
Reflections of Wonder (Devotional)

Angelus Assignments Includes:
Interview in Hell
Interview on Earth

Children's Books:
Little Stories for Little People
Traveler's Tales
The Adventures of Zack and Mira
The Adventures of Paul and Dana
(A House on the Beach)
The Monster of Mystery Valley

www.ingramcontent.com/pod-product-compliance
Lightning Source LLC
Chambersburg PA
CBHW060240100426
42742CB00011B/1596